# GENDER : PROBLEMS AND POLICIES

*2nd Revised and Enlarged Edition*

# GENDER
## PROBLEMS AND POLICIES

*2nd Revised and Enlarged Edition*

*Edited by*

K.R. Gupta

**ATLANTIC**

**PUBLISHERS & DISTRIBUTORS (P) LTD**

Published by

**ATLANTIC**

**PUBLISHERS & DISTRIBUTORS (P) LTD**

7/22, Ansari Road, Darya Ganj, New Delhi-110002
Phones : +91-11-40775252, 23273880, 23275880, 23280451
Fax : +91-11-23285873
Web : www.atlanticbooks.com
E-mail : orders@atlanticbooks.com

Branch Office
5, Nallathambi Street, Wallajah Road, Chennai-600002
Phones : +91-44-64611085, 32413319
E-mail : chennai@atlanticbooks.com



ISBN 978-81-269-1801-0



Printed in India at Glorious Printers, A-13, D.S.I.D.C.,
Jhilmil Industrial Area, Delhi-110095

# Preface

India has witnessed wide gender inequalities since its early history owing to social set-ups, economic conditions and religious practices, which resulted in a gap between the position of men and women in society. During the British rule no attempt was made to improve the status of women as the government followed its exploitative policies rather than committing itself to bring about any social development. Though the landmark legislations like abolition of *sati* and child marriage attempted to remove these social evils, the implementation was slow and difficult in the complex web of Indian society. In general, the condition of women remained poor.

After the achievement of Independence in 1947, the Indian government set out to achieve the main objectives of poverty alleviation, removal of social inequalities and realisation of fast economic growth. The Constitution, adopted in 1950, ensures gender equality as a fundamental right and even empowers the state to adopt measures of positive discrimination in favour of women. Several programmes, policies and laws have since been made for empowerment of women. India has also ratified various international conventions and human rights instruments committing to secure equal rights of women, for example, Convention on Elimination of Discrimination Against Women (CEDAW). Notwithstanding, there still exists a wide gap between the envisaged goals, constitutional provisions, legislation, policies, plans, programmes and the reality regarding the status of women in India.

It is said that women hold half of the sky. There is thus an urgent need for improving the access of women to national resources so that they can realise their potential and actively participate in national development. It is necessary to understand the various aspects of gender inequality in India and the multitudes of problems the women are facing in our society.

*Gender: Problems and Policies* is comprised of papers contributed by erudite scholars in the field of women's studies. Vibhuti Patel studies the integration of women in development in the globalised world. There exists a relationship between international trade and women's work which not only promotes gender equality but also removes global poverty. There are large numbers of poor, and the desperately needy women, looking for work within the narrow confines of a socially imposed inequitable demand for labour and strict taboo on mobility. Globalisation has helped in solving these problems and thus bears the promise and possibilities of furthering women's rights and well-being.

Nishta Paul studies the plight of the underprivileged girl child in India in the context of the interplay of several historical, social, cultural and political factors. She concludes that the state has an extremely important role to play in creating a suitable environment for promoting gender equality through education and strengthening the supportive legal framework ensuring universal access to education.

Housing rights have been a major concern of the women's movement in India. When women's groups started providing support to women in distress, it was relatively easier to find jobs and school admission for children. The most difficult task, however, was to get an accommodation for women who are victims of violence, desertion, and rejection from natal or matrimonial families. The article "Women and Housing Rights" urges us to understand women's housing needs from the point of view of women's right to dignified life.

The article by Bhabani Shankar Nayak and Geeta Sinha depicts the patriarchal practice of Indian democracy and under-representation of women in Indian Parliament. It analyses the Women's Reservation Bill for 33 per cent reservation of seats for women in the Indian Parliament and the debates around it. Parthasarathi Mondal draws attention to the liberal development thinking and gender. He explores the views of Amartya Sen, John Rawls and Ludwig Wittgenstein regarding social transformation and suggests that addressing gender concerns is an essential ingredient for development.

Elected women representatives in urban self-government bodies have made their presence felt after the 74th Amendment in the Indian Constitution in 1994. Now we have provision for 33 per cent women in municipal bodies. However, not much is provided in the municipal budgets for the upliftment of urban poor women. Since budget is an important tool in the hands of state for affirmative action for improvement of gender relations and reduction in gender gaps, the budgeting policies need to keep into consideration the gender dynamics operating in the economy and society. Thus, the article, "Cities, Gender Budgeting and Civic Governance" underscores participating approaches to pro-poor budgeting.

The focus of the article "*Fasting, Feasting*: Foods, Consumption and Politics of Power" is to see how food-related practices reflect power imbalances in gender relations. Arpana Nath analyses how food-related practices impact women as homemakers and play a crucial role in the formation of gendered identities. Pallav Mukhopadhyay studies the problem of gender inequality in West Bengal and identifies the hurdles in the way of expansion of education of women in the state. The study, however, is representative of the whole country as the problems faced in West Bengal are encountered in most of the other Indian states as well.

Apart from these well-researched articles, this anthology contains National Policy for the Empowerment of Women (2001), giving its objectives, policy prescriptions and operational strategies. It also apprises the readers of "Ujjawala"—a scheme for prevention of trafficking and rescue, rehabilitation and reintegration of victims of trafficking for commercial sexual exploitation. The objectives of the scheme, target beneficiaries, implementing agencies, eligibility conditions and patterns of assistance have been mentioned. The book also contains various articles of Convention on Elimination of Discrimination Against Women (CEDAW) which throw ample light on the technical aspects relating to gender discrimination and suggest appropriate measures to be taken by the states parties to improve the situation.

The Sexual Harassment of Women at the Workplace (Prevention and Redressal) Bill, 2004 has also been included in the book. The bill provides for the prevention and reddressal of sexual harassment of women at workplaces, or arising during, or out of the course of their employment and matters connected thereto, in keeping with the principles of equality, freedom and liberty as enshrined in the Constitution of India. Besides, the book contains the objectives, target groups, implementing agencies and other aspects of Scheme of Short Stay Homes for Women and Girls. Several new schemes for the upliftment of women were launched during 2001 which was observed as Women's Empowerment Year. The book also includes a list of major events like seminars, summits, exhibitions, teleconferences, workshops and conventions held to bring about a change in the environment which will be conducive to develop self-confidence and assertiveness among women.

Vibhuti Patel in her article, "Gender Gap and the Development Goals", accentuates the fact that values like freedom, equality, solidarity, tolerance, respect for nature and shared responsibility can be achieved if a rights-based approach is adopted to development, both within the UN system and at the country level, that prioritizes equity, profound social changes and sustainability, rather than simply the achievement of narrow quantitative targets.

In another article, "Gender Inequality and Development", Vibhuti Patel states that women's studies have challenged the conventional indicators of development that focus on higher education, industrialisation, farm mechinsation, etc. With the changes in society, the definition of gender equality and empowerment has changed. There is need to address more subtle issues like various forms of discrimination against women; patriarchy that has been well entrenched in our social system; control of women's sexuality and fertility; market, mobility and women; and proper implementation of policies for the welfare of women.

The last article, "Gender Sensitization", focuses on the need for gender statistics in formulating policies and programmes. Census data is very useful in this regard. The census is now also directed towards areas that show abnormal gender parameters like sex ratio, literacy and female work participation, by developing special gender modules and training strategies for sensitisation of census functionaries.

The book is of paramount importance for understanding the problems of gender inequalities in India and in formulating the right policies for women's empowerment. Researchers, teachers and students of social science, women's studies, development studies, India's demography and those concerned with gender equalities will find it highly useful.

**K.R. GUPTA**

# Contents

# Globalisation, Women and Work*

1

*Vibhuti Patel*

## Introduction

Globalisation (G) in the 19th and in the first half of the 20th century symbolised colonialism and in the later part of the 20th century symbolised neo-colonialism. Economic G used slave and indentured labour to build the empires of today's prosperous countries. In the 21st century, G has been categorised as free trade, unfettered markets and integration of economies of the nation states in the world capitalism. This neo-liberal agenda is driven by the enlightened self-interest of transnational corporations and multinational corporations and has resulted into highly uneven effects on across class, caste, gender, ethnicity and race. The rich countries of the west want G to involve removal of all barriers to trade and movement of capital, but they oppose unhindered and unfettered global movement of workers. The Indian capitalists don't like the issue of LABOUR STANDARDS (child labour, occupational health, social security, etc.) to be a trade issue at WTO, as within the country, they are trying to curtail workers' rights 'to cut the cost' and be competitive in the world trade.

In the rapidly changing world, ideologies are giving way to practical economics, business sense and market compulsions. World economies are converging into a global village economy. Rapid technological progress in communication and transport sectors, have made movements of goods, services, capital, professional and workers extremely fast. National economic

* http://www.europe-solidaire.org

reforms are guided by the global economic order defined by the world capitalism.

### Women and Structural Adjustment in India

In response to a mounting burden of debt leading to a balance of payment crisis, the Government of India (GOI) adopted a structural adjustment programme (SAP) in 1991 officially declared as New Economic Policy. It included reductions in public investment, devaluation, cutting food and fertilizers subsidies, dismantling of public distribution system, the reduction of budgetary provision for developmental planning/social sector, capital intensive and 'high-tech' productive activities, economies in government expenditure, an increase in the bank rate, insurance charges and rail tariffs. Simply put, the policy aimed at capital, energy and import-intensive growth with the help of 4 "Ds"—devaluation, deregulation, deflation and denationalisation. The mainstream economists call this process as "economic reforms".

This policy has intensified the processes pursued in the last decade and a half (mainly in the post-emergency period), as a result of a new international division of labour between the advanced capitalist economies and the post-colonial economies of Asia, Africa and Latin America as per Washington consensus in 1992. The national and multinational corporations in the USA and Europe realised that the best way to reduce the wage-bill and to enhance profit rates was to move industrial plants to poorer countries like India, Sri Lanka, Bangladesh, Indonesia, Philippines, Thailand, etc. The cheap labour of 'docile', 'nimble fingered' and 'flexible' Asian women—the last colony was found to be most attractive step to enhance profit margins. This policy was given the appealing title of 'Integration of Women in Development'.

The new strategy of 'Integration of Women into Development' meant in most cases getting women to work in some income-generating activities, integrating women into market oriented production and thus integrating women into the world market economy. It was not meant that women should expand their subsistence production and produce more for their consumption—for their own food and their clothes. Income-generation in this approach meant money income. Money income could be generated only if women could produce something, which could be sold. People who could buy these products belong to the upper strata of economic hierarchy.

## The Impact of Globalisation on Women Workers in India

It is crucial to understand relationship between international trade and women's work. Does it promote gender equality or global poverty?

Women of the third world are seen as the most flexible of the world's labour force. The lower supply price of these women provides a material basis for the induction of poor working-class women into export industries such as electronics, garments, sports goods, food processing, toys and agro-industries. Working class women are rigorously socialised to work uncomplainingly, under patriarchal control, at any allotted task however dull, laborious, physically harmful or badly paid it may be. There are large numbers of poor and desperately needy women looking for work within the narrow confines of a socially imposed, inequitable demand of labour and strict taboos on mobility. These women have become ideal workers for this kind of international division of labour.

Economic globalisation, deep economic restructuring across countries and neo-liberal macro-economic policies have led to increasing informalised and decentralised processes of production, transforming labour markets and the world of work in the industrialised and the developing countries. In the name of flexibalisation; social security and statutory protection to workers have been dismantled.

In the export-oriented industries, the production of leather goods, toys, food-products, garments, diamond and jewellery, piece-rate female labour is employed, working from sweatshops or from home or from stigmatised labour markets. In a similar way, the women of ethnic minorities—south Asians, Afro-Caribbeans, Puerto Ricans and Mexicans living in the industrialised countries have been used as cheap labour by the world capitalism since the early 1980s. They face triple oppression as they are subjected to race and colour prejudices as well as class exploitation. The relationship between the formal sector and the decentralised sector is a dependent relationship where the formal sector has control over capital and markets and the 'informal' sector works as an ancillary. G is enjoying piggy ride over the backs of millions of poor women and child workers in the margin of economy.

In India, 96 per cent of women work in the decentralised sector, which has a high degree of labour redundancy and obsolescence. These women have less control over their work and no chance for upward mobility because of temporary, routine and monotonous work. In the agrarian sector, the cash crops—fruits, mushrooms, flowers and vegetables, are replacing the traditional subsistence crops where women had important role to play. This process has also intensified immiserisation of the working women in rural areas and has created tremendous food-shortages (Patel & Karne, 2006).

**Health-care**: Studies on intra-household distribution of resources reveal that among the poorer households with gross malnutrition and nutritional deficiency, the deficiency among girls and women was 25 per cent more than among men. National Family Health Survey, 2006 has revealed that Anaemia among Indian women is around 50-60 per cent. High rate of inflation leading to high price of pulses, cereals and vegetables, non-availability of safe drinking water to the poor masses has proved to be extremely detrimental to women's health. For every three men using health-care facilities in India, only one woman does so. According to the 2001 census, the sex ratio showed there were 933 women for every 1000 men in India. In the 0-19 age group, the death rate of girls is higher than boys. In this context, budgetary-cuts in public health expenditure have dire consequences for working class women and girls in India. In the budget, funds for the treatment of tuberculosis, malaria, phyleria and goitre eradication programmes have been reduced drastically.

The inadequate funds for the rural sanitation programme in each and every budget in the post-reform period for provision of clean water, toilets and sewerage has given rise to higher incidents of water-born diseases and has increased the burden of women in terms of nursing. Also, the reduction in the quota of clean water resources by 38 per cent in the urban areas and 36 per cent in the rural areas has increased the drudgery of working class women who have to stand in long queues for many hours to obtain one bucket of water.

**Women in the Unorganised Sector:** Ninety-four per cent of the total women workers are in the 'informal' (dependent) sector. The NEP reinforces the trend of informalisation for the female workforce. The formation of a 'flexible' labour force is the key concept of NEP. A shift from a stable/organised labour force to a flexible workforce has meant hiring women on a part-time basis and the substitution of highly paid male labour by cheap female labour. The NEP provides congenial state support for the large corporate houses who are closing down their big city units and using ancillaries who employ rural and tribal unmarried girls (without responsibilities for families and children) on a piece-rate basis. Home-based work by women and girls is easily legitimised in the context of increasing insecurity in the community life due to criminalisation of slums, riots and massive displacements and relocations. Subcontracting, home-based production, family labour system, and the payment of wages on a piece-rate basis, are jobs earmarked for women. This is called an increase in 'efficiency' and 'productivity' of labour.

In the name of increasing marginal efficiency of financial capital, there have been attacks on women's access to credit, extension services and input subsidies.

**Employment Profile in Agriculture**: The employment elasticity of output in agriculture has reduced to 0.64 per cent. Reduction of subsidy and credit in agriculture has affected small and marginal farmers negatively. Unemployment and underemployment in the rural areas have gained serious proportion because, in the NEP, schemes for rural development and rural industrialisation have not been given any importance. Massive scams in implementation of National Rural Employment Guarantee Scheme prevent absorption of the backlog of the unemployed and the new additions to the labour force. More that 66 per cent of workers working under NREGS are poorest of the poor and most vulnerable-female headed households.

**Part-time Work for Women:** The government finds it difficult to dismiss permanent staff in public sector enterprises, as they are well organised, vocal, articulate and visible. To create an ideological justification for segmentation in the labour market on the grounds of gender relations, a debate on the issue of part-time work for women employees has begun. The argument in favour of it is that working women shoulder the burden of domestic duties as well as office-work, so a reduction of working hours will give them some relief. It deprives women of promotion and responsible assignments, as well as providing a weapon to discriminate against women, by projecting women as "supplementary earners". Moreover, often the most strenuous part of work is commuting back and forth, and whether a person works part-time or full-time, the same amount of time and energy is spent on commuting.

The argument in favour of part-time work for women does not question the existing gender-based division of labour in the family. It throws the whole burden of child-care and housework on the individual woman. The long-standing demand for the socialisation of family functions to be supported by the state is also negated here. The women's movement in India has suggested that the best way to reduce the double burden for women is to inculcate the ethos of housework shared between both male and female members of family, the provision of cheap and safe eating facilities, child-care centres that provide both custodial care and developmental inputs for children, and better transport facilities, etc.

**Environment and Forest Development:** The most ironic impact of the SAP is on the environment and forest development. In last few years, the environment has become one of the most debated political issues. At the Rio Summit, government organisations (GOs) and non-government organisations (NGOs) from India made their presence felt by making passionate presentations. Collection of fuel, fodder and water, livestock-raising and kitchen gardening take away 4-5 hours of women's labour for unpaid care economy.

Women are employed in wasteland development, social forestry and desert development programmes on a large scale. Smokeless 'chullas' have been enthusiastically promoted among rural and urban poor women because they are less harmful to women's health. The Government's budget for funding this project has reduced by 18.5 per cent.

In the context of a wood-fuel crisis, alternate energy resources like biogas and solar energy equipment gain major importance. The Government, however, has reduced the budget for these alternate energy sources by 26.3 per cent and 25.4 per cent respectively. Further funds allocated for research on alternate energy resources have been reduced by 26.3 per cent. On the one hand, a resource "crunch" is created where environmentally regenerative programmes are concerned while on the other hand, millions of rupees are made available for controversial mega projects like the Sardar Sarovar and Special Economic Zones.

**Feminisation of Poverty:** Studies have shown that the burden of poverty falls more heavily on women than on men. The inequality in income and consumption levels between women and men. Of the total households, around 11 per cent are supported by women's income alone. In other words they are 'female-headed households' (FHH) i.e., households supported totally by widows, single unmarried women, deserted or divorced women. The female headed households are the poorest of the poor. The combined effects on these households of price rises, reduced quotas for PDS, reductions in health-care facilities and educational facilities are deplorable. The fact that the FHH and poverty go hand in hand has been established.

Children of the FHHs will suffer more from nutritional deficiency and inadequate primary health care facilities and cuts in expenditure for the primary and non-formal education. State support to FHHs had been one of the central demands of the women's movement since 1975. In the National Perspective Plan (NPP) for Women (1988-2000), the GOI had responded quite positively. But the SAP has worked against the objectives of the NPP.

**Sex-tourism as an Integral Part of Globalisation:** Sex-tourism in India has reached massive proportions with globalisation. A new type of publicity material for foreign-tourists shows scantily dressed women waiting for tourists at the beach or in the foyer of five star hotels. Worsening economic conditions force young, poor and lower middle class women to become prostitutes—either for survival or by brute force. In last two decades, rich men from the Middle-East, Scandinavia and Western Europe have been the main clients of the sex-industry. Now it is being geared up to accommodate an international clientele. This subject needs serious examination. The available literature on Gender implications of SAP in other Asian, African and Latin American countries has also neglected this issue.

## Girl Child Labour

In rural areas, their struggle to collect fuel, fodder and water will become sharper. In the urban areas, the number of girls working in the informal/unorganised sector for precarious wages has increased. Multinational corporations operating in the Free Trade Zones (FTZs), Special Economic Zones (SPZs) and the Export Processing Zones (EPZs) of India employ girls in their production units or hire them on piece-rate basis for home-based work. High production quotas create mental and physical stress among the workers. Chemical hazards, improper ventilation and lack of health and safety provision in the EPZs make these girl-workers victims of respiratory ailments, burns, ulcers, deteriorating eyesight. Young unmarried girls are of primary interest to the MNCs and TNCs, they will not fight for their rights because of family pressure to earn money. "Catch them in loop" is the motto of the MNCs and TNCs. Using girl-child labourers is the cheapest way to increase the profit margin. Corporate houses follow the same practice. Many of them have closed down their large units in industrial towns and cities using instead tribal and rural girls and paying them on a piece-rate basis. Hindustan Lever Ltd., Godrej and multinational pharmaceutical industries have begun to use this employment strategy.

## Conclusion

As already mentioned, the SAP has increased women's drudgery and hardship in the struggle for survival. The inflationary impact of the SAP reduces the purchasing power of a household which in turn increases unpaid labour of women. For example, buying cheaper food requires more time for procuring, cleaning and preparation. The unpaid labour of women for cooking, cleaning, caring and doing those chores which augment family resources (like collection of fuel, fodder, water, looking after live-stock, poultry farming and processing of agricultural goods) is regarded as elastic by the IMF stabilisation and the World Bank SAP. The reduction in paid work for women makes women hunt for the cheapest resources for sustenance of the household. Casual employment of urban working class women in the organised manufacturing industry (textile is a glaring example) has forced thousands of women to eke out their subsistence through petty trading activities (officially known as an 'informal sector' occupation).

The SAP has forced working women into the unorganised sector, thus depriving them of their trade-union rights. By doing this, the women fall outside protective labour laws such as The Maternity Benefits Act (1961), The Employees State Insurance Scheme, Factories Act (1948), Equal Remuneration Act (1976), The Bombay Shops and Establishment Act (1984), The Plantation Labour Act and the Child Labour (Prohibition and Regulation) Act, 1976.

In response to imposition of structural adjustment programmes and stabilisation policies coupled with neo-liberal globalisation at the behest of International Monitory Institute, women's movements across the national boundaries have to challenge the Neo-liberal Development Paradigm. World Social Forum and Regional Social Fora have provided democratic platforms for reflections on a just, sustainable and caring Global Economy. These deliberations have convinced us that **Another World is Possible** and globalisation also bears the promise and possibilities of furthering women's rights and well-being. Gender sensitive strategic thinking can address practical and strategic gender needs of women. For example, more women in more areas of economic activities can be gainfully and justly employed. Information technology can enable women throughout the globe to share strategies, successes and stress-free and safe life. We should not forget that there is North in the South and there is South in the North. So we must strive for global solidarity and sisterhood of all women who are oppressed and exploited, degraded and dehumanised by the patriarchal class structure. Universal labour standards ensuring just wages, occupational safety and social security must be the central issues of the women's movement.

## REFERENCES

Vibhuti Patel (2002). *Women's Challenges of the New Millennium*, Gyan Publications, Delhi, 2002.

Vibhuti Patel and Manisha Karne (2006). *The Macro Economic Policies and the Millennium Development Goals*, Gyan Publications, Delhi, 2006.

# Gender Inequality in Education

*Nishta Paul*

2

## Introduction

Epitomising the life of '*sacrifice*' and '*hardship*' is the story of a young girl, Bina Kumari of Baridhi village in Bihar. Forced to drop out of school at the tender age of 9 years, she stays at home, undertaking the care of her siblings and other domestic responsibilities. As ironic as it may seem, Bina's father actually claims very high motivation for the education of boys and girls. His eldest daughter remains out of school, while her younger siblings are all enrolled in primary schools. Her future, of a marriage at the tender age of 13 years has been determined, and little hope remains for any form of independence from this life of labour, for the little girl.[1]

The plight of the underprivileged girl child in India should not be analysed in isolation. Instead the study must be attempted in context of the interplay of several historical, social, cultural and political factors. Examining the historical context of the problem of the declining status of the girl child, it may be ascertained that the over all position of women began declining during the Brahminical period, when several restraints were imposed on them restricting their mobility and confining them to the domestic spheres. Conditions in the subsequent centuries deteriorated. It was during the end of the nineteenth century, when the need for education of women was realized. Measures adopted during the later years, proved insufficient and at the time of independence the government was faced with the formidable task of educating a large section of the uneducated, illiterate population.

As widely accepted the nation has legal and political commitments to achieve gender equality in education. Recognising the moral and instrumental value of the right to education, it was included as a fundamental right within the constitutional framework of India.[2] Examining the special position of the girl child with regard to discrimination faced by the girl child in enrolling and attending schools, the problem was found rooted in a wider socio-economic and cultural context. Therefore, the government undertook several policies to improve accessibility to education, at least during the early years of the child's life. It has been widely perceived that bridging the gender gap in education will provide an effective solution to the problem of gender equality. The researcher seeks to re-examine this contention in course of the paper.

India has been successful on the front of ensuring gender parity, through the provision of basic facilities, necessary for the purpose of ensuring full enrollment of the girl child. To improve accessibility in the right to education, the government needs to undertake concerted efforts to target special groups. In this paper, the researcher has sought to examine gender parity and gender equality based concepts. The primary argument addressed in the second section of this paper is that in exploring the dimensions of the education right, a broader view must be adopted. The researcher asserts that the right to education, through ensuring the access to education is the first aspect of the issue of gender equality. The larger framework that draws upon the rights agenda must be allowed due consideration in the process of policy decision-making, to ensure complete justice to the girl child.

## SECTION I

### Gender 'Inequality' in Education

Conceptual debates on gender inequality in Indian society have been prevalent for a very long time. To come to a conclusive definition of 'Gender Inequality' is problematic, primarily because it is difficult to quantify inequality. This concern is further enhanced as the fact arises, that the status of inequalities changes over a period of time. It is in this context, that gender differentials become important.

## Measuring Gender Inequality

Gender differentials in health, education and employment, such as the *Gender-related Development Index* (GDI) and the *Gender Empowerment Measure* (GEM)[3] used as indicators of gender bias, are essentially measurable manifestations of gender inequality.[4] These indicators do provide a useful insight of the scenario of gender inequality, though there are deeper concerns regarding the gendering of roles that must be kept in mind.

Unequal gender relations may arise due to domestic violence, stress as well as cultural practices of exclusion. These factors, not only promote unequal gender relations but also impact gender related development outcomes. It has been argued that irrespective of the overall socio-economic background, in most cases views on femininity come in conflict with the goals of education, which are directed towards *survival* and *unity*. Although education emphasizes on independence and promotes a spirit of enquiry, traditional notions of femininity seek; to create a docile and submissive character of the girl child.[5] Typically a girl child is assigned with home-oriented tasks, which include cooking, cleaning and taking care of young ones. Studies indicate that these attitudes were more rigid in North India, where both domestic and economic responsibilities compelled the girl child to drop out of school.[6]

## Achieving Gender Parity in Primary Education

Goal 3 (*Target 4*), of the *Millennium Development Goals*, explicitly provides that gender disparity must be eliminated by the year 2015, at all levels of education. A special emphasis has been laid on eliminating gender inequalities at the level of primary and secondary school education.[7] Recent statements of development goals have drawn a clearer distinction between achieving outcomes of gender parity and gender equality in education. Achieving gender parity in education, in terms of relative stocks of education held by men and women has been emphasized upon, as it affects growth prospects, for India.

Improving the educational level of the girl child has a favourable impact on economic growth as well.[8]

### Reducing the Gender Gap

The report of the *11th Plan Working Group Report*, has reported a reduction in the gender gap at the primary stage. Statistics indicate that gender gap in terms of enrollment has improved from 5.5 points in 2002-03 to 4.2 points during 2005-06.[9] It is pertinent to note that the gender-gap for marginalized groups of society, specifically the schedule class and schedule tribe group is significantly higher. In fact the gender gap for the Schedule Tribe groups, as of 2004-05 stands at 6.1 which is almost 1.5 points greater than the gender gap for all groups.[10] Rural girls belonging to these disadvantaged communities constitute a bulk of the illiterate population. They suffer from the triple jeopardy of '*caste, class, and sex*'.[11]

### Increasing Enrollment Levels of the Girl Child

Achieving gender parity in education has been identified as an essential attribute to fulfilling the goal of Universalisation of Education. Progress on enrollment of girl child in education is an important indicator on the status and prospects for achieving gender parity. Recent statistics reveal that enrollment rates for the girl child, as a group at the level of primary school in India, have improved from 43 per cent to approximately 47 per cent during a period of three years.[12] Provision of the mid-day meal scheme and other supplementary support schemes such as anganwadis have encouraged parents to send their children to schools. States such as Rajasthan, North Karnataka as well as Chhattisgarh reported an improvement in girl's enrollment on account of provision of hot cooked meals in primary schools.[13] The low improvement in the enrollment rate at the upper primary level is still a cause for concern.

### Focused Interventions: Gender Parity in Education

The PROBE study conducted in 5 specific states in North India, reports that a significant percentage of parents are interested in the education of the girl child. The response of parents is not uniform however, suggesting that attitudes of parents affecting girl child enrollment in schools, differ not only on an economic basis but also on a regional and social basis. In the case of the boy child, the employment object is a powerful motivation for parents to ensure the enrollment of the boy child in schools. An economic argument for female disadvantage in primary education is that the opportunity costs of the girl child's time are greater as she spends a higher time on domestic work as compared to boys. This argument explains the lower enrollments and greater rates of drop-outs among girls, especially in the upper primary stages.[14]

## Social Dimension of the Problem

Reaching a social consensus on the issue of necessity for the education of the girl child can act as an impetus to increasing the participation of girl children in primary schools. This relies on the premise that parents' views on education do not indicate their independent stand; rather it is a reflection of the views of the community in which they reside.[15] Parental attitudes towards girl child education, especially, are highly interdependent. The role of the community in promoting the value of education assumes greater importance. For example in Kerala, parents take it as self-evident that going to school is what is expected of children. Therefore, enrollment rates are particularly high in the state.[16]

## Gender Division of Labour

Deeply rooted in the complex dichotomy of male versus female role, it can be argued that certain feminine characteristics and qualities are associated with the girl child. This gender typing of tasks begins very early in life.[17] The commonly perceived roles that women are expected to play have strong implications for female education. Since the girl child is perceived to undertake domestic work in her role as a housewife, the social expectations from female education appear 'pointless' to many parents. Taking from this assumption, Dreze asserts that benefits from female education are less clearly perceived and less strongly valued as compared to returns from male education.[18]

Efforts directed towards motivating parents and informing them about the need for sending every child to attend school, indicate the possibility of a social consensus on the need for the girl child to attend school. In this respect the researcher has proposed community involvement and community based action at the grass-roots level, as necessary to ensure successful participation of the girl child.

## Focused Interventions: Recommendations

Girl child education has been identified as an area of key focus in recent times, however, concerted efforts need to be made on pursuing more group/communities and locations specific policies. The situation of the girl child across the group is not uniform. Examining the statistical data obtained on the status of enrollment of girl children could reflect on the existing *caste-gender-spatial* perspectives.

- ***Schedule Castes and Schedule Tribes***: Girls belonging to clearly identify disadvantaged social groups such as the schedule castes, schedule tribe, minority groups as well as other backward classes face an inherent disadvantage in terms of accessibility by virtue of their position.[19] In fact, female child belonging to certain tribal communities have been identified as groups facing the greatest discrimination.
- ***Rural Urban Divide***: The rural/urban divide is especially significant for female child as well as adolescent. This relates to community perceptions, parental attitudes, as well as perceived economic benefits of education.[20] Parents in fact prefer to send their girl child to sub-standard government schools providing education free of cost, whereas the boy child is often enrolled in private schools, which normally charge fees. This can be traced to the fact that education is treated as an *investment*, which may bring better employment prospects for the boy. The motivation for getting the girl child married is find her better marriage prospects. Disadvantaged castes however admit that finding educated husbands for their daughters was difficult, and therefore chose to engage their young daughters in the household work.

Motivation levels of parents, in response to girl child education, have significantly changed over the past few decades.

Education is viewed as necessary for the girl child, in order to equip her with knowledge and the requisite skills to face life. The challenge for the government lies in understanding the situation of different socio-economic groups, as well as the hardest to reach groups, in both urban and rural areas. Special needs for these groups must be mapped and plans must be outlined accordingly. The state must give due consideration for funding and strengthening the formal school system for the girl child, in order to ensure that girls have a greater chance for completing at least primary school education.

## SECTION II

### Moving Towards Gender Equality

Gender parity has been described as a concept that focuses more on quantitative aspects, such as the relative proportion of girls and boys participating in primary schools.[21] The focus is, therefore, on the aspects of access to education, which is the first step towards achieving equality in terms of participation. Gender equality encompasses a larger framework that draws upon the rights agenda. In this regard the researcher proposes a rights based argument, for achieving gender equality. This actually gains prominence in the light of the argument, that a committed shift towards the creation of gender equality in education can create a wide range of associated benefits for economic growth.

The researcher has proposed that effective measures must be undertaken to ensure not only the fulfillment of the right to education, but also include the dimensions of the right within education as well as the right through education. The researcher has proposed that the wider scope of this approach, in the context of ensuring a good education, is viewed as a powerful force for bringing about wider social and economic changes.

### Right to Education

The 86th amendment to the Indian Constitution, during the year 2002, recognized the Right to Education of a child between the ages of 6-14 years, as a fundamental right, within the ambit of the right to life, within the scope of Article 21.[22] The state has defined its responsibility of providing free and compulsory education to all children, within the specified age group, indicating its commitment to the fulfillment of the Millennium Development Goals.

**Ensuring Access with Equity**

The thrust of the right to education, as clearly outlined in the Right to Education Bill, 2005 has been to ensure equitable participation in the process of primary schooling. In this context both access and equity become important concepts.[23] The state has the responsibility to provide for access to primary education through adopting the rights based equity-oriented approach.

In context of the right to education, it may be stated that the goal of equity is ensuring equality of opportunity, which implies creation of opportunities for learning for all those endowed with similar capabilities. Co-relating the concepts of equity and access, in respect of the education of the girl child the following propositions have been made.

- ***Physical Accessibility***: The supply of physical infrastructure is the first step in ensuring increased access to primary schools. Efforts in improving accessibility must be directed towards providing greater number of classrooms as well as teachers. The problems of physical accessibility are significantly low, the primary argument has been to identify select districts and states where the enrollment rates are low due to inadequacy of infrastructure or distance related accessibility problems.[24] The state should follow a uniform policy in respect of basic infrastructural requirement.
- ***Creating a Physical Environment***: Advancing the argument for uniformity in access to education it can be stated that the state's role extends to providing gender-aware infrastructure for ensuring girl's full participation in schooling. Proper latrine facilities especially separate toilets for boys and girls must be recognized as a fundamental requirement.[25] It's necessary to provide adequate sanitation facilities in order to ensure maintenance of hygiene as well as prevent overcrowding, due to increased enrollments in

the schools. Countries such as Bangladesh made remarkable progress in closing gender gaps by ensuring basic conditions of sanitation and provision of drinking water facilities were satisfied.

- ***Improvement in State Functioning***: The first two dimensions of the right to education, relating to creation of infrastructure have been adequately discussed.[26] Changing state practices wherein patronage based placement policies are replaced with policies based on merit can create a change within the system. The role of the state must be recognised and improvements in state run educational institutions must be envisaged for ensuring equality of educational opportunity.

## Rights in Education

The second dimension of the education right, the right in education assumes importance in relating equity and quality concerns.[27] This can be achieved by actually improving the quality of schooling experience for the girl child. The larger objective has been defined as creating education institutions that are places of learning, growth as well as empowerment for the girl child. A dual approach has been suggested herein to ensure the fulfillment of the conditions mentioned above:

- ***Creating a Safe and Equitable School Environment***: The role of the teacher, in creating a gender sensitive learning environment, cannot be further emphasized upon. The teacher acts as the interface between the education system and the learner, and therefore is entrusted with the huge responsibility of not only ensuring that learning takes place within the environment, but becomes accountable for creating a secure environment within which arouses the interest of the girl child in the learning process.

Change in the attitude of the teacher through greater gender awareness and sensitization is a prerequisite to achieving this condition. Teacher training processes must emphasise on addressing issues of gender awareness.[28] If these mechanisms do not induce a change in the behaviour of the teacher in the classroom, then the need for impositions of controls or forms of state interventions through stricter monitoring control becomes necessary.

- *Sexism in the Curriculum*: The Class – 3 Hindi textbook used in Uttar Pradesh, uses illustrations to represent various professions. Men are represented as doctors, engineers, teachers and kings. On the other hand women are represented in subordinate positions, owing to standardization of feminine roles.[29] This form or gender role stereotyping reflected in the school curriculum reinforces conservative views about the role of women in society. As the education imparted in a school environment affects the perceptions of the child, it can be stated that such gender stereotyping can undermine the confidence of the girl child and lead her to develop a dim view of her capabilities. The first step to ensuring gender equality must therefore emphasise upon imparting education that forces the girl child to question her position in society, and eventually allows her to assert her independence, in the interest of responsible decision-making.

**Right Through Education**

What is entailed by the requirement of Equity? Examining aspects of equity as proposed earlier, it requires fulfilling the requirement of equality of opportunities as well as equality of outcomes. Provision of equitable quality schooling is expected to produce equitable outcomes in terms of achievement in education. This dimension of rights goes beyond the ambit of provision of creation of capacity and improvement of quality of education, for ensuring gender equality.[30] It is proposed that gender equality can be affected only when the outcomes produced through the process of education, enable overcoming gender related barriers in all spheres of life for women. Furthermore, enhancing the awareness levels of the girl child, can affect her participation in social, economic and political processes, resulting in a more equitable society.

In fact statistics reveal that where gender participation is equal girls tend to out perform boys. However, they are unable to convert this academic edge over boys into greater equality in other spheres of life.[31] Encouraging the pro-active participation of the girl child creates a sense of confidence as well as independence and proves successful in affecting gender participation in society.

## Conclusion

***Hunnar*** (skill), ***hisab*** (accounts) and ***himmat*** (determination and self-will), as proposed by the father of a young Muslim girl, have been identified as all necessary ingredients for the development and successful participation of the girl child, achievable only through education. This is the true reflection of hope and aspirations of new generation parents residing in rural and urban area.[32]

The state has an extremely important role to play in enabling the creation of a suitable environment for promoting gender equality through education. The Indian government has undertaken legislative and policy reforms, in respect of making investments in the redistribution of resources. Necessary resources for female education have been targeted, and special measures have been undertaken in order to reduce inequity in education.

The existence of a supportive legal framework is very crucial to improvement in equality in education. A compulsory schooling legislation is necessary, however it will not suffice, unless the government provides more broadly based rights protection.[33] Women must enjoy non-discrimination and protection of their fundamental freedoms, ensuring fulfillment of their economic and social justice. Mainstreaming of women within institutions, can be achieved by including their specific interests within legislations, policies and programmes, will ensures that men and women benefit equally.[34]

To conclude the researcher recommends that the performance of duties as well as obligations of the government, in respect of the rights relating to attainment of education, arising within the human rights framework, must be made mandatory. Need for the implementation of the right to education, would entail immediate measures to be taken by ensuring universal access and availability of education, even in the most remote parts of the country. The larger objective of the right must be to ensure that the framework of the right is adapted to create a suitable environment, leading to the safe and healthy growth of the girl child.

## NOTES

1. The Probe Team, 'Public Report on Basic Education in India', 31 (1st ed., New Delhi: Oxford University Press, 1999).
2. EFA Global Monitoring Report - 2005 (Washington D.C.: World Bank, 2005), www.worldbank.org.
3. These are important indicators of Gender Bias popularized through the UNDP Human Development Report of 1995.
4. Ratna Sudarshan, 'Educational Status of Girls and Women', *The Gender Gap in Basic Education*, 39 (Ed. Rekha Wazir, London: Sage Publications, 2000).
5. *Ibid.* at 90.
6. *Supra* note 5.
7. *Supra* note 2, at xii.
8. UNESCO, EFA Global Monitoring Report - 2004, www.efareport.unesco.org.
9. Ministry of Human Resource Development, Chapter on Elementary Education (SSA & Girls Education) for the 11th Plan: *Working Group Report*, 5, www.planningcommission.nic.in.
10. *Id.*
11. Sujata Reddy, 'The Social Context of Elementary Education in Rural India', *Azim Premji Foundation Report*, May 2007.
12. *Supra* note 8.
13. *Supra* note 11, at 3.
14. *Supra* note 11, at 38.
15. *Supra* note 1, at 23
16. *Supra* note 1, at 24
17. *Supra* note 11, at 41.
18. *Supra* note 1, at 41.
19. *Supra* note 1.
20. *Supra* note 1.
21. *Supra* note 5.

22. *Supra* note 5.
23. *Supra* note 1.
24. *Supra* note 8.
25. *Supra* note 8.
26. *Supra* note 5.
27. *Supra* note 8.
28. *Supra* note 8
29. *Supra* note 1.
30. *Supra* note 8.
31. *Supra* note 8.
32. *Supra* note 5.
33. *Supra* note 8
34. *Supra* note 8.

# Women and Housing Rights*

*Vibhuti Patel*

3

## Introduction

Housing Rights have been major concern of the women's movement in India for over two decades. When women's groups started providing support to women in distress, it was relatively easier to find jobs and school-admission for children. The most difficult task was to get an accommodation for women victims of violence, desertion, rejection from natal or matrimonial family and cheating by their relatives.

Women's Movement has been doing advocacy work about housing rights for women since 1980. Says Ms. Neera Adarkar, an Architect and a trustee of *Majlis*, Bombay, "In the beginning, I saw myself as an architect. But after being a practicing architect, who was dealing with building construction activities for a number of years, I have started critiquing my profession. Housing and other environments with which we worked have to follow certain norms as they affect our lives on a daily basis. We take our built environment (house-community-city) for granted. We think that this environment exists, but actually, it is built by men. We have to ask ourselves questions such as,

'Do we as women, utilize space differently?'

'Can we create environments which are more gender sensitive?'

'Can we make policy makers and planners who are working at the state level understand the politics of built environment and gender rules?'

---

* http://www.europe-solidaire.org

'What are our alternatives to the existing approach adopted by Sight and Service Schemes (SSS) and Slum Rehabilitation Schemes (SRS)?'

'What interventions can we make in the city planning which involves physical access, economic access and social access?'"

**Women's Right to Housing (WRH):** WRH is linked with women's right in property, land and inheritance. As primary user of housing, women's stakes and requirements are the highest in housing. For women, beyond shelter, housing is a place of employment, a place for social interaction, a place for childcare and a refuge from social instability and sexual violence.

**Special Needs of Female Headed Households (WHHs):** In the peaceful areas of India, 1/10th of the households are headed by divorced, deserted and single women. In our country, in the conflict prone areas, over 30 per cent households are headed by women. In WHHs women shoulder main economic responsibilities including house hunting. Even if they have money, they face hurdles while looking out for a rented place or a house on an ownership basis. Nearly one-third of households worldwide are now headed by women; in certain parts of Africa and Latin America, as many as 45 per cent are FHH. The households headed by women tend to be poorer than male headed households. United Nations Centre for Human Settlements (UNCHS) (Habitat) estimates that at least 600 million people in the cities of developing countries live in shelters that are life—or health—threatening.

**Women's Rights to Stay in Parental and Matrimonial Homes:** In the last 20 years, many women have filed petitions in the High Courts and the Supreme Court of India demanding wife's right to live in the matrimonial home and daghter's right to stay in the ancestral home. As per Mitakshara laws applicable in the Hindu Code, only sons get coparsonary rights over ancestral property as they are considered *Karta*. Lata Mittal challenged Mitakshara laws applicable to Hindu daughters who are deprived of right to stay in the ancestral home.

**Housing and Women's Identity:** Women's identity is entwined with a house but housing's identity as a capital investment and the largest outlay in the household budget lies with male head of the household. Whether women are or aren't property owners, their place of sphere is considered to be within the house. Even, this cult of domesticity does not help women as it perpetuates low status of women. Market economy devalues domestic work and the mainstream planners and policy makers consider it 'non-work' and invisibalise women's housing concerns.

**Gender Bias and Housing Problems:** The gendered construct of social and economic relations within and outside the household and deeply entrenched patriarchal attitudes in the civil society discriminate against women in virtually every aspect of housing, be it policy development, entitlement in government projects, control over household resources, right of inheritance and ownership and even the construction of housing.

**Emerging Issues:** There is a need to focus on housing in terms of "personal meanings" as well as affordability, women's role and the housing industry. The state must take affirmative action to empower women in exercising their housing rights because men as property owners enjoy privileged position and control housing delivery system. Moreover, general subordination of women is also reflected in women's lack of representation in higher echelons political bodies. Societal restrictions reinforce women's status as second-class citizens. As a result, women professionals in the housing industry i.e., engineers, architects and agents have to sub-serve the interests of male-dominated construction industry.

**Gender Aware Approach:** Gender-neutral approach in housing goes against women's interest. Hence there is a need to introduce gender aware approach in housing that takes women's strategic and practical needs, concerns and rights into consideration. For that, we will have to sensitize all stake groups in the housing industry i.e., land surveyors, builders, developers, designers, financiers, mortgage bankers, lawyers, credit unions, government officers, material suppliers, real estate brokers, appraisers, contractors, interior decorators, gardeners, landscape architects and cooperative societies. In the language of economics, both, supply side-production, construction, management, maintenance, rehabilitation and the demand side community groups, consumer forum and cooperative societies should be sensitized about women's housing rights.

**Gender Audit of Syllabi for Engineering, Architecture and Interior Designing:** Public-private split in the syllabi of construction related academic disciplines needs to be questioned. The syllabus should emphasize that as a physical structure, the house is a site for multi-tasking-house work (cooking, cleaning, caring), home-making and wage-labour for majority of women all over the world. A house layout influences and affects gender roles among household members and therefore mirrors change in society's concept of the family. Designing of house should promote the ethos of shared housework by men and women members of the household.

**International Human Rights Law on Security of Tenure:** A person is said to have a secure tenure if he/she is protected from being removed arbitrarily and involuntarily from their homes and lands. Tenure is secure if it is protected by legislation rather than protected merely through customs and traditions.

**Threat to Women's Security of Tenure (WST):** Circumstances and conditions that threaten WST are:

- **Gender biased laws** preventing women from owning, inheriting, purchasing, leasing, renting, bequeathing housing, land and property.
- **Judicial Interpretation of the Law:** No explicit forbidding of WRH in gender-neutral laws, still they create obstacles for WRH because of male-chauvinistic interpretation of the gender neutral laws. General statements are considered to be applicable to only men.
- **Land and Housing Systems** as they grant titles to private property to "Heads of Households" who are often deemed to be men.
- **Customary Laws, Traditions, Attitudes:** Many cultures and customs don't grant women's independent existence. In several cultures women staying alone, without male protection are punished severely due to sexist attitudes.

Customary laws are not codified. In polygamous and polyandrous communities, shared community values go against individual women leading independent life.

**Domestic Violence:** Domestic violence challenges security of tenure of women by generating fear, tension, insecurity among women victims and their minor children. Violation of WRH can be both the cause and the consequence of violence against women, particularly in case of domestic violence.

### Financial and Material Barriers

Major hurdles faced by women in the housing market are due to gender-biased policies in financing for housing, availability of services, material and infrastructure, affordability, habitability, accessibility, location and cultural adequacy to handle political economy of housing. Women face major difficulties in securing loans for purchase of good quality housing. It is not easy for single women or WHH to get rental housing. Even if they manage to get rented homes, they have to face harassment of various sorts. Unmarried single women are perceived as threat to sexual morality. In the absence of old age homes for women, the plight of women senior citizens is deplorable. Many destitute women start staying on the pavements or railway platforms.

**Indian NGOs and WRH**: Two decades of Debate—Two positions:

1. **WRH independent of male ownership and control** because women's land-use priorities are different from that of men.
2. **Joint Titles**—majority of poor masses hardly manage to have one house. Hence, separate house for women is a non-issue.

The Felt Need:

Need for a training manual to deal with the modalities of attaining WRH.

Experiences of SEWA and SPARC:

*SEWA*: inclusion of women's name in the title to property before granting loans for housing. As monetary benefits accrue to the family, the husband/father and family members accept the proposal of joint titles to land/house.

*SPARC*: Supports Mahila Milan (MM), network of pavement dwellers, assists MM to get recognition and support from the settlements, skills and training, makes resources available for the low cost housing.

**State and Civil Society Initiatives**

Progressive states have empowered women by granting housing rights, e.g. Building societies in Sweden and England; Unions in Germany; Self-help Groups & Cooperative Enterprises in Canada, Central and Latin America, Africa and Asia.

The enlightened nation states accept societal responsibility for women's housing and the rest live it to individual women to fend for themselves.

**Witch-hunting of Women Exercising Right to Housing**

- *Bhootali* (Maharashtra), *Dayeen* (Bihar)—Widowed/ divorcee Dalit/Tribal women.
- *In the latest Koombha Mela* 60000 women were deserted by their family members.
- ***Sarpanch, Talati and Tahasildars*** taking advantage of illiterate women.
- In Algeria and West African countries FFHs were burnt. International Committee of Women Living Under Muslim Laws.

**Crucial Conventions for WRH**

- The Universal Declaration of Human Rights, 1948
- The Elimination of All Forms of Discrimination Against Women (CEDAW), 1979
- The housing rights of Refugees, 1951
- The Housing Rights of Indigenous People (Not yet adopted)

They are DIRECTED AT GOVERNMENTS

## The UN on Forced Eviction

"Women...and other vulnerable individuals and groups suffer disproportionately from the practice of forced eviction. Women in all groups are especially vulnerable given the extent of statutory and other forms of discrimination which often apply in relation to property rights (including home ownership) or rights of access to property or accommodation, and their particular vulnerability to acts of violence and sexual abuse when they are rendered homeless" (UN Committee on Economic, Social and Cultural Rights, Sixteenth Session, 1997).

**Displaced Population due to Natural as well as Man-made Disasters:** Women victims of natural disasters such as floods, earthquakes and social disasters such as caste, communal, ethnic conflicts and war.

There are three approaches adopted by people-oriented architects to handle the issue of shelter:

1. *Legal approach*: It deals with ownership rights and tenure, right to matrimonial property of married women, right to ancestral home for an unmarried daughter. Hema Dandekar's study of Charcop's Sight and Service Scheme reveals that in this scheme there is no bar against women owning a house. Loan facilities given for buying a flat depend upon the repaying capacity of women.

2. *Social approach*: House as a unit is related to family structure. It gets reflected in a housing policy. Women and Shelter Group had done advocacy work in these regards. After 1993, some of us made interventions in changing the scenario. We took responsibility to reconstruct the destroyed homes in the riot-affected areas near Mahim utilising Times of India funds. For this we had to run from pillar to post. We had to face an extremely communal attitude of the entire bureaucracy. After three-four months, we managed to get a plot of land/*pattas* in Dindoshi. We had to meet the collector a couple of times to see to it that the *pattas* given to riot-affected people are in the name of women because women use these *pattas* for subsistence while men use them as commodity in the market.

3. *Physical planning of a house*: Patriarchal values get reflected in the physical planning of a house. Rules and regulations, by-laws have been stipulated by the Urban Development Department. In BDD chawls, all spaces allocated for community have been used by men where women feel constrained. In slum projects and sight and service projects, kitchen and toilets are clubbed together. 'Kitchen and toilet' are treated as isolated spaces while women beneficiaries of slum development projects don't like it. Architects from MHADA don't listen to the women's point of view. Ventilation is not considered to be all that important. A small study of slums and chawls in Bombay showed that women emphasized a separate space in the community that is exclusively used for washing clothes and making *chapatis* (Collective kitchen). *Nagari Nivara* Trust headed by Mrunal Gore and Baburao Sawant is dealing with a mass housing project for five thousand people. In this, we have made a provision for a space in the community, which is exclusively used, for women's activities. Even, the ownership titles are made in the name of women. There is a need for a shelter home for women in distress and a *creche* within each plot. SPARC, Bombay has managed to get *balwadi* and community hall included in their project areas. As per the FSI regulation, while zoning and city planning, 'public' is separated from 'private' but in actual reality women's lives are not compartmentalised like this. We need to critique the existing housing policies, demystify technical language and conduct surveys to understand how women's lives are affected by the urban development. To bring changes in the by-laws which are gender sensitive and people friendly, the lawyers and architect will have to work in collaboration. We need to raise consciousness among the students of architecture, more than fifty per cent of who are women. When I ask the students of architecture the question regarding home-based professions, they identify women home-based professionals as providers of *crèche* facilities, dance-teachers or beauticians, while male home-based professionals are identified as engineers, doctors, chartered accountants and management consultants. Many women architects are going to be home-based professionals and they have to redesign the existing patterns of houses, keeping in mind both house-work and professional duties. The same applies to their women clients

who are shouldering double burden. Advantages of keeping kitchen-space near drawing/living room are many:

(a) Women don't feel isolated from rest of the happenings in the outside world.

(b) All members of the family start taking interest in kitchen cabinet. They get encouraged to share housework.

(c) It ensures cleanliness of the kitchen area, as it is visible.

## Conclusion

Women's housing needs must be understood from the point of view of women's rights to dignified life. They should not face any discrimination in exercising their housing rights due to their caste, race, age, religion and ethnicity. State and civil society initiatives must facilitate the process of women's empowerment through exercising WHRs. The local self-government bodies should reserve 10 per cent of all houses/flats/industrial units/ shops in the market places for women. Schools of Architecture, Engineering Colleges and Institutions for Interior Designing should organize capacity building workshops and training programmes for women. Gender sensitization of the decision-makers in the housing industry and the elected representatives of the mainstream political bodies should be given top priority. For formulation of gender-sensitive policies, experts on the subject should be inducted in the apex bodies of urban, rural and tribal housing projects.

## REFERENCES

Jeemol Unni (1999). "Property Rights of Women: Case for Joint Titles to Agricultural Land and Urban Housing", *Economic and Political Weekly*, Mumbai, May 22-28.

Neha Madhiwala (2005). "Right to Shelter and Development for Women", SAMYUKTA, Thiruvananthapuram, Vol. V, No. 1, January.

Vibhuti Patel (2002). *Women's Challenges in the New Millennium*, Gyan Publications, Delhi.

Website— www.cohre.org.

# The Practice of Patriarchal Democracy in Post-Colonial India: A Study on Women's Reservation Bill for the Representation of Women in the Indian Parliament

4

*Bhabani Shankar Nayak* and
*Geeta Sinha*

## Introduction

History of the world undoubtedly reveals that the quest for liberty, equality, justice and fraternity, was one of the defining events of the twentieth century history for decolonization and establishment of democracy. The Indian Freedom Movement against British colonialism was a part of this larger philosophy of decolonization and democracy. The principles of liberty, equality, justice and fraternity had dominated the ideas of Indian freedom struggle. This struggle reiterated the commitment towards the empowerment of the socially and economically marginalized people of India; i.e., the women, dalits and tribal populations. The ethos of this struggle was to bring these disadvantaged groups into the mainstream and achieve an egalitarian order in its bicameral parliamentary form of democracy. The legacy and visions of Indian freedom movement was reflected in the post-colonial Indian Constitution[1] that guarantees equal rights to all citizens, irrespective of race, gender, religion, and other considerations. The Constitution of India not only laid the foundation stone for a democratic set up in India but also prohibits discrimination on the basis of race, ethnicity, gender, caste, and religion. It also allows universal adult franchise, thereby making the Indian democracy representative and the largest in the world as well. The Constitution of India has also provided "Directive Principles of State Policy"[2] and made it obligatory guidance for the government to ensure these ideas while formulating public policy.

However, even after more than half century of independence and fifty-five years of adoption of Indian Constitution, the visions reflected in the 'Preamble to the Constitution of India' has remained but a daydream until now and the promise has not yet been achieved in many fields. In the process of parliamentary democratic practice, the objectives and visions of the Indian Constitution have largely been ignored. The history of practice of democracy in India certainly reveals that one of the major failures of Indian parliamentary democracy is the quest for gender equality and justice which was one of the defining events of our time. Although there has been a growth of political consciousness among the women in India, Indian democracy has failed by and large to change the patriarchal political institutions and its culture into democratic one.

This paper is based on the secondary data and an extensive literature review on the women's empowerment and representation in Indian democracy. The paper is divided into three parts to focus my study and put forth my arguments in a systematic way. The first part reveals the marginalised social, economic and political condition of women in the post-colonial India. This will lead into the second part, which deals with the essence of political power through the representation of women in Indian democracy for the empowerment of women. Special attention will be paid to a reflection on the reality of women's representation in the Indian Parliament from 1952 to 2004 to locate under representation of women in Indian Parliamentary democracy. This section argues that a special provision in the form of reservation of seats in the Indian Parliament is necessary for the equal representation of women, which can make Indian democracy truly representative of gender. The third and final part will locate the patriarchal nature on the debates on women's reservation bill, which has yet to be passed by the Parliament of India.

## The Condition of Women in Post-Colonial India

The condition of women in India in both the colonial and post-colonial periods has always been an issue of concern for the state and any development institution. Yet, even in the twenty-first century, the condition of women in India is still deplorable. The mere mention of 'women's issues' in the Indian context conjures up images of dowry, domestic violence, sati, child marriage, sexual harassment, rape, widowhood, witchcraft, incest, wife-beating, discrimination, rights, quotas, gender, sexism and feminism. The list of problems and issues of women seems endless in India. Although the post-colonial Indian State managed to bring remarkable change for women in many fields[3] but it has failed by and large to transform the Indian patriarchal society[4] to a gender sensitive society. The basic and underlying issue of equality, liberty and justice in relation to gender invariably gets ignored. In this way the discrimination remains a fact of life for women in India. The disadvantageous condition of women is also reflected in the political sphere. The powerlessness of women in the family hierarchy of India and existing gender biases restrict mobility, education and acquisition of skills, ensuring that they can't earn an adequate income.[5]

The economic deprivation is putting women in socially disadvantageous positions. These issues are nothing but the outcomes of the existence of feudal and patriarchal society. The disadvantaged condition of the women in India has led various activists and development agencies[6] to work for women's empowerment. Women's empowerment consists of four dimensions, each of which are equally important: the cognitive (critical understanding of one's reality), the psychological (feeling of self-esteem), the political (awareness of power inequalities and the ability to organize and mobilize) and the economic (power to generate independent income) (Stromquist, 1995 cited in Stomquist, 2002:23). It was the felt need of the activists and development agencies to work for the emancipation of women through some affirmative action.

One of the affirmative actions to address the issue of women's empowerment was to bring forward the women explicitly in the field of politics, which would also trigger their empowerment in different aspects. One of the major focuses is on the subtle strategies of politics, whereby women seek small but important changes in their personal lives. The triumphs in the field of political power increases 'personal power and power within' that can lead to individual empowerment. Ultimately it leads to the involvement in formal political activism, or 'power with and power to' as well (Desai as cited in Parpart et al., 2002:15-16). Lukes (1974:23-24) rejects "the notion that power is simply control over institutions and resources, and argues instead that power is wielded by controlling the agendas and thinking of others". The analysis moves further by rejecting the notion that power is something held by individuals or groups (and not others). It is argued that it permeates society, power is fluid and relational and exists in the everyday relationships of people and in institutions. Such power can lead to repressive practices that are expressed in disciplined bodies, actions and thoughts and discourses (Foucault, 1979, 1991; McNay, 1992).

Many feminists have questioned the concept of power as simply power over people and resources. An arena of politics that has been particularly important for understanding the concept of public power as power over has been that of the state. Feminist scholars have addressed this issue in terms of both the institutional power of state to privilege some (male) interest over others (female) and its capacity to maintain gender inequalities (MacKinnon, 1987). The inequality in the representation of women in politics gives space to the male-dominated politics to control the state powers, which further aggravates the gender differences.

**Position of Women in Indian Politics**

Women have not been able to make a remarkable position in the political sphere. They have been very much confined to the private arena, which is none other than the household and care sector (Devi, 2003). The involvement of women in politics not only leads towards gender sensitive society but also expands the horizon of politics. "By expanding the definition of politics to encompass both the public and the private spheres—indeed, by asserting that the two were mutually constitutive—feminists were able to show how women, far from being absent from the political sphere, were very much present as an 'absence'—that their exclusion from the public was necessary for the private and the public to be dominated by masculine interests and power. By insisting that 'experience' was an important starting point of knowledge, feminists have sought to contextualize the basis of politics itself" (Scott, 1992 as cited in Rai, 2002:2).

Furthermore, Table-1 and Table-3 (Annexure) reveals the increase in participation of women in different parliamentary elections. Comparatively women are contesting more in the elections than earlier but still there is a decline in the winning women candidates and thus representation in the parliament. Again, Table-2 and Graph-1 (Annexure) depicts the picture about the decline in voting percentage of women over the years. It has declined from 58.60 per cent in 1984 election to the 53.30 per cent in 14th Lok Sabha election during 2004 whereas Table-4 (Annexure) deals with the declining of percentage of women's vote and declining success rate of women in different elections. So, when it comes to leadership and winning in the elections then women are far behind from their counterpart male candidates. Even in the national political parties, women are far behind in decision-making and representation (Table-5). This reflects the patriarchal structure in Indian politics that is inherited from its society and culture. "Feminism offers that only politics can transform women's world into a more humane place and deal with global issues like equality, development and peace, because it asks the right questions: about power, about the links between the personal and the political; and because it cuts through race and class. Feminism implies consciousness of all the sources of oppression: race, class, gender, homophobia, and it resist them all. Feminism is the call for action" (CCIC, 1987:8).

In the political participation sphere, the women have essential roles to play particularly as voters and political representatives. A progressive step on the voting front was taken in the form of adult franchise, which was granted in the year 1937. The Constitution of India guarantees equal rights to men and women as voters and citizens. The picture is too grey when we look at the statistical data in terms of voters' participation, representation and leadership.

### Representation of Women in Indian Democracy

It is necessary to gain a solid understanding of the historical background of the basis of the current demand for one-third reservations for women in the state assemblies and in the Union Parliament. It is a necessary precondition for the justification behind the demand. Although the issue of the reservation for women originated during the nationalist movement against British colonialism during 1920s but the idea was put into the back seat. It was felt that these reservations for women would weaken the demand for universal adult franchise and the national movement for freedom as well. "The public, official language of politics especially before a colonial government had to be a language of equality and for fundamental rights of citizenship irrespective of sex, caste, religion or creed" (John, 2000:3 as cited in Raman, 2002).

The leading nationalistic organisations and women organisations like the All India Women's Conference, the Women's Indian Association and the National Council of Women in India, the Home Rule League, the Indian National Congress and the Muslim League had supported this opinion. In 1932, a Joint Memorandum on the Status of Indian Women from the all-India women's organisations to the Franchise Committee was set up at the end of the Second Round Table Conference and expressed their demand for universal adult franchise "irrespective of any property or literacy qualification, with no expedients such as nomination or reservation of seats" (Menon, 2000). This was again reiterated in the Karachi session of the Indian National Congress, 1931, which called for equality before the law, irrespective of religion, caste, creed or sex, universal adult franchise and women's right to vote, represent and hold public office.[7] However, the British administration sought to provide the right to vote for women in the urban areas. The British administration thought that the urban women could represent the women in India better. It was opposed by all nationalistic and women organisations (*ibid.*).

The colonial and post-colonial understandings of politics in India provide further insights for the study in gender and politics. Nationalist movement engaged with modernity took the form of a 'complex inter-relationship of contest and collusion between indigenous patriarchal norms and those held by (colonial) administrators (Sangari & Vaid, 1993:7). The 15th August,

1947 had heralded an era of independence and democracy in India after its long struggle against British colonialism. It is important to note that there was a consensus in the national movement on the issue of affirmative action or reservation for the women. There were many special provisions in the Indian Constitution[8] for the women's participation, representation and share in Indian democracy.

The setting up of the *Committee on the Status of Women in India (CSWI), 1974* was a landmark in the history and debate of women's representation in post-colonial Indian politics. The demand for greater representation of women in the political sphere was only considered after the setting of the CSWI. Before the set up of this Committee, the women's movement focused on the socio-economic issues of the women in India. This was regarded as the primary cause of the political marginalisation of women (Kishwar, 1996). "While the women's movement engaged with the project of redefining politics by imbuing it with feminist analysis based on the dictum 'the personal is political', this project focused largely on the improvement of access to participation in this redefined politics" (CWDS, 1994:19-25). The *CSWI* has submitted its report in 1976 that reflected two notes of dissident voices. The dominant opinion was opposed to the reservation for women. The basis of the opposition was that women's reservation in parliament would be retrogressive and would contradict the principles of equality guaranteed in the constitution. The arguments against reservations followed that reservations for women would be a departure from the constitutional principle of equality; women's interests cannot be isolated from the economic, social and political interests of groups, strata and classes in the society and linked to this was the notion that women are not a community, they are heterogeneous category; and systems of special representation for women may spiral into similar demands from other groups and interests and thus threatening national integration. The *Towards Equality Report* (1974) has also rejected the idea of reservation in political institutions on similar grounds, even though the Committee painted a bleak picture on the status of women and recommended a statutory for all women panchayats to look after the welfare of women (GOI, DSW, 1974).

Moreover, there was a strong argument in favour of women's reservation in the *CSWI Report (1974)*. The arguments in favour of reservations dealt with the difficulties of women to gain entry into male-dominated political parties that reservations for women would ensure a significant presence that would enable women to act as an important pressure group; and the presence of a critical mass of women would heighten the sense of responsibility among women, thus ensuring that women's interests would be adequately represented. This report also noted that in spite of equal rights and universal adult suffrage guaranteed by the Indian constitution, women's presence in the parliament had been declining steadily (*see,* Table-1) over these years. Thus, there is a strong base for the reservation of women in politics is a necessary precondition for the empowerment of women and achievement of gender equality and justice. As a result this, the *National Perspective Plan for Women* (1988-2000) by the *Department of Women and Child Welfare (DWCW)* has strongly recommended a 30 per cent reservation in the local government (Menon, 2000).

Despite more than five decades of Indian democracy, the share of women in the Union Parliament has not exceeded eight per cent (*see* the Table-1). The 73rd Constitutional Amendment in 1992 has given a formal constitutional recognition to local self-governance units, i.e. panchayats in India. Most significantly, it reserved 33 per cent of seats for women. The introduction of the 81st Amendment Bill (Kannabiran, 1997) and indeed the legislative changes in the form of the 74th Amendment act, demonstrated the importance of women's political representation in Indian politics (Kishwar, 1996). The success of the women's movement in placing the issue of political under representation of women on the agenda of the political parties and governments is perhaps the result of the 'troubling impasse' (Omvedt, 1993:97) that the women's movement faced in the 1990's.

## Locating Patriarchal Debates in the Women's Reservation Bill

### *The Women Reservation Bill*

The Women's Reservation Bill[9] proposed legislation to reserve 33.3 per cent seats in Parliament and state legislatures for women and was drafted first by the H.D. Deve Gowda-led United Front government. The Bill was introduced in the Lok Sabha on September 12, 1996. The bill was reintroduced in 1998 but lapsed following the government's fall during the same year. It was resurrected in December 1999, but has continued to create opposition in the Lok Sabha, the lower house of the parliament (Menon, 2000 and Kishwar, 1996). The present status of the bill remains as a draft bill in the Ministry of Law. The Ministry of Law has prepared two drafts of the Women's Reservation Bill. The first bill envisages reservation of 33.3 per cent seats for women within the existing strength of the two Houses of Parliament. The second bill calls for increasing the strength of the two Houses by 33.3 per cent. The existing 545 seats in the Lok Sabha will increase to 900 if this draft of the Bill is enacted. Though it has been introduced in Parliament several times since then, the Bill could not be passed because of lack of political consensus.[10]

### The Debates on the Women's Reservation Bill

The advocates for the Women's Reservation Bill say it would lead to gender equality in Parliament, resulting in the empowerment of women as a whole. Historically, the Bill's supporters say, women are deprived in India and that increased political participation of women will help them fight the abuse, discrimination, and inequality they suffer from. However, various political parties have staunchly opposed it because they fear many of their male leaders would not get a chance to fight elections if 33.3 per cent of seats are reserved for women (Kishwar, 1996). The Bill has also been opposed by politicians from the socially and economically marginalised classes. They argue that reservation would only help women of the elitist groups to gain seats, therefore causing further discrimination to the poor and backward[11] classes. The vocal opponents of the bill, which include the Rashtriya Janata Dal[12], the Samajwadi Party[13] (both centre-socialist), and along with some constituents of the opposition under the banner of the National Democratic Alliance (NDA) of the ruling coalition, led by the Hindu nationalist Bharatiya Janata Party (BJP).[14] The entire debate on women's reservation bill is patriarchal by nature as it revolves around caste and minorities; the very basis of a different mode of patriarchy in India. It upholds caste inequality and projects the politics of identity.

However, the left political parties like the Communist Party of India (Marxist), the Communist Party of India (CPI) and the Congress Party consistently support the bill in its present form. Their basic argument is to allow the bill to be passed first in its present form and that only after some years of the implementation of the bill should there be a change or modification of the bill in order to suit the needs of the marginalized and under represented communities and categories of women. The present situation demands to pass the bill as the women's representation in parliament in proportion to the women population is under representation. Thus, the bill is vital for the representation of women in Indian democracy.

## The Causes and Consequences of the Opposition to the Bill

In a short time after the implementation of reservation of seats for women in local and district level electoral processes, women have shown their potential to wield power effectively at the village and local levels and challenge feudal traditions (Mohanty, 2001). This is one of the reasons why the passage of the Women's Reservations Bill, which seeks to reserve 33 per cent of all seats in the national parliament and state assemblies to women, has been repeatedly blocked in the parliament. The consequence of the opposition to the Women's Reservation Bill has put it in the Ministry of Law as a draft only.

## Conclusions

The failure of Indian parliament to pass the women's reservation bill reflects the patriarchal practice of Indian parliamentary democracy, which is a product of its patriarchal social structure reflecting in politics and its institutions. Even after more than five decades of practice of parliamentary form of democracy, India has yet to recover from its patriarchal hangover. Although the post-colonial Indian state is responsible for the mass participation of women in Indian electoral and other democratic processes yet there is a decline in the representation of women leadership in Indian parliament. This means that there is a growth of women voters but not women leaders to uphold the issue of gender. The empirical evidences in this paper show that although there is mass participation of women in different elections and in the voting. But there is a decline in leadership both in the political parties and in the parliament of India. This reflects a sign of the existence of the patriarchal political culture in Indian democracy.

This paper advocates for an increased level of participation of women in Indian parliamentary politics and government by participating in leadership. It is not just about conceptualizing the issues of the role of women in Indian parliamentary politics that is important, but also to work towards the empowerment of women in India. It is about the mass participation of women in Indian politics at all levels. It points to implication about both the quality and quantity of women's participation and representation by which the patriarchal form of parliamentary democracy in India can be transformed into a place of gender sensitivity, gender justice, equality and liberty. At the same time it needs to be represented by all categories of women. However, at this phase of the movement to transform patriarchy, women's unity needs to be stressed rather than shifting the approach from united women's unity to caste, colour, religion and region based approach. This deconstructionist approach[15] is a sinister design developed by the patriarchal parliamentarian (members of Indian Parliament) to weaken women's representation in Indian politics and in the Indian parliament. Women's representation is designed to enter into democratic institutions of the country is important on the grounds of social justice and legitimacy of the parliamentary democratic system of India. However, it does not easily transform the patriarchal system into democratic one that upholds the idea of women's freedom and equality. Moreover, in long run, it can work as an institutional agency to empower women and transfer the patriarchal parliament into a democratic one. The Women's Reservation Bill for the Representation of Women in Indian Parliament is a necessary precondition for the empowerment of women in India and the representation of women in the Indian Parliament towards the transition of a gender just and truly representative democracy in general.

## NOTES

1. The legacy of Indian freedom struggle and the vision of the Constitution of India is reflected in its 'Preamble to the Constitution of India' which read as follows: "We, the people of India, having solemnly resolved to constitute India into a [Sovereign, Socialist, Secular, Democratic, Republic] and to secure to all its citizens: JUSTICE, social, economic and political; LIBERTY of thought, expression, belief, faith and worship; EQUALITY of status and of opportunity; and to promote among them all, FRATERNITY assuring the dignity of the individual and the [unity and integrity of the Nation]; In our Constituent Assembly this twenty-sixth day of November, 1949, do hereby Adopt, Enact and give to ourselves this Constitution."
2. The Part IV of the Constitution of India constitutes the Directive Principles of State Policy (Article-36 to Article-51) which is not to be enforced by any court, but the principles therein laid down are nevertheless fundamental in the governance of the country and it shall be the duty of the State to apply these principles in making laws. It says to make special provision and take special care for the weaker sections of the society like Schedule Castes, Schedule Tribes, Women and Children while making and implementing law.
3. The post-colonial Indian state made many provisions in it legal system to protect the interests of women like universal adult franchise; universal education, anti dowry law, law against domestic violence, end sexual abuse in the work place, etc. are some of the examples of progress towards a gender just society in India.
4. Patriarchy is an ideology that manifests and institutionalizes male dominance over women in a society through their control over power, authority and institutions. Thus, it enforces inequality and discrimination based on gender (*see* Lerner, 1986, 239). The Indian society replicate all the tenets of patriarchy in many forms. The one form of patriarchy is political where men controls the political power and institutions thereby making gender discrimination in voting, elections and representation in Indian democracy.
5. *see*, Report on women workers by the National Commission on Self-Employed Women, 1987.

6. Both state and central government agencies like the Ministry of Women Affairs, Department of Women and Children Welfare, National Commission for Women, many NGOs from United Nations to National and local level works towards the empowerment of the women in India. The activists and political organisations like the All India Democractic Women's Association, All India Women's Organisation and National Women Human Rights Organisation are some of the examples which are working towards the women's empowerment.
7. *Indian Journal of Gender Studies*. Vol. 6, No. 1, Jan.-June, pp. 129-33.
8. Article 15(3) of Indian Constitution lays down the basis for the state making special provisions for women and children. While Article 14 confers on men and women equal rights and opportunities in the political, economic and social spheres. Article 15 prohibits discrimination against any citizen on the grounds of religion, race, caste, sex, etc. Similarly, Article 16 provides for equality of opportunities in matter of public appointments for all citizens. Articles 325 and 326 of the Constitution of India guarantee political equality—equal right to participation in political activities and right to vote respectively. The Directive Principles of State Policy (DPSP) directs the state to make special arrangements for the upliftment of the women. These are some of the important articles provided by the Indian Constitution to ensure gender equality in all spheres of life.
9. The Women's Reservation Bill aims at providing reservation for women at each level of legislative decision-making, starting with the Lok Sabha, down to state and local legislatures. If the Bill is passed, one-third of the total available seats would be reserved for women in national, state, or local governments.
10. In a democratic set up like India, the government needs majority to pass any bill or in enacting any law. In all other bills, the government follows this principle of majority support to pass bills, the annual budget, educational bills and other sensitive bills like North East Region of India but what is the need of political consensus to pass women's reservation bill is yet to be clarified. The government has majority to pass the bill but still both the government during NDA regime and the present United Progressive Alliance (UPA) regime, the government says it needs political consensus to pass the bill. Why and what is the need of political consensus to pass the bill? Is it the way to stop the bill and put it in the cold storage?
11. The term 'backward' is a derogatory term but it is used here as an administrative term used by the Government of India.

12. The Rashtriya Janata Dal (RJD) under the leadership of the present Central Railway Minister, Mr. Lalu Prasad Yadav says that the Bill 'would deny adequate representation to other sections of society'. He favours 10 to 15 per cent reservation for women. 'My party is not opposed to women's reservation, but the case of Dalits, backward classes, Muslims and other religious minorities should not be overlooked', is his argument.
13. The Samajwadi Party under the leadership of Mr. Mulayam Singh Yadav favours making it mandatory for political parties to give 10 per cent of election tickets to women. His argument is that if inadequacy of representation is the issue, why not reservation for Muslim women (there are only two in the present Lok Sabha)? If 33.3 per cent reservation for women is added to the already existing 22.5 per cent for scheduled castes and tribes, more than 55 per cent of seats in Parliament would be reserved. This would not be fair to other sections of the population is his basic argument.
14. The Bharatiya Janata Party (BJP) claims that the bill should include a sub-quota for Other Backward Classes and Muslim women. Otherwise they argue that the quotas will only promote the interests of the elite.
15. During the colonial regime the demand for special provision for women was opposed by all sections of nationalist force as it was felt that it may weaken the national struggle for freedom. The same argument can be extended to the present Women's Reservation Bill which demands for 33 per cent of reservation for women in Indian parliament. Any sub categorisation of women will weaken the demand to pass the bill. Again the categorisation of women on the basis of their region, religion and caste will divide the larger issues faced by women in India. There is much in common problem faced by the women in India. One such common problem is the under representation of women in Indian politics and alienating women from their political power. Thus, the political representation of women in parliament is a larger issue and any attempt to divide women is nothing but will weaken the demand for reservation. Thus it is a deconstructionist approach. The special provisions for the rural, marginalized, minority and lower caste and class women within the women's reservation bill can be looked into after the implementation and pass of the bill in Indian parliament. See, Sangari (1995) for a detailed discussion on the post-modernist/ deconstructionist approach as the multiple forms of patriarchies in India and its impact on women's unity and achievements in India.

## REFERENCES


Centre for Women's Development Studies (CWDS) (1994). *Confronting Myriad Oppressions: The Western Regional Experience*, New Delhi: CWDS.

Canadian Consortium for International Cooperation (CCIC) (1987). "Feminist Perspective on Development", *Discussion paper of the CCIC Inter-Agency Working Group on Women and Development.*

Devi, U.S. (2003). New Capitalism and Politics of Care Work, *Economic and Political Weekly (EPW)*, July.

Foucault, M. (1991). *The Foucault Reader: An Introduction to Foucault's Thought,* ed. P. Rainbow, Harmondsworth: Penguin.

—— (1979). *Discipline and Punish. The Birth of the Prison,* Harmondsworth: Penguin.

Government of India (GOI) (1974). Department of Social Welfare, *Towards Equality, Report of the Committee on the Status of Women in India (CSWI)*, New Delhi: GOI.

Government of India (GOI) (2004). *Constitution of India*, New Delhi: GOI.

Kannabiran, V. and Kannabiran, K. (1997). "From social action to political action: Women and the 81st Amendment." *Economic and Political Weekly,* 1 February, pp. 196–97.

Kishwar, M. (1996). "Women and Politics: Beyond Quotas." *Economic and Political Weekly,* Vol. 31, No. 43, 26 October, pp. 2867–74.

Lerner, G. (1986). *The Creation of Patriarchy*, Oxford University Press, New York.

Lukes, S. (1974). *Power: A Radical View,* London: Macmillan.

MacKinnon, C. (1987). *Feminism Unmodified: Discourses on Life and Law,* Cambridge, MA: Harvard University Press.

McNay, L. (1992). *Foucault and Feminism: Power, Gender and Self,* Cambridge: Cambridge University Press.

Menon, N. (2000). "Elusive Woman: Feminism and Women's Reservation Bill." *Economic and Political Weekly,* 28 October.

Mohanty, B. (2000). *The Daughters of 73rd Amendment*, New Delhi: ISS.

National Commission on Self-Employed Women (1997). *Report on Women Workers,* New Delhi: GOI.

Omvedt, G. (1993). *Reinventing Revolution: New Social Movements and the Socialist Tradition in India.* New York: ME Sharpe.

Partpart, J., Rai, S. and Staudt K. (eds). *Rethinking Empowerment—Gender and Development in a Global/Local World*, Routledge: London.

Rai, Shirin M. (2002). *Gender and the Political Economy of Development: From Nationalism to Globalization.* Cambridge: Polity Press.

Raman, V. (2002). "The Implementation of Quotas: Asian Experiences", "The Implementation of Quotas for Women: The Indian Experience", *A paper presented in the workshop hosted by International Institute for Democracy and Electoral Assistance (IDEA)* in Jakarta: Indonesia.

Sangari, K. and Vaid, S. (eds.) (1993). *Recasting Women: Essays Indian Colonial History,* New Delhi: Kali For Women.

Stromquist, N. (2002). Education as means for empowering women, in Partpart, J., Rai, S. and Staudt, K. (eds). *Rethinking Empowerment—Gender and Development in a Global/Local World*, Routledge: London.

## ANNEXURE

## (Tables and Graphs)

**Table-1: Participation of Women in National Elections**

| Election Year | Voting of Men | Voting % of Women | Total Seats Contested by Women | Total Seats Won by Women | % of Seats Won of the Contested Seats | Total Seats | % of Women Members |
|---|---|---|---|---|---|---|---|
| 1952 | 53.00 | 37.10 | 51 | 23 | 45.09 | 499 | 4.40 |
| 1957 | 56.00 | 38.77 | 70 | 27 | 38.57 | 500 | 5.40 |
| 1962 | 62.10 | 46.63 | 68 | 35 | 51.47 | 503 | 6.70 |
| 1967 | 66.70 | 55.48 | 66 | 31 | 48.43 | 523 | 5.90 |
| 1971 | 69.70 | 49.15 | 86 | 22 | 27.50 | 521 | 4.20 |
| 1977 | 65.62 | 54.96 | 70 | 19 | 25.70 | 544 | 3.40 |
| 1980 | 57.69 | 51.22 | 142 | 28 | 19.70 | 544 | 5.14 |
| 1984 | 63.61 | 68.17 | 421 | 159 | 28.30 | 544 | 7.90 |
| 1989 | 70.90 | 43.90 | 189 | 28 | 14.80 | 525 | 5.30 |
| 1991 | 52.56 | 47.42 | 307 | 33 | 10.75 | 503 | 6.60 |
| 1996 | — | — | — | 40 | — | 543 | — |
| 1998 | — | — | — | 43 | — | 543 | — |
| 1999 | — | — | — | — | — | — | — |
| 2004 | — | 53.64 | 355 | 45 | — | 543 | — |

*Source*: PIB, Different Reports of Election Commission of India, Government of India.

**Table-2: Voting % in Lok Sabha Elections**

| General Election | Year | Male | Female | Total |
|---|---|---|---|---|
| 1st | 1952 | - | - | 61.2 |
| 2nd | 1957 | - | - | 62.2 |
| 3rd | 1962 | 63.31 | 46.63 | 55.42 |
| 4th | 1967 | 66.73 | 55.48 | 61.33 |
| 5th | 1971 | 60.90 | 49.11 | 55.29 |
| 6th | 1977 | 65.63 | 54.91 | 60.49 |
| 7th | 1980 | 62.16 | 51.22 | 56.92 |
| 8th | 1984 | 68.18 | 58.60 | 63.56 |
| 9th | 1989 | 66.13 | 57.32 | 61.95 |
| 10th | 1991 | 61.58 | 51.35 | 56.93 |
| 11th | 1996 | 62.06 | 53.41 | 57.94 |
| 12th | 1998 | 65.72 | 57.88 | 61.97 |
| 13th | 1999 | 63.97 | 55.64 | 59.99 |
| 14th | 2004 | 61.66 | 53.30 | 57.65 |

*Source*: "Turn Out Lok Sabha 1952-2004", Election Commission of India, New Delhi.

**Table-3: Participation of Women in the Lok Sabha and Rajya Sabha**

| Election Year | Women Members in Lok Sabha | | | Women Members in Rajya Sabha | | |
|---|---|---|---|---|---|---|
| | No. of Seats | No. of Women | Percentage | No. of Seats | No. of Women | Percentage |
| 1952-57 | 499 | 22 | 4.4 | 219 | 16 | 7.3 |
| 1957-62 | 500 | 27 | 5.4 | 237 | 18 | 7.6 |
| 1962-67 | 503 | 34 | 6.7 | 238 | 18 | 7.6 |
| 1967-71 | 523 | 31 | 5.9 | 240 | 20 | 8.3 |
| 1971-77 | 521 | 22 | 4.2 | 243 | 17 | 7.0 |
| 1977-80 | 544 | 19 | 3.4 | 244 | 25 | 10.2 |
| 1980-84 | 544 | 28 | 5.1 | 244 | 24 | 9.8 |
| 1985-90 | 544 | 44 | 8.1 | 245 | 28 | 11.4 |
| 1990-91 | 529 | 28 | 5.3 | 245 | 24 | 9.7 |
| 1991-96 | 509 | 36 | 7.1 | 245 | 38 | 15.5 |
| 1996-97 | 537 | 34 | 6.3 | 245 | 20 | 8.2 |
| 1997-98 | 545 | 40 | 7.3 | 245 | 19 | 7.8 |
| 1998-99 | 545 | 44 | 8.1 | 245 | 19 | 7.8 |
| 1999-04 | 545 | 48 | 8.8 | 245 | 20 | 8.2 |

*Source*: Election Commission of India, Government of India.

**Table-4: Women Contestants in Lok Sabha Elections 1952-1996**

| Election Year | Women Contestants in Lok Sabha Elections 1952-1996 | | |
|---|---|---|---|
| | Contestants per Seat | % of Share among Contestants | % of Success Ratio |
| 1952 | 0.10 | 2.7 | 43.1 |
| 1957 | 0.14 | 4.4 | 38.6 |
| 1962 | 0.14 | 3.4 | 50.0 |
| 1967 | 0.13 | 2.8 | 47.0 |
| 1971 | 0.17 | 3.1 | 25.6 |
| 1977 | 0.13 | 2.9 | 27.1 |
| 1980 | 0.26 | 3.1 | 19.7 |
| 1989 | 0.29 | 2.9 | 27.7 |
| 1991 | 0.37 | 3.1 | 14.3 |
| 1991 | 0.60 | 3.7 | 12.0 |
| 1996 | 0.90 | 3.4 | 7.9 |
| Average | 0.30 | 3.2 | 28.5 |

*Source*: CSDS Data Unit, New Delhi.

**Table-5: Women's Participation in Political Party Committees**

| Name of the Party | Women | Men | % of Women |
|---|---|---|---|
| Congress(I) | 2 | 17 | 11.7 |
| BJP | 8 | 62 | 12.5 |
| JD | 3 | 25 | 12.0 |
| CPI(M) | 3 | 58 | 5.1 |
| CPI | 2 | 18 | 11.1 |

*Source*: Coordination Unit (1995) of the above political parties.

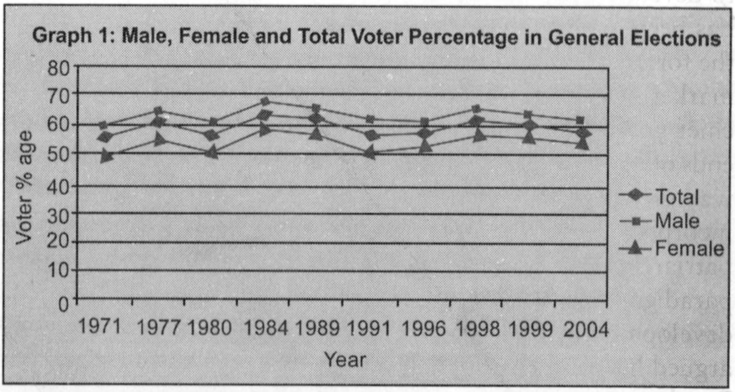


*Source*: Based on the data provided in the Table-4 in the Annexure.

# Sen, Rawls and Wittgenstein: Liberal Development Thinking and Gender

5

*Parthasarathi Mondal*

## 1. Introduction

The rapidity and complexity of social transformation across the world economy today has intensified the debate on the nature of development. In a time when the call for the establishment of a world order based on market economy is strident the quest for a free and just society appears as welcome temperance. The crying need to pay heed to the deprivations, tribulations and demands of those marginalized by social exclusion has been an intimate ingredient of this quest. There is recognition that development planning and the development process generally has not acknowledged women's contribution to development, and that the impact of development on women has been inadequately studied. Amartya Kumar Sen has been at the forefront of broadening the debate beyond the borders of the market sufficiently enough to make human well-being as the chief goal of development. For Sen, freedom is the means and ends of development. Sen has based his arguments in an important way on capabilities of people. This has lent his theorizing to an incorporation of the urgent concerns of those handicapped by patriarchy and disability within the framework of a neo-liberal paradigm. His thinking has been crucial to gender analysis in development. It is important to bear in mind here that Sen has argued his case keeping the theory of justice developed by John Rawls as his main point of reference. The nature of this relationship is important for the potential in Sen's enterprise.

A careful reading of their works especially in reference to each other reveals certain tensions. This paper seeks to explore the tensions as they pertain to the project of forming a free and just society as an essential ingredient for development. The implications of these tensions for addressing gender concerns are then teased out. It is argued that Sen's framework of justice based on capability demands of him theorization at a level which appears to exceed the scope of the stated objectives of his work. A similar shortcoming dogs the feminist improvisation of Sen's approach. This difficulty arises perhaps from an appropriate reading of Rawls' philosophical enterprise having elided Sen. Our ability to take Sen's approach to development as an alternative is thus somewhat compromised.

From within development economics, Sen's work is well acknowledged as providing the necessary corrective to a development strategy, which is largely based on economic growth, should take. His work is thus located within the development approach of rights, justice and freedom. Sen argues that the traditional concerns of development economics, viz. industrialization, rapid capital accumulation, mobilization of underemployed manpower, and planning and an economically active state, continue to be relevant and important no matter what neo-classical development economics has to say (Sen 1983, 745-53). However, the "...real limitations of traditional development economics arose not from the choice of means to the end of economic growth, but in the insufficient recognition that economic growth was no more than a means to some other objectives" (Sen 1983, 753).

Sen brings in redistributive and welfare concerns to bear on the predominant neo-classical model of development economics in such a way that not only the social correlates of economic development are examined in their full import but also the goal of growth being an improvement in living standards is not lost sight of. Sen's main contention is that income and growth is not as good a measurement of development as an expansion in a person's "entitlements" which refer to the alternative bundles of commodities which he can enjoy within the context of opportunities available to him (Sen 1983, 754-56). Further, these opportunities are significantly affected by the nature and degree of political arrangements available to secure them (Sen 1983, 757-60). Hence it is by surveying the entitlements and the development in the "capabilities" in the person which ensue, within the context of political arrangements that one arrives at a better understanding of development.

The capability approach is sensitive to human diversity because it accounts for interpersonal variations in the conversion of commodity features into functionings. These variations can be because of personal, social or environmental factors but the variation which has captured the imagination of several advocates of the capability approach is that of gender. Gender discrimination is all-pervasive in almost all societies and is one of the factors influencing income and other commodity conversions. Accordingly application of the "capability approach" has led to the discovery of sex bias and "missing women" in developing nations which in turn is helpful in explaining the poorer performance of women compared to men in a number of functionings such as mortality, morbidity, nutrition, health and literacy. The neglect of gender issues and the correlative key entitlements in the development process has been highlighted by thc *Human Dcvelopment Reports* of the United Nations Development Programme which have been conceptually guided by Sen and his late colleague Mahabub ul Haq. However, long years of teasing out the nitty-gritty of the capability approach have led Sen to discuss, in his later work, development in the context of freedom.

Sen's argument of development as freedom (Sen 2006a) is considered today to be at the forefront of economic philosophy and development thinking within the liberal paradigm. Development is seen as a process which removes most of the obstacles to a person who is trying to enjoy a life of freedom according to what is valued by him. Conversely a deliberate attempt to expand the scope of freedom in the different sectors of society facilitates the process of development. This approach, it is contended, helps in focusing on the role that development measures or means play in promoting human freedom. The linkage between the means and ends of development become clearer. In that sense, this approach is broader than theories advocating economic growth, industrialization, technological advance or modernization as the royal road to development.

However, Sen can be seen as stating that focusing on development as freedom allows us to direct our investigations more towards the goals of humanity rather than towards the means often adopted for reaching those ends. Freedom is seen as instrumental to development. A discussion of the specificities of the instrumentation of development then becomes necessary. Sen identifies these instrumental freedoms as "...economic opportunities, political freedoms, social facilities, transparency guarantees, and protective security" (Sen 2006a, xii).

The role of these instrumental freedoms is further related to the issue of individual agency. The extent of freedom which a person enjoys is constrained by the extent and nature of these instrumental freedoms played out in the life situations of the person. Freedom actually enjoyed is then to be understood in terms of the capabilities of persons. Development, therefore, becomes a process of enhancing capabilities.

"Five distinct types of freedom, seen in an 'instrumental' perspective, are particularly investigated in the empirical studies that follow. These include (1) political freedoms, (2) economic facilities, (3) social opportunities, (4) transparency guarantees and (5) protective security. Each of these distinct types of rights and opportunities helps to advance the general capability of a person. They may also serve to complement each other. Public policy to foster human capabilities and substantive freedoms in general can work through the promotion of these distinct but interrelated instrumental freedoms" (Sen 2006a, 10).

The import of instrumental freedoms and agency for gender is well brought out by Sen in the discussion on "women's agency and social change" (Sen 2006a, 189-203). The personhood of women acquires full status only when they become agents of change in their own lives rather than being mere enjoyers of well-being as recipients of welfare measures. Greater agency for women helps at the outset in removing inequities which prevent well-being, viz. independence of livelihoods, literacy and education (Sen 2006a, 191). Another crucial area where agency plays a role in women's well-being is in child-bearing and child-rearing. Gender equity is facilitative of freedom also in spheres of women's lives beyond these immediate concerns:

> "The same applies to many other areas of economic, political and social action, varying from rural credit and economic activities, on the one hand, to political agitation and social debates, on the other. The extensive reach of women's agency is one of the more neglected areas of development studies, and most urgently in need of correction. Nothing, arguably, is as important today in the political economy of development as an adequate recognition of political, economic and social participation and leadership of women. This is indeed a crucial aspect of 'development as freedom'." (Sen 2006a, 203)

Now Sen pitches his version of freedom in terms of capabilities against the utilitarian welfarists and against the notion of justice in terms of access to and holding of primary goods as held by Rawls. It is largely in the debate with the theory of justice—justice as fairness—developed by Rawls that Sen articulates his capability approach as a correct evaluative procedure for assessing the freedom and justness of a society. He says that "By far the most influential—and I believe the most important—theory of justice to be presented in this century has been John Rawls' 'justice as fairness'" (Sen 2002, 75).

Sen sees these differences in the way they each place importance on different things in order to assess whether a society is just or not. The concern of both the approaches is justice but the information bases of evaluating levels of justness are different (Sen 2002, 73-87). Sen's approach to justice is articulated more directly in terms of 'freedom' and 'capability' whereas Rawls approaches justice in terms of 'fairness' and 'primary goods'. The shift from 'justice' to 'freedom' is apparently based on the shift from 'primary goods' to 'capability'. Sen acknowledges the potential for freedom in Rawls' theory of justice but complains that Rawls' freedom as based on primary goods is not as constitutive of freedom as is freedom based on capability (Sen 2002, 80). Rawls has discussed this charge rather well in *Justice as Fairness: A Restatement* (2003) (hereafter *JFR*) (Rawls 2003, 168-76). His claim is that primary goods do include or acknowledge certain basic human capabilities.

The paper however shall set out to explore the proposition that the theory of justice as freedom (hinging on capabilities) built by Sen, as a critique of the theory of justice as fairness (hinging on primary goods) constructed by Rawls, is constrained by the contingent nature of Sen's propositions. The success of the capability approach becomes contingent upon the flowering of liberal democracies in societies which are as yet not that. A similar contingency persists with the elaboration and engendering of the capability approach provided by feminist economics. This imposes the further demand that Sen's theory specify how liberal democracies are to be set up in different societies. Sen does make an effort at specification by enumerating the "instrumental freedoms". However, as he considers the instrumental freedoms as both the means and the ends to freedom and liberal democracy, it appears that we are left with almost no effective or feasible guidelines on how to engender liberal democracies in societies of different and diverse natures.

It is further argued in the course of the next few pages that this difficulty in Sen arises probably from his having missed considering an important reading of the philosophical nature of Rawls' enterprise. One of the main guiding philosophical traditions in Rawls can be seen as that of Ludwig Wittgenstein and Sen's critique of Rawls does not appear to acknowledge this. The upshot of all this is that our opportunity to take Sen's work as a contender for an alternative approach to development gets constricted.

This situation perhaps could be linked to Sen's seeming to have not acknowledged the flow of the Wittgensteinian tradition in his own work. Amiya Kumar Bagchi has alluded to the Wittgensteinian roots of some of Sen's work (Bagchi 1999, 91-92). The plot thickens when Sen himself notices the contribution of economic thinking to Wittgenstein's work (Sen 2003, 1240-55) and acknowledges Wittgenstein as "arguably the greatest philosopher of our times" (Sen 2006b, 3). An exploration of the Wittgensteinian element in Sen's work could raise some interesting questions for the argument presented here but let us make it the subject of another discussion. For the moment it is more important to pay close attention to the debate between Sen and Rawls. I begin with a discussion of some strands in Rawls' thinking.

## 2. Metaphysics, Politics and Primary Goods

### *2.1 Some Ways of Looking at Rawls*

The widespread response to Rawls as a philosopher (in politics) has led to the core his work to be read and defined in myriad ways. I take up here a few readings, by way of illustration, which are helpful in indicating the Wittgensteinian quietism in Rawls. This largely pertains to the reticence in matters of philosophical import and a self-imposed limit to expectations. Rawls' work has been seen as contributing to the debate in that part of contemporary moral and political philosophy which insists on considering our moral and political principles as interpretations of our socio-political and economic practices. Gilbert Harman (Harman 2003, 1-19) has identified three trends in moral and political philosophy in the last fifty years, namely the interaction taking place between scientific and philosophical studies of morality with emphasis on philosophical psychology of morality and evolutionary aspects of morality, the attempt to use intuitions of particular cases to arrive at new moral principles, and the effort to work out negotiated settlements of particular judgements and principles.

The last trend, exemplified by Rawls' work, is characterised as "rejecting special foundations". In contrast to the advocates of special foundationalism the general foundationalism of Rawls assumes that a person's beliefs and methods are foundational because they are the grounds of beginning any process of justification. "In deciding what to believe, we are to start where we are with all our beliefs and inferential methods, adjusting them to each other in case of conflict, trying to make them cohere. Key principles within general foundationalism are conservatism, coherence, and simplicity" (Harman 2003, 2). The process followed is thus one in which one has to attempt a coherence between one's considered intuitions of particular cases with one's considered general principles and *vice versa*. This process should continue until one reaches a worldview whose constitutive beliefs and principles are in accord with each other. This process is stretched to parties outside oneself so that, through reasoned interaction between general foundationalists, "overlapping consensus" on principles of justice and governance in pluralistic societies is achieved between citizens. This is Rawls' reflective equilibrium. The salience of this concept in Rawls' thinking is indicative of the centrality of a set of principles for justice based on *praxis* rather than on metaphysical claims.

In a somewhat similar vein, Henry Richardson (Richardson 1999, ix-x) has identified three intertwining concerns which mark Rawls' work. The objective of Rawls' ethics has been to arrive at practical solutions in controversial situations when there are disagreements between people and the corresponding social arrangements. The emphasis is on workable propositions, on feasibility. However, resolution of the disagreements is to be worked out through efforts at reasoned justification. Sufficient conditions of justifiability for any proposition or principle has to be attempted by all parties concerned so that the results are widely accepted and respected. The third concern suggested is that the practical justification of ethical principles subsumes a recognition that "all principles are open textured, and hence stand in need of interpretation or specification" (Richardson 1999, x). This concern is supposed to be inspired by the Wittgensteinian teachers of Rawls, namely Norman Malcolm and Max Black. Thus keeping the question of philosophy open in a discussion of justice and its principles moves Rawls towards the search for feasible postulations.

However, the pragmatism sensed in the political philosophy of Rawls has been read in two opposite directions. One interpretation, such as given by Thomas Pogge (Pogge 1989), contends that Rawls' work could be seen as not having done adequate homework in preparing feasible ways of reforming the deficiencies in the justness of existing institutional arrangements in our society. Rather, especially in the later writings, the discussion has veered off towards the philosophical or metaphysical underpinnings of the theory of justice. Apparently

Rawls shifts his attention from pragmatism to metaphysics. This movement away from the "primacy of the practical" is clearly evident in Rawls' participation in the debate between him and his libertarian and communitarian critics: "...he has made every conceivable effort to accommodate the moral positions of others, even where such accommodation has diluted the central moral statement of his own conception of justice" (Pogge 1989, 4).

The second interpretation agrees that the changes in course in the development of Rawls' thinking have been occasioned in large part by his debate with the libertarians and communitarians but it comes to the opposite conclusion. It sees Rawls' pragmatism as a retreat from a comprehensive doctrine of the moral good to a plan to suit current political purposes. Emphasis, allegedly more in Rawls' later writings (e.g. Rawls 1985, 1987, 1988, 1989, 1993, 1999 and 2003), on the construction of principles of justice and governance from our social practices and on the need to construct only those moral principles which are of a practical nature has been seen as the abandonment of a possible ethical theory deriving inspiration from Kant which was hinted at in Rawls' earlier works (e.g. Rawls 1972, 1975a, 1975b and 1977). In between these two sets of works lie a set of writings (e.g. Rawls 1980 and 1982) which, while engaging with Kant, try to begin taming the universal nature of Kant's moral theory (which had permeated much of the earlier writings) and make them rooted to the values of liberal democratic societies.

The tension in Rawls regarding Kantian metaphysics has also been noticed by the feminist Martha Nussbaum who, in a rich analysis of Rawls' position on categories which are not taken to be ordinary or normal entities in considerations of justice (e.g. persons with disability and nonhuman animals), show how they can be traced to Rawls' adherence to the Kantian concept of the person which splits personhood and animality (Nussbaum 2007a, 127-40). It is held that although Rawls does not overtly subscribe to the metaphysical elements in Kant or to the Kantian "two-worldview" regarding normal persons, he is led to a position where such 'special' categories or entities "fail to qualify for equality".

However, irrespective of its sequence, direction and nature, Rawls' work from the earliest writings has exercised restraint in terms of philosophical boldness—he states that the principles of justice are procedural in nature because the effort is to reach a consensus from within existing social practices and not from other philosophical premises (Rawls 1951). Principles of justice are to be derived from a hypothetical agreement reached on the basis of the barest information but this information is confined to the laws of the nature and society as we know it.

What emerges as significant is that in the whirlpool of debate with his critics whilst trying to develop a practical conception of justice and its justifications, Rawls takes Kant as a north star. Whether he is to be seen as moving from a comprehensive or universal doctrine of justice to a politically expeditious one or as moving from the concern with institutional justness to esoteric philosophical discussions, or whatever be the nature of the tension between Rawls and metaphysics, an interpretation of Kant is found lurking in the background. In what follows therefore a rough sketch of developments in Rawls' thinking as they engage with Kant is made.

### *2.2 Rawls' Kantianism*

Section 40 of the *TJ* is titled "The Kantian Interpretation of Justice as Fairness". At first sight the main Kantian conceptions used by Rawls are autonomy, rationality, and the categorical imperative although their derivability from Kant has been questioned (Johnson 1974, 58-66). A well-ordered society is peopled by autonomous citizens. This is the autonomy emulated from the rationally autonomous parties in the original position. When these citizens act according to the principles which the parties in the original position would choose under what Rawls calls "fair terms of cooperation" the citizens enjoy the autonomy which was prized by Kant as the moral ideal. Further interaction is based not only on mutual self-respect and reciprocity with a clear idea of benefits and burdens but also on a public conception of this mutuality.

The parties in the original position also act rationally. This is because they accept the principles of justice knowing full well that even though they have to reach at their decision from behind the veil of ignorance, they will have chosen such principles which would lead to the best possible deal for themselves irrespective of what is revealed about their socio-political and economic background after the veil is lifted. On this basis, Rawls contends, citizens who take themselves to be rational can adopt these principles of justice.

Kant makes a distinction between categorical imperative and hypothetical imperative. When one acts on the desire for a specific end he is said to be motivated by hypothetical imperative but when he is spurred on by goals which concern the whole of humanity he is taken to be motivated by the categorical imperative. In other words when one is acting under categorical imperative one is willing a moral law as a principle governing the actions of all rational beings. It is possible thus to do this and move away from hypothetical imperative only when we abstract ourselves away from our interpersonal differences.

So here we have a person who is a free and equal rational being who is careful enough to will as principles which can be willed by all. Clearly Rawls is making an effort to mould his social contract on a Kantian understanding. The *TJ* was followed by a series of writings which, while constituting a response to the many critics of *TJ*, also gave Rawls the opportunity to elaborate his linkages with Kant. For instance, in 'A Kantian Conception of Equality' published in 1975 (Rawls 1975a), Rawls contends that the veil of ignorance could be seen as an incorporation of a Kantian idea in his scheme in the sense that the requirement of the parties to deliberate on the principles of justice without any knowledge of the parties' background is similar to Kant's notion of negative freedom which meant the freedom to act independently of contingencies. Thus in the original position knowledge of only the most general laws governing nature and society is permitted. Rawls also draws a parallel with Kant's conception of positive freedom. Positive freedom is possible because the parties in the original position deliberating on principles of justice are free and equal moral persons. Secondly the principles of justice have a content consonant with the view of free and equal moral persons because:

> "...these principles express, on their public face as it were, the conception of the person that is realized in a well-ordered society. They give priority to the basic liberties, regard individuals as free and responsible masters of their aims and desires, and all are to share equally in the means for the attainment of ends unless the situation of everyone can be improved, taking equal division as the starting point. A society that realized these principles would attain positive freedom, for these principles reflect the features of persons that determined their selection and so express a conception they give to themselves." (Rawls 1975a, 265-66)

These developments in Rawls' interpretation of Kant in the search for a theory of justice and its principles however are always done with a certain realization on the limits of their universal applicability. As the earlier works show there is awareness in him that the roots of the principles must lie in existing social practices and our knowledge of the general laws of nature and society, and should not be reduced from other higher-order principles. He takes this up again in 'The Independence of Moral Theory' in 1975 (Rawls 1975c) where he distinguishes moral theory from moral philosophy. The former is part of the latter but it is concerned more with forming arrangements which would give expressions to our notions of the right and the good. Moral theory then is somewhat independent of other branches of philosophy such as epistemology, philosophy of mind, and metaphysics. The impulse to remain within the boundaries of existing societies in the formation of principles of justice is evident in 'Fairness to Goodness' (1975) (Rawls 1975b) and 'The Basic Structure as Subject' (1977) (Rawls 1977) where Rawls concentrates on questions of justice in the institutional arrangements of large-scale societies whose members cooperate and thereby argues against the alleged asocial conception of a person in his theory. His contention is that the principles are sought to be constructed out of associative or cooperative processes already in operation amidst persons in society. Hence his individuals are not atomic creatures but social inhabitants in society.

This restrained Kantian project, as it were, gets carried forward in his writings to follow with the caveat that now the attention shifts from principles of justice derived from society as such to principles of justice derived from and appropriate to certain specific societies, namely liberal democratic constitutional states. In 'Kantian Constructivism in Moral Theory' (1980) (Rawls 1980) Rawls finds the Kantian understanding of the person as appropriate to his present concerns. The concern is that in liberal democracies like America there is no agreement on how to organize institutional arrangements such that they would conform to the freedom and equality of citizens (Rawls 1980, 305). In this search the Kantian notion of the person is helpful. This is so because such a person is both free and equal. In addition he is capable of ensuring the best bargains for himself in any situation of negotiation and at the same time he wills those first principles of justice which can also be willed by other rational persons like him. The former is called the Rational and the latter the Reasonable by Rawls. The sense of mutuality and reciprocity of the Reasonable form the context of the Rational and thereby subsumes it. Without conceptions of the good persons would not know why they should cooperate. In this manner the free, equal, rational and moral person becomes the means and ends of social cooperation (Rawls 1980, 306). The aim of a theory of justice here should be to formulate or construct the principles of justice from the common sense manifest in social cooperation between such pérsons. If necessary a process of critical reflection of the sense of tradition may be initiated so that the deeper bases of social agreement are brought to light.

This is, admits Rawls, a slightly different proposition from deriving principles of justice from hypothetical or imaginative arrangements even if they were to be public in nature (Rawls 1980, 306). It, therefore, becomes plainer that what we are now looking for in social cooperation amongst people is the mechanism of agreement or the procedure through which justice is secured. Procedural justice has therefore even less traffic with comprehensive moral doctrines (Rawls 1980, 304).

In 'The Basic Liberties and Their Priority' (1982) (Rawls 1982) Rawls makes it clear that he is not out to postulate the priority of liberty as such but of certain specific liberties. These liberties are to be specified at the levels of the original position, and of constitutional, legislative and judicial procedures. At each stage the Reasonable subsumes and restrains the Rational: the parties in the original position are constrained by conditions of reasonableness, these principles are applied to select a constitution, legislators make laws in accordance with the constitution, and the judiciary has to interpret laws prepared within the demands of the Reasonable. Hence although a person acts rationally at every stage his rationality gets circumscribed by reasonableness. Taken together, these two papers argue how a project drawing inspiration from the work of Kant helps in overcoming the tussle between freedom and equality and yet in a contextualized way, without reference to assumptions of reality or human nature and so on. In a sense the writings of this period may be seen as marking the transition from the search for a universal theory of justice applicable to society *per se* through justice as fairness for liberal democratic societies only to a political conception of justice and its principles which avoids the need to discuss global philosophical or metaphysical concerns.

In the later writings which follow Rawls has been widely interpreted as taking a stance which rejects the Kantian spirit of his work in the early and middle periods. The principles of justice as fairness are now seen as being moral in the specific sense of being worked for our political, economic and social institutions only. The focus is on the mere basic structure of society. In this sense the principles of justice are political: "...since justice as fairness is intended as a political conception of justice for a democratic society, it tries to draw solely upon basic intuitive ideas that are embedded in the political institutions of a constitutional democratic regime and the public traditions of their interpretation" (Rawls 1985, 390). This also means that they are not part of any comprehensive moral or metaphysical doctrine. The history of a modern democratic state compels any conception of justice and its principles to "...allow for a diversity of doctrines and the plurality of conflicting, and indeed incommensurable, conceptions of the good affirmed by the members of existing democratic societies" (Rawls 1985, 390). A political liberalism is thus based on toleration.

Accordingly, Rawls now has something to say about Kant:

> From this conclusion it is clear what is problematic with the liberalisms of Kant and Mill. They are both general and comprehensive moral doctrines: general in that they apply to a wide range of subjects, and comprehensive in that they include conceptions of what is of value in human life, ideals of personal virtue and character that are to inform our thought and conduct as a whole. Here I have in mind Kant's ideal of autonomy and his connecting it with the values of the Enlightenment, and Mill's ideal of individuality and his connecting it with the values of modernity. These two liberalisms both comprehend more than the political. Their doctrines of free institutions rest in large part on ideals and values that are not generally, or perhaps even widely, shared in a democratic society. They are not a practicable public basis of a political conception of justice, and I suspect the same to be true of many liberalisms besides those of Kant and Mill. (Rawls 1987, 427)

Interestingly the distancing from Kant and Mill is accompanied by a distancing from Hobbes as well, that is from liberalism as a *modus vivendi* arrived at by the falling together of group and individual interests which are coordinated by constitutional arrangements. This is in contrast to the political conception of justice wherein the consensus is moral in nature: "...it includes conceptions of society and of citizens as persons, as well as principles of justice, and an account of the cooperative virtues through which those principles are embodied in human character and expressed in public life" (Rawls 1987, 432).

This dalliance with Kant does have the salutary effect of enriching a contemporary account of justice from within the social contractarian tradition. However, it is not able to equip itself adequately in order to be able to overcome a basic rupture which has dogged liberal thinking since time immemorial, or so it is thought. As noted earlier, protestations apart, Rawls is read by feminists to be dependent on the Kantian conception of person which holds that in order to qualify for personhood the individual should be in full possession of his reason and moral powers. Rationality sets normal human beings apart from not only nonhuman animals but also from people who have physical and mental disabilities. This has important moral implications: "...Kant denies that we have any moral duties to animals.... What is true of animals is bound to be true of all beings who lack the rather complex capacity for moral and prudential reasoning that in Kant's view is characteristic of mature human beings" (Nussbaum 2007a, 131). In Rawls such a Kantian personhood has the very real potential of puncturing the delivery of justice as fairness.

> "Indeed, people with severe mental impairments appear to be those 'scattered individuals' (*TJ* 506) who, lacking the moral capacities to some essential minimum degree, fail to qualify for equality. Moreover, just as Kant and Rawls explicitly deny that reciprocity and relations of justice, hold between humans and nonhuman animals, so, too, they are required to hold that there is no reciprocity, in the requisite sense, between 'normal' human beings and people with severe mental impairments. Rawls defines reciprocity as a relation between citizens understood in terms of the Kantian conception of the person" (*PL* 16). (Nussbaum 2007a, 133)

In other words, Rawls' formulation of the normal person as the subject and object of justice as fairness seemingly poses a problem for the social contractarian tradition in two ways.

> The contract doctrine seems unable to accommodate their [i.e. those with mental impairments and disabilities] needs for special social attention, for reasons of social productivity and cost that pertain to all people with impairments. But they are disqualified from citizenship in a deeper way as well, because they do not conform to the rather idealized picture of moral rationality that is used to define the citizen in the Well-Ordered Society. (Nussbaum 2007a, 135)

Matters become complex when the split personality is seen in conjunction with Rawls' approach to gender. It is dogma today that the family is the site of both cooperation and conflict. The family is both a public institution as well as a sphere of the most intimate privacy. These private values are likely to be sacrificed if made the substance of public debate but it also cannot be denied that the family has a formative influence on the development of our personhood and as such constitutes what Rawls calls an element in the basic structure of society. Now Rawls' position is seen to be stating that on account of the family being a part of the basic structure of society the principles of justice apply to it although the principles do not apply to the "internal life of families" (Nussbaum 2000, 271). "Thus, the family need not obey the Rawlsian difference principle, with regard to its internal distribution of resources and opportunities; nor need it obey the priority of liberty, with regard to basic political and religious liberties. On the other hand, the fact that its members are part of a society in which the lives of all citizens are governed by institutions based on these two principles will regulate, in many ways, what can and what cannot go on there" (Nussbaum 2000, 271). This makes it difficult for Rawlsian justice as fairness to provide for equality for women (and also children) in families. Justice as fairness does not appear to be adequately gender sensitive after all. Therefore, it is posed that Rawls' inability to take justice to the doorsteps of the physically and mentally impaired on account of a Kantian affair is extended to the arena of gender when justice of fairness tends to give women short shrift in the delivery of justice and equality.

### *2.3 Metaphysics and Politics*

To begin with, then, the sense that one gets from this discussion is that Rawls' is appropriating Kant in a way that would secure for him the basis for justice in the social practices of the intrinsically moral person which would thus enable him to avoid taking recourse to comprehensive moral doctrines in order to bulwark his conception of justice, without having to debate the veracity of the global doctrines. The nature of this enterprise is manifest in the shifts taking place in Rawls' thinking, namely the shift from the search for principles of justice which are true for human society *per se* (and thus not derivable from non-human society higher-order principles) to principles which are true only for human society of a particular sort (i.e. liberal democratic societies) to principles which may or may not be true but are—all importantly—arrived at by reasoned public agreement between citizens of liberal democratic societies. What however remains problematic in this peculiar appropriation of Kant is the stress on a personhood which excludes women and the disabled form the sphere and concerns of justice.

Interestingly however it is the shifting to the political conception of justice—the last shift—which appears to be the clue to another narrative which runs concurrently to the main story-line in Rawls' work, that is, a theory of justice. In discussing the principles of justice Rawls is also constantly engaged in an enterprise which is philosophical in nature and which is of no less important than his discussions on justice. Rawls can be read as doing philosophy in his own style and following a particular philosophical method. Put the other way round, following a particular philosophical method helps Rawls to develop his own style of philosophy.

This is characterized by the manner in which he addresses the question of metaphysics. The method that he follows is that of ducking the question of metaphysics. Philosophical method eschews metaphysics mainly by avoiding discussions of truth claims. The overview of Rawls' Kantianism shows how the ground is shifted from a discussion on what exists as true to what can be consensually achievable in particular human societies. The grounds for the principles of justice are shifted from universal human society to liberal democratic societies to political consensus in liberal democratic societies. What is going on underneath these shifts in justice as fairness is that philosophy as a discussion of what exists or what is true is shifted to philosophy as what is true in liberal democratic societies to philosophy which no more discusses truth-claims of any sort but focuses on more pragmatic concerns. In this manner the question of deciding truth-claims are avoided without having the need to deny their existence.

This procedure takes his philosophy towards the political, that is, it transforms his philosophy to a political one. Hence

Rawls could be read as a special style of doing philosophy in which addressing the question of metaphysics through a unique method (viz. by ducking the question of metaphysics) makes philosophy political. That is, in developing a methodological stance of agnosticism towards metaphysics philosophy becomes political. In 'Justice as Fairness: Political not Metaphysical' (1985) Rawls declares:

> In this discussion I shall make some general remarks about how I now understand the conception of justice that I have called 'justice as fairness' (presented in my book *A Theory of Justice*). I do this because it may seem that this conception depends on philosophical claims I should like to avoid, for example, claims to universal truth, or claims about the essential nature and identity of persons. My aim is to explain why it does not. I shall first discuss what I regard as the task of political philosophy at the present time and then briefly survey how the basic intuitive ideas drawn upon in justice as fairness are combined into a political conception of justice for a constitutional democracy. Doing this will bring out how and why this conception of justice avoids certain philosophical and metaphysical claims. (Rawls 1985, 388)

The grounds for philosophy as political or philosophy as metaphysics not discussed have been foregrounded in several parts of Rawls' work. As noted above 'The Independence of Moral Theory' argues how much of moral theory is only a part of moral philosophy and how it is somewhat independent of metaphysics (Rawls 1975c, 286-88). What is moral theory?:

> Moral theory is the study of substantive moral conceptions, that is, the study of how the basic notions of the right, the good, and moral worth may be arranged to form different moral structures. Moral theory tries to identify the chief similarities and differences between these structures and to characterize the way in which they are related to our moral sensibilities and natural attitudes, and to determine the conditions they must satisfy if they are to play their expected role in human life. (Rawls 1975c, 286)

Moral theory, therefore, has its own subject matter which has to be investigated for its own sake. Moreover, those parts of the other arenas of philosophy (viz. epistemology, theory of meaning, or metaphysics) which are relevant to moral philosophy (e.g. "the analysis of moral concepts, the existence of objective moral truths, and the nature of persons and personal identity") are dependent on an understanding of the structures of substantive moral conceptions and their relations to moral sensibility. Thus the traditional understanding that moral philosophy or ethics is dependent on clarification of issues at the higher semantical, epistemological or metaphysical levels is not quite correct. Just as, for instance, the theory of meaning became sensible after the underlying structure of its logical apparatus was explicated, so it is that the study of underlying structures of moral theory will give us the truth of moral philosophy. Hence Rawls can be seen here as arguing a case for an autonomous domain of studying moral sensibilities which at the same time is aware of its relationship to moral philosophy and the other domains of philosophy. The argument is not to deny that metaphysics etc. has any role in a discussion of moral sensibilities and their structures but that it is a relatively far off concern for the purposes here. The beginnings of doing philosophy in ambivalence towards metaphysics had begun.

Rawls' strategy of avoiding metaphysics in a discussion of morality and justice by analogy to logic is to be found again in one of his earliest writings—'Outline of a Decision Procedure for Ethics' (1951). Here the quest is for a rational procedure which would enable an adjudication of competing interests. Rawls is in search of certain criteria which shall be able to mark such a method or procedure (Rawls 1951, 1). The concern is only with a reasonable method and nothing beyond that.

> "The original question has been framed the way it is because the objectivity or the subjectivity of moral knowledge turns, not on the question whether ideal value entities exist or whether moral judgements are caused by emotions or whether there is a variety of moral codes the world over, but simply on the question: does there exist a reasonable method for validating and invalidating given

> or proposed moral rules and those decisions made on the basis of them?" (Rawls 1951, 1)

Therefore, the point towards which Rawls is straining is not that there is no such thing as philosophy but that philosophy is political and it is not metaphysics. That is, in the process of understanding the structure of our substantive moral conceptions and in the search for criteria to assess the validity of moral claims, philosophy becomes characterized not by metaphysics but by the political. In following the method of eschewing metaphysical questions philosophy becomes political in style. The philosophical method is one of mere description and of eschewing explanation of hidden layers of reality.

Rawls is able to advocate this position by adopting the stance of quietism as developed by Wittgenstein in his discussions on the nature of philosophy. The central point of Wittgenstein is that "philosophy simply puts everything before us, and neither explains nor deduces anything. Since everything lies open to view there is nothing to explain. For what is hidden, for example, is of no interest to us" (Wittgenstein 1988b, 50e). The Wittgensteinian quietism however gets circumscribed when Rawls' justice as fairness is thought to belie certain metaphysical or universalist elements in its assumptions of personhood which are seen, in turn, as facilitating the exclusion of women and the disabled from within its ambit.

### *2.4 The Quietist Wittgenstein*

Wittgenstein is normally taken to be a part of the legacy of analytic philosophy and logical positivism which usually liked to see itself as taking up and developing certain parts in Kant's writings, namely those which were more amenable to a philosophy of language and logic (Hylton 1992 and Coffa 1998). The ground on which they can be compared is their response to metaphysics. Both Wittgenstein and Kant were interested in restricting the scope of metaphysics. However, whereas Kant's exertions were directed towards re-establishing the importance of metaphysics Wittgenstein took the extreme step of making the raising of metaphysical questions appear irrelevant and thus ended up with philosophical quietism.

Philosophy was considered to the 'queen of the sciences' which is the repository of ultimate truths or essences. Even after the discovery of the empirical world by the experimental sciences philosophy hung on to the idea that its truths were more profound than those of the rest. This special province was metaphysics whose hidden knowledge was still accessible by the traditional methods of analysis, reflection and inference. Wittgenstein felt that this claim of philosophy was untenable.

However, his contention was that most metaphysical questions in philosophy were nonsense because they are logically indistinguishable from incoherent talk. Importantly, Wittgenstein wanted to see him saying that philosophical statements are logically incoherent without at the same time having the need to propose alternative answers about reality or by adducing to any theory of meaning. "Most of the propositions and questions to be found in philosophical works are not false but nonsensical. Consequently we cannot give any answer to questions of this kind, but can only point out that they are nonsensical..." (Wittgenstein 1988a, 19). Philosophers tended to think that there are problems objectively out there which they have to set out to discover. Wittgenstein, on the contrary, thought that there are no objective problems which have to be discovered from the depths by trained experts. Most of the time those problems arose precisely because we misunderstood the nature of things. Hence "...it is not surprising that the deepest problems are in fact *not* problems at all" (Wittgenstein 1988, 19). For Wittgenstein, therefore, it was only wise that we should simply ignore most philosophical questions and statements and let them lie. This was to be the hallmark of the philosophical method. "Instead of teaching doctrines and developing theories, Wittgenstein came to think, a philosopher should demonstrate a technique, a method of achieving clarity" (Monk 1991, 297). Accordingly "What we cannot speak about we must pass over in silence" (Wittgenstein 1988a, 74), we must remain quiet. A difficulty in this entire process (which shall not be addressed here) is the extent to which Wittgenstein follows his pronouncements on philosophical method while he himself is doing philosophy. Crispin Wright has noted that "...a *real* integration of Wittgenstein's official conception of philosophy with his own practice is something which has so far eluded even the best commentary" (Wright 2001, 439).

The concern with philosophy as method arises out of Wittgenstein's unhappiness with his early work largely defined by the logical atomism of the *Tractatus-Logico Philosophicus* (1921) (hereafter *TLP*) (Wright 2001, 439) and the 'verificationist phase' immediately following it. During his fascination with verification "...Wittgenstein believed that most of the things people would call 'propositions' are not properly so-called. Genuine propositions must be capable of truth or falsehood, which, for Wittgenstein, meant the same thing as conclusive verification or conclusive falsification in terms of the given. A 'proposition' is, therefore, in effect, a prediction that some particular contingent event will take place in my life; it will be verified if the event takes place, falsified if it does not" (Coffa 1988, 250).

But what had Wittgenstein said in the *TLP*? Very broadly, first, the purpose of this work was to "elucidate the essence of any possible *language*, to clarify the nature of any form of representation" (Baker and Hacker 2000, 34). The investigation of language thus became the correct subject matter of philosophy and not traditional metaphysics because it went beyond the limits of sense. Accordingly logic became the study of the essential properties of symbols and not the study of language-independent concepts, laws and judgements. However, the concerns of metaphysics were to be found in the sentential or propositional nature of a language. Second, an important contention was that any possible language is governed by a complex system of logical rules (Baker and Hacker 2000, 34-35). One type of rules determines the modes of combinations of atomic propositions while the other concerns names: "the combinatorial possibilities of names mirror the combinatorial possibilities of the objects which are their meanings and the proposition pictures the state of affairs which it represents" (Baker and Hacker 2000, 35). This relation is ineffable and mental.

There are several important implications of these two concerns (Baker and Hacker 2000, 35-36). The logical structure of the rules governing our language is hidden from view and is not to be discovered in our daily linguistic practices. Secondly, these underlying rules operate independent of human activities. Further, the correct analysis of a proposition may be hidden. Fourthly, when a person has mastered a language it means that he has implicit knowledge of the rules of logical structure.

These concerns were largely overturned later by Wittgenstein himself in the *Philosophical Investigations* (hereafter *PI*) (Wittgenstein 1988b). In reformulating his philosophy Wittgenstein resolved these concerns into five core theses (Pitcher 1972, 171-87). One of the theses was that "the world is all that is the case" (Wittgenstein 1988a, 5) and that it can be divided not into things but into atomic facts. "The world is the totality of facts, not of things" (Wittgenstein 1988a, 5) and "the world divides into facts" (Wittgenstein 1988a, 5). However, Wittgenstein later contends that how a thing divides up or what are its ultimate constituents do not depend so much on reality—such that one account becomes right and the others wrong—as much on the purposes the dividing up is supposed to serve or the viewpoint from which the dividing is being done. Hence the world can be divided up into facts or things or events as equally alternative ways of division. "An account of the world in terms of things, an account of the world in terms of facts and an account of the world in terms of events is just an account of one world in three languages" (Wisdom 1972, 174). Accordingly each proposition has not one final analysis but radically different analyses.

The second assumption challenged is that every proposition has a determinate or definite sense. "When a proposition expresses it expresses in a determinate manner, which can be set out clearly; a proposition is articulate" (Wittgenstein 1988a, 13). The sense of a proposition is the situation which it describes and a situation must be taken to exist as part of the world. As such a proposition can have only one specific sense. The real logical form of the proposition is buried in it and can be brought to light by analysis. However in reality many propositions are indeterminate and somewhat vague and yet we manage to keep up communication. Hence a working proposition is good enough and does not require in-depth analysis.

This encourages Wittgenstein to question analysis itself. Analysis is supposed to be the process through which the meaning or sense of a proposition is made clear. However a consideration of any number of propositions shows that often analysis—breaking down of the one proposition into its constituents—does not necessarily express things better than what is there in the original proposition. Hence analysis is not the only way of conveying the meaning between words. Analysis is further constrained by the fact that its ability to decompose complex things into its simplest constituents is hampered because nothing is absolutely simple. What is simple and what is complex is contextual.

Thirdly, the earlier conception of meaning is questioned. The meaning of a name was supposed to be the object which it denotes. "A name means an object. The object is its meaning" (Wittgenstein 1988a, 12). Here the confusion is between the bearer of a name with the meaning of the name. Wittgenstein realizes later that what corresponds to the name is its bearer and not its meaning. "The meaning of a name...is given by the various descriptions which apply to the bearer of the name and enable one to identify it" (Pitcher 1972, 181). Hence the meaning of a name and what it applies to—its bearer—are quite different and cannot be identified with one another.

It can be said further that since absolute simples do not exist and since there is no identification between name and object the contention that elementary propositions are pictures of reality also does not hold. This is how Wittgenstein argues his case while distancing himself from the picture theory of reality in the *TLP*. As elementary propositions do not exist and as indestructible simple reality does not exist picturization becomes impossible.

The fifth thesis questioned is the one that the link between language and the world is through meaning or the mental act of intending: "...a person speaks or writes the propositional sign and, in addition, performs the mental act of intending (meaning) the different words to stand for certain specific objects, of intending (meaning) the propositional sign to describe just one specific situation, and no other" (Pitcher 1972, 184). This proposition is based on the difference between saying something and meaning it, and saying something without meaning it. But it is extremely difficulty to say something and mean something else. "Make the following experiment: *say* 'it's cold here' and *mean* 'it's warm here'. Can you do it?—And what are you doing as you it? And is there only one way of doing it?" (Wittgenstein 1988b, 140e). Similarly it should be possible to mean something without saying anything. This again is very difficult (Wittgenstein 1987, 42-43). These are some of the reasons adduced by Wittgenstein to say that he was wrong about language, mind and world in his early phase.

These difficulties constitutes for Wittgenstein difficulties in understanding the "logic of our language" (Grayling 1988, 68). "Most of the propositions and questions of philosophers arise from our failure to understand the logic of our language" (Wittgenstein 1988a, 19). However, the solution lies in not devising an alternative philosophical theory of language or of something else but to make them irrelevant by showing how it is our misunderstandings which generated these issues as problems. This method will dissolve away our misconceptions and the tensions which they generate, resulting in peace and quiet of mind. Philosophy and its method are thus therapeutic: "The philosopher's treatment of a question is like the treatment of an illness" (Wittgenstein 1988b, 91e).

The key then is to look into the workings of our language. This can be done by studying the grammar or in-depth logic of a linguistic activity rather than by studying its surface logic. Philosophy becomes a grammatical activity (Grayling 1988, 69). However, the rules of this grammar are not universal as in the logical syntax of the *TLP* but they are "...rules of particular languages at particular times, characteristic of particular forms of representations" (Baker and Hacker 2000, 40). Grammatical study or the study of the logic of our language means that our philosophical activity is limited to describing the nature of arrangement of terms in our linguistic activity. It does not mean the search for underlying causes of our linguistic activity.

Philosophy is thus a descriptive activity and not an explanatory one (Grayling 1988, 69).

Explanation is the process used by science to justify its propositions with hypotheses and empirical examination. In science reality is hidden—in the sense that it is not observable—and theories are postulated to see if the hidden reality can be dug up. In order to activate the theories conjectures or hypotheses are made and verified against reality. This decides whether our theories give us a purchase on hidden reality (i.e. makes them observable) or some other theories are required. Wittgenstein says it is a mistake for philosophy to proceed as if it were science.

> "It was true to say that our considerations could not be scientific ones. It was not of any possible interest to us to find out empirically that, contrary to our preconceived ideas, it is possible to think such-and-such—whatever that may mean. (The conception of thought as a gaseous medium.) And we may not advance any kind of theory. There must not be anything hypothetical in our considerations. We must do away with all *explanation*, and description alone must take its place. And this description gets its light, that is to say its purpose, from the philosophical problems. These are, of course, not empirical problems; they are solved, rather, by looking into the workings of our language, and that in such a way as to make us recognize those workings: *in despite of* an urge to misunderstand them. The problems are solved, not by giving new information, but by arranging what we have always known. Philosophy is a battle against the bewitchment of our intelligence by means of language." (Wittgenstein 1988b, 47e)

Wittgenstein illustrates this by elucidating the workings of our language. The objections raised to the received theory of language as discussed in the core five theses show how language has been misunderstood. In searching for indestructible reality behind names and propositions we have searched for the essential properties of language. By now we know how mistaken we are to have understood language in this way. Instead of reading language by rearranging what already lies open to view we have erected hidden realities and sought to dig deep to excavate these hidden essences (Grayling 1988, 70-71). Questions have been formulated in us through our desire to penetrate phenomena in linguistic analysis. As looking for hidden depths of language are incorrect our questions arising from this quest are also wrong. "We feel as if we had to *penetrate* phenomena: our investigation, however, is directed not towards phenomena, but, as one might say, towards the '*possibilities*' of phenomena" (Wittgenstein 1988b, 42e). The working of a language is the working itself—the working of a language can be understood by the working itself and not by looking for something hidden behind them.

Language is not stuck to one form of reality, that is, it does not display a single underlying logical structure. We do so many different sorts of things with language that one cannot but be struck with its variety and multiplicity. "It is interesting to compare the multiplicity of the tools in language and of the ways they are used, the multiplicity of kinds of word and sentence, with what logicians have said about the structure of language (Including the author of the *Tractatus Logico-Philosophicus*.)" (Wittgenstein 1988b, 12e). It is a multifarious activity, the various parts of which is related to each other and is not bound by a unitary theory of meaning. "We see that what we call 'sentence' and 'language' has not the formal unity that I imagined, but is the family of structures more or less related to one another. But what becomes of logic now? Its rigour seems to be giving away here..." (Wittgenstein 1988b, 46e). Meaning of a word is contextualized by the language-game of which it is a part of then and not the object which it denotes (Grayling 1988, 71-73). It is the practice of a word which gives it its meaning. "Here the term 'language-*game*' is meant to bring into prominence the fact that the *speaking* of language is part of an activity, or of a form of life" (Wittgenstein 1988b, 11e). Thus "...understanding language means *knowing how to use it*" (Grayling 1988, 76).

One of the assumptions which the rejection of the five theses of the *TLP* implies is that our use of language is governed by rules. Language operates according to "a structured system of strictly defined rules (the rules of logic) which function automatically" (Grayling 1988, 77). The activities which form the framework of the possibility of following a rule are "teaching, explaining, justifying and criticizing, evaluating and defining rule-governed activities" (Baker and Hacker 2000, 47). The output of the application of these rules is meaning. A person understands the meaning of a word when he masters the rules which govern its use. The focus on language-games however indicates that the rules in language are not part of a single unitary grammar but are somehow related to the way a word is practiced. Rules are thus contextual to the language-game in question and are thus not independent of us. Hence there is no one rule in language but a multiplicity of rules.

Here Wittgenstein exhorts us to study further the implication of rule-following in language-games, that is, of the nature of rules not as in the rejected unitary model of the *TLP* but of rules in language-games. Rules have the danger of appearing objective, that is, of being understood as having a power to dictate whether what we are doing is correct or not independent of our practice of it. In other words, they acquire a capacity to tell us what to do. Read in this sense, rules also often are able to determine what the outcomes of their application are supposed to be. Wittgenstein contrasts this sense of rules with rules followed in language-games being rules which arise out of public practice: "What Wittgenstein emphasizes is the crucial fact that what *constitutes* a rule is *our collective use of it*: rule-following is a general practice established by agreement, custom, and training. Therefore, although rules indeed guide us and afford us with our measures of correctness, they are not independent of us and hence do not constitute a coercive standard imposed from outside our rule-following practices themselves" (Grayling 1998, 80-81). "A rule stands there like a sign-post..." (Wittgenstein 1988b, 39e) and so interpretation is not the only way of grasping a rule. In most cases we simply respond to our training and in doing so participate in an established practice.

"But how can a rule shew me what I have to do at this point? Whatever I do is, on some interpretation, in accord with the rule." That is not what we ought to say, but rather: any interpretation still hangs in the air along with what it interprets, and cannot give it any support. Interpretations by themselves do not determine meaning.

"Then can whatever I do be brought into accord with the rule?"—let me ask this: what has the expression of a rule—say a sign-post—got to do with my actions? What sort of connexion is there here?—Well, perhaps this one: I have been trained to react to this sign in a particular way, and now I do so react to it.

But that is only to give a causal connexion; to tell how it has come about that we now go by the sign-post; not what this going-by-the-sign really consists in. On the contrary, "I have further indicated that a person goes by a sign-post only in so far as there exists a regular use of sign-posts, a custom" (Wittgenstein 1988b, 80e).

Accordingly rule-following in language-games become customary practices which are thus public and not some hidden mental activity (as claimed by the link between language, mind and world in the *TLP*) (Grayling 1988, 81-82). There is no such thing as a private language. "And hence also 'obeying a rule' is a practice. And to *think* one is obeying a rule is not to obey a rule. Hence it is not possible to obey a rule 'privately': otherwise thinking one was obeying a rule would be the same thing as obeying it" (Wittgenstein 1988b, 81e). In other words it is not that a person follows a certain rule and then behaves accordingly but that his behaviour is the rule (i.e. the rule in practice). Therefore, a study of the logic of language—philosophy—does not have to look for hidden rules but study the manifest language behaviour which is the rule manifest in practice.

Secondly, while these rules are practices they are also social practices. That is, they exist in the community as a result of agreement in the community regarding their existence. Members of a community have to come to an agreement as to what would constitute rules of language. Accordingly rule-following once again becomes a public matter and there can be no private rule-following. Whether I am following a rule can be checked not by appeal to some underlying universal logic of language but by appeal to public criteria. By extension we can say that one knows that one is following a rule only when one is practicing a rule according to the publicly agreed upon criteria. Hence such rules are their own justification and they do not need any independent or external objective criteria to assess truth-claims: "...one is *not* following a given rule if one's activity fails to conform to the community's practice in that case" (Grayling 1988, 82).

Does it then mean that the rules which are agreed to are true? Wittgenstein answers this by incorporating another element in the explanation. He says that because linguistic practice reflects a multiplicity of things which we do as human beings agreement in rules refer to an agreement broader than an agreement between mere opinions. Agreement on the meaning of a word is more than the collective opinions or dispositions of the community—it is a consensus on action. Agreement refers to the sharing of a "form of life". Here Baker and Hacker have read Wittgenstein as saying that different epoch and cultures have different forms of life (Baker and Hacker 2000, 243). These distinct cultures have their own distinct conceptual structures and forms of representation. What does Wittgenstein mean by form of life?

"...it is the underlying consensus of linguistic and non-linguistic behaviour, assumptions, practices, traditions, and natural propensities which humans, as social beings, share with one another, and which is therefore presupposed in the language which they use; language is woven into that pattern of human activity and character, and meaning is conferred on its expressions by the shared outlook and nature of its users.... Thus a form of life consists in the community's concordance of natural and linguistic responses, which issue in agreement in definitions and judgements and therefore behaviour. Because the 'foundation', so to speak, of the practices which language-use consists in is the form of life into which that language is woven, it follows for Wittgenstein that questions about the ultimate explanation or justification of the concepts embodied in our thought and talk very soon *come to an end*—what justifies our usages is the shared form of life underlying them, and that is that: no more either need be or indeed can be said" (Grayling 1988, 84-85).

Therefore to ask philosophical questions in terms of metaphysics is a wrong thing to do. Cora Diamond (along with the likes of James Conant, Tom Ricketts and Warren Goldfarb) has, however, cautioned us against a pervasive mistake in the readings on philosophical method especially with reference to the substance and import of the *TLP* (Diamond 1996a, 13-38). She notes that there is a tendency to understand Wittgenstein as holding a realist position in the early work (largely the *TLP*) and an anti-realist position in the later work (largely the *PI*). Most of the foremost interpreters of Wittgenstein—F. Ramsey, Bertrand Russell, G.E.M. Anscombe, Norman Malcolm and Max Black—were subscribers to this tendency and contended that the *TLP* puts forward substantive claims about a language-independent reality. The realist position reads the *TLP* as claiming that the objects which make up the world are bound in fixed ways independently of language. Language mirrors this nature of things "in what it makes sense to say". These metaphysical features undergird the logical syntax of language. Language can never express them although they are there. The contention is here that Wittgenstein develops an anti-realist position in the *PI*. Now Diamond claims that "these readings of early and later work depend, both of them, on failure to take seriously what Wittgenstein says about philosophy itself. Both readings take for granted that there is a genuine philosophical question whether there are or are not metaphysical features of reality underlying structural or logical characteristics of language, and they see Wittgenstein as giving first one answer and then another" (Diamond 1996a, 18).

Diamond contends that the critique by the *PI* of the *TLP* lies precisely in mentioning that there is no philosophical problem. She argues out her case with two main points. First, the later Wittgenstein can be read as saying that the *TLP* does not make the contention that there is a reality underpinning the logical structure of our language no matter how unsayable it is: "...it is not, not really, his view that there are features of reality that cannot be put into words but show themselves. What is his view is that that way of talking may be useful or even for a time essential, but it is in the end to be let go of and honestly taken to be real nonsense, plain nonsense, which we are not in the end to think of as corresponding to an ineffable truth" (Diamond 1996b, 181).

Second, in this sense therefore, our propositions do not become metaphysical. Rather our propositions become metaphysical when we as philosophers (when we as persons doing philosophy) demand that they should be subjected to logical analysis, that is, they are to be rewritten in such a way that the logical relations already inhering in them become clearly visible. Subtending this is the belief that our propositional structure is inherently and already logical. Hence it is this requirement imposed on our propositions which make the act of imposition—philosophy—metaphysical. In other words philosophy creates or raises the shadow of a problem when it is not at all there. Furthermore it is only when we understand this way of looking at the *TLP* from the *PI* that we realize what Wittgenstein meant when he said that philosophy raises problems when they are not there and that therefore it is best to eschew (such a philosophy) and let things lie. At the least, the mind will get peace and be at rest. The only purpose of philosophy is to recognize the limits of philosophy and thus effect a therapy.

However P.M.S. Hacker, who is contemporary heir to the 'language-independent reality' reading and is of the opinion that one is left with some ineffable truths after the ladder is thrown away, calls this interpretation a "post-modernist defence" (of the value of the *TLP*) and feels that it is mistaken (Hacker 2000). He contends that the argument neglects the evidence in the other writings coterminus with the *TLP* which seems to go against it, and further, passages from the *TLP* are quoted selectively (i.e. passages are not plain nonsense when it suits the argument and those passages which further their argument are exempt from the "post-modern" analysis). Moreover, the distinction made in this argument between metaphysical truths which are considered plain nonsense and those which are "transitional" nonsense is problematic. Hacker believes that Wittgenstein's philosophical assertions may be nonsense but they are important nonsense because they can be used to understand the reality behind the logical syntax of language. Throwing them away as useless after having thus used them does in no way therefore reduce their importance or lead to the denial of reality behind language. Ian Proops argues that there are indeed substantial philosophical doctrines in the *TLP* which were later denied by the *PI* and other later writings, and it cannot be claimed that Wittgenstein has claimed that everything is nonsense and that all of it has to be thrown away (Proops 2001).

The clue to the Hacker-Diamond debate and the way forward is to be found, I think, in Marie McGinn's account: "On the other reading, far from being a work of metaphysics, *TLP* represents the 'unfolding of a therapeutic strategy'...the so-called philosophical perspective is an illusion. The upshot of this journey is that we are no longer tempted to ask or answer philosophical questions, but willingly confine ourselves to the realm of what can be said, the propositions of natural science" (McGinn 1999, 492). Diamond's therapeutic or quietist reading gives more space to science than to philosophy as the originator of new knowledge and understanding. This is important given that most analytic philosophy has come to accept and even propagate some version or the other of naturalism as the main ontological and epistemological paradigm. Diamond's interpretation has the further advantage of creating space for naturalism without making the assertion or denial of metaphysics necessary. The metaphysical or philosophical question is itself considered to be a non-question: philosophy becomes irrelevant because it is not now necessary to take a stand on whether there are or there are not metaphysical truths.

Being able thus to acknowledge the force of nature without having to take a metaphysical position appears to be a good option for one to take in the contemporary tussle beginning to take place within analytical philosophy—between the widely accepted paradigm of philosophy being naturalist and non-metaphysical and the attempts of some analytical philosophers to re-open the question of metaphysics. Rawls can be read as an attempt to work out this option through the realm of politics. He is trying to say that raising the issue of metaphysics in order to show that metaphysics is not there is itself metaphysical. There is no need to raise the bogey that metaphysics is there and that it is false and that therefore we have to remove it. Hence metaphysics or philosophy raises non-problems in its body and thereby itself becomes nonsensical. Metaphysics or philosophy has to remain quiet. In ethics, metaphysics or philosophy remains quiet by becoming political philosophy. In political terms this position can be understood as stating that:

> What is crucial here is that philosophical attempts at justification *not usurp* what is *for us* (as citizens) to accomplish. (Pohlhaus and Wright 2002, 804)

### 2.5 How is Rawls a Quietist?

In 'Justice and Fairness' (1958) Rawls states that the "fundamental idea in the concept of justice is fairness..." (Rawls 1958, 47) and the two principles of justice are the ones which specify justice as fairness. The two principles of justice, which are considered to be only a *part* of a comprehensive vision of the good society and are derived from the original position under conditions of the veil of ignorance, are "...first, each person participating in a practice, or affected by it, has an equal right to the most extensive liberty compatible with a like liberty for all; and second, inequalities are arbitrary unless it is reasonable to expect that they will work out for everyone's advantage, and provided the positions and offices to which they attach, or from which they may be gained, are open to all" (Rawls 1958, 48). However these principles of justice become most effective only under conditions of fairness. When free persons, having clear ideas of what are their legitimate claims, having no greater power over each other and engaged in a joint activity with competing claims, agree to these principles as being mutually acceptable does this particular conception of justice appear fair. "It is this notion of the possibility of mutual acknowledgement of principles by free persons who have no authority over one another which makes the concept of fairness fundamental to justice" (Rawls 1958, 59). Justice and its principles, therefore, make sense only when it is perceived as fair.

Now one of the central assumptions here is that a person is acting on the basis of his self-interest. Rawls is nonetheless at pains here to distinguish between a general theory of a person being self-interested from a person being self-interested in contexts of justice (Rawls 1958, 55-59). That is, he is trying to say that the issue of justice arises mainly when arbitration of competing claims have to be made and in such situations it is but natural to expect a person to argue from the point of protecting his self-interest only. This, however, does not mean that a person acts in all instances in his life from self-interest.

However, as Brian Barry notes, there is a significant shift in the understanding of personhood by the time Rawls writes the *TJ*: "...emphasis now rests on the desire to act justly being a central aspect of human development, a natural (and reflectively supported) extension of love for particular people and loyalty to particular associations. The desire to be just and co-operate in the maintenance of a just society is something that a man cannot frustrate except at the cost of stunting his moral nature, which is the most important part of himself" (Barry 1975, 2-3). The shift comes close on the heels of a growing importance of Kant in Rawls' work, viz. in the *TJ*. Kant becomes central as an armament to elaborate the social contract tradition against the claims of the utilitarians. Kant also acquires importance for his contributions to social and political theory (Barry 1975, 3-4).

Rawls' main statement on the importance of Kant to his work in the *TJ* is in § 40 which he titles "The Kantian Interpretation of Justice as Fairness" (Rawls 1972, 251-57). Justice as fairness is considered to be in consonance with the ethics of Kant, especially as they pertain to the notions of autonomy, rationality and categorical imperative. Now Rawls seems to be saying that these ethical principles of Kant are not to be understood as being based solely on universal or metaphysical assumptions. Care must be taken to read his ethics not from his works on moral philosophy but mainly from the works on politics and political theory. "It is a mistake, I believe, to emphasize the place of generality and universality in Kant's ethics. That moral principles are general and universal is hardly new with him.... It is impossible to construct a moral theory on so slender a basis..." (Rawls 1972, 251). He repeats this view in the footnote on the same page: "To be avoided at all costs is the idea that Kant's doctrine simply provides the general, or formal, elements for a utilitarian (or indeed for any other) theory.... One must not lose sight of the full scope of his view, one must take the later works into consideration" (Rawls 1972, 251). What are we to make of this?

Traditional metaphysics which was popular during Kant's time claimed that it was possible to know certain basic or foundational things about the world without having the need to take recourse to experience. It accordingly argued for such independent realities such as soul, world and God. Kant argued that the traditional proofs offered for "rational psychology", "philosophical cosmology" and "rational theology" respectively were unsound. We have no access to the human soul or self as a thing in itself but only what we appear to ourselves as, mediated by experience. Similarly the arguments given for several metaphysical propositions regarding the world—the world has a beginning, there is something simple, there is an absolutely necessary being, etc.—were flawed because they derived from the principles of reason wherefrom it is possible to both prove and disprove them. Again in the case of rational theology Kant said that the imagined perfection of God did not have much of an empirical purchase and that the ontological argument for God was eventually based on experience and was thus not a proof.

Now despite the compelling evidence of experience Kant did not go along with full-blown empiricism to claim that all knowledge can be reduced to sensations. It is not that we know the so-called laws of nature as they are in nature. Nature does not contain the laws. The laws through which we understand nature are constructions of our mind. This means that that the stimuli of nature are ordered and thus made sense of by the principles of our mind. These principles operate within the contexts of space and time, and certain *a priori* concepts or categories. In other words any sense experience that we know of is categorical and spatio-temporal. We do not and cannot know sensory experience otherwise. Hence, although the force of experience teaches us to shy away from the attractions of traditional metaphysics we at the same time do not have the privilege of knowing nature or things as they are—we know the world only through the spatio-temporal and categorical frameworks of the mind. The "noumenal" world or the world of things-in-themselves is unknowable. The upshot of this is that neither the metaphysics of tradition nor the metaphysics of experience is knowable by us. Therefore, true knowledge is based on these "synthetic *a priori*" principles of mind. In sum the claims of traditional metaphysics and that of its opposite empiricism are abandoned and conceptual experience is acknowledged. Traditional metaphysics is given up without giving up all metaphysics. This was Kant's metaphysics, worked out as "metaphysics as a science".

> "In order that as a science metaphysics may be entitled to claim not mere fallacious plausibility but insight and conviction, a *Critique of Reason* must itself exhibit the whole stock of *a priori* concepts, their division according to their various sources (Sensibility, Understanding, and Reason), together with a complete table of them, the analysis of all these concepts, with all their consequences, especially by means of the deduction of these concepts, the possibility of synthetical cognition *a priori*, the principles of its application and finally its bounds, all in a complete system. Critique, therefore, and critique alone, contains in itself the whole well-proved and well-tested plan, and even all the means required to accomplish metaphysics, as a science...." (Kant 1990, 139-40)

It is this understanding of metaphysics that Kant takes to the realm of morals. Like the scientific world the moral world too is subtended by principles which are not servants of the contingencies of nature and at the same time are not derived from metaphysical entities like soul or God. These principles are called "practical synthetic *a priori* judgements". These principles underlie all moral decisions and arguments. There is a slight twist however. Whereas in the natural order it is not possible to know the noumenal world, in the moral order it has to be assumed that a person has free will in order to enable him to take moral decisions. This implies knowledge of the noumenal world in the realm of morals. Hence a person is not only influenced by experience and its causal laws—the phenomenal world—but also by free will which belongs to the noumenal world.

Although free, the will becomes moral only when it is willed for duty's sake and not for self-interest (i.e. to merely satisfy a desire) which may or may not be in accordance with duty. The freedom of the will is shaped by the status of autonomy of the will. When one acts on the basis of desire or on the basis of something which is subjective or contingent, that is, with the aim of gaining the object towards which the action is leading the will is supposed to be heteronomous. The will becomes autonomous only when it acts in accordance with the moral law, that is, when it performs duties for duty's sake. Hence although intrinsically free the will acquires a higher desirable quality—autonomy—when it acts only for duty's sake. This autonomous will is true freedom. "The *autonomy* of the will is the sole principle of all moral laws and of the duties conforming to them; *heteronomy* of choice, on the other hand, not only does not establish any obligation but is opposed to the principle of duty and to the morality of the will" (Kant 1956, 33).

Another way of assessing the moral worth of the will is to see if a person wills what he wills to be universal law. It is extremely difficult though to ascertain empirically if an action has been done from duty. However, we can make sense of the dynamics of morality only if we assume a universal or metaphysical proposition that only acts done for duty's sake are morally worthy. Only if it is assumed that there is such a principle can we assess the moral worth of a person's actions because a person's volition is notoriously fickle and thus cannot form the base of estimating its worth. This is an *a priori* ideal and it is this which is called the "categorical imperative".

Kant breaks down the categorical imperative into three main formulae, the first of which is "Act only on the maxim through which you can at the same time will that it should become a universal law" (Kant 1964, 88). The second maxim is "Act in such a way that you always treat humanity, whether in your own person or in the person of any other, never simply as a means, but always at the same time as an end" (Kant 1964,

96). The third maxim is "...the Idea of the will of every rational being as a will which makes universal law" (Kant 1964, 98).

The first two formulae lay out very well our obligation to act keeping others or the universal in mind but the last formula of autonomy is significant because it establishes the conditions of our freedom. True, we must think of others and be responsible for ourselves but we must also be masters of ourselves. We have the freedom to give ourselves our laws so long as we satisfy the condition that the laws are applicable to all rational beings. We are a law unto ourselves. In other words, morals are formed and not dictated because we are free to formulate our own morals. Hence morality presupposes freedom. However, as we will formulate laws for ourselves keeping the universal moral law in mind our freedom consists in it being in tune with universal freedom. Accordingly, therefore, Kant calls freedom the "supreme principle of morality". These then are the fundamental *a priori* principles of the realm of morals. They constitute for Kant the metaphysics of morality. This metaphysics is *a priori* but at the same time not prisoners of traditional metaphysics: it is not God's commands but our autonomy which is the basis of our morality.

Now the metaphysics of morality is related to the realm of politics: "For Kant, a theory of politics (which, for him, amounts in the main to a metaphysics of law) is inevitably a part of the metaphysics of morality. This is so because politics deals with the question of what we ought to do in our social and political context, or in other words, it is concerned with establishing criteria by which we can settle public conflict of interests" (Reiss 1991, 20). In other words there are principles or laws which underpin all that happens in the realm of politics. However, these principles do not claim to arbitrate disputes in the inner life of a person. These principles are meant to arbitrate only in cases of one's duty towards others. Thus the principles which guide the settlement of matters when conflicts of interest take place in public constitute the political law or metaphysics of politics. Hence the metaphysics of politics is about morals but it is about public morals only. "On the one hand, ethics and politics overlap. On the other hand, moral and political duties are clearly different.

Political duties are not perfect duties towards oneself, but only what Kant call perfect duties towards others, whose non-performance is wrong and whose performance may therefore be enforced" (Reiss 1991, 20). Therefore, the principles of politics are substantially principles of right, principles which enable us to decide whether our public actions are right or wrong. The principles of politics or justice enable us to ascertain whether we are discharging our duty for the sake of duty, that is, willing our actions to be universal laws. In effect the principles of justice are the principles of law. Now what does this do to autonomy and categorical imperative?

The metaphysics of morals have established that we are our own masters—we are free and autonomous. However, in the realm of politics where we are dealing with the adjudication of only public morality, we become free to pursue our own ends of which we are capable provided they do not curtail similar freedom of others. That is, we are free to pursue our interests so long we adhere to the universal principles of law. This leads us to the central principle of right: "Every action which by itself or by its maxim enables the freedom of each individual's will to co-exist with the freedom of everyone else in accordance with a universal law is *right*" (Kant 1991a, 133). Therefore:

> The universal principle of right is basically only an application of the universal principle of morality, as laid down in the Categorical Imperative, to the sphere of law, and thus also to the sphere of politics. But since it is morally necessary to realise external freedom, we can be compelled by others to carry out our duty of entering civil society. But we do not have to become morally better to enter it; for the political problem must be capable of solution not only by good men, but even by 'a nation of devils (so long as they possess understanding)'. (Reiss 1991, 23)

This implies that, for the political sphere, it does not matter whether in my inner life I am treating human beings as ends in themselves and not as means or whether I am willing actions which are universal—that is, whether I am moral or not—so long I follow the law and thus contribute to the securing of external freedom in society. I might have the most selfish motivations for my actions but so long as I follow the law (i.e. play according to the principles of politics or justice) I am fine in the domain of politics. In other words the principles of justice secure for me only my external freedom. This in contrast to the metaphysics of morals which secure my internal freedom.

Metaphysics of morality thus restrained to the public sphere becomes morality of politics. The sphere of justice is connected to moral philosophy because it deals with the public morals of a person in society, but at the same time it is not concerned with promotion of morality but only with the securing of external freedom of a person through the law. The moral concern with autonomy and freedom is there in politics but it is restricted to public autonomy. There are three specifications of a publicly restrained metaphysics of morality; viz. a person is free, equal and self-dependent (Reiss 1991, 24-27). Man is free because he agrees to get coerced by laws to which he would have agreed. Laws are then not commands of the sovereign to his subjects but edicts which are given by the people unto themselves through the sovereign. In this sense acceding to public laws constitute man as his own law-maker and thus a person who is actually free from coercion, who is free. Second, the fairness of public law increases when everyone is made equal before the law. Last, no man should be dependent on others for formulating his public morals or legislation—he should be independent. This clearly shows that the sphere of politics seeks and itself becomes a further curtailment of metaphysics.

"Men are free, equal and self-dependent. This statement is derived from the idea of freedom. For if all individuals are free, they must necessarily be equally so; for the freedom of all individuals is absolute and can only be universally and equally restricted by law. Each free person must also be self-dependent. The idea of freedom entails the individual's autonomy, for it postulates the individual's power of exercising his will independently, uninhibited by improper constraint" (Reiss 1991, 25).

In sum then metaphysics remains in politics but in a highly restricted mode. Justice is adjudicated on the basis of some higher-order principles, principles which universally subtend all decisions and actions related to right, but which are not only not of the unknowable realm but are also only tenuously moral. These principles therefore handle autonomy or freedom—"the supreme principle of morality"—only in terms of its operation in the public sphere. Justice knows nothing about a person's autonomy outside his functioning in the public sphere of society, that is, outside his life as a citizen. No further 'inner' or 'deeper' level sources of the principles are discovered or are relevant here. Autonomy in the context of justice is only public autonomy or external freedom. Further external freedom is autonomy through voluntary submission to coercion.

When therefore Rawls is, in the context of justice and its principles, pointing towards Kant's political works he is usually read as hinting that metaphysical principles may be allowed to subtend any notion of justice but even these metaphysical principles need to be restrained by moving them away from comprehensive doctrines of the traditional metaphysical sort or even those of moral philosophy. The grounds for justice as fairness can be argued out in metaphysical terms but in a much restrained way. This also means saying that although comprehensive metaphysical doctrines do not form the grounds of justice as fairness the principles of justice are nevertheless derived from some metaphysical assumptions.

Rawls brings in Kant in the context of autonomy whilst discussing the nature of decision-making in the original position. The principles of justice as fairness constitute freedom because they are arrived at by individuals who in the original position have no idea of the consequences of their decisions. The decisions are taken autonomously and not heteronomously.

"Kant held, I believe, that a person is acting autonomously when the principles of his action are chosen by him as the most adequate possible expression of his nature as a free and equal rational being. The principles he acts upon are not adopted because of his social position or natural endowments, or in view of the particular of society in which he lives or the specific things that he happens to want. To act on such principles is to act heteronomously. Now the veil of ignorance deprives the persons in the original position of the knowledge that would enable them to choose heteronomous principles. The parties arrive at their choice together as free and equal rational persons knowing only that those circumstances obtain which give rise to the need for principles of justice" (Rawls 1972, 252).

However, as Rawls says that the individuals in the original position are there to promote their interests in the best way they can, Oliver Johnson (Johnson 1974, 61-62) is of the opinion that the nature of motivations of the individuals in the original position is not changed by the veil of ignorance—only the conditions under which the decisions are reached have changed: "Each man's decision, in other words, still has as its basis in want or desire" (Johnson 1974, 62). The conclusion is thus that the 'autonomy' of the original position under the veil of ignorance is not 'Kantian autonomy': it is heteronomous.

This argument appears to miss Rawls' usage of Kant. Rawls is trying hard to find a way of grounding decisions of the right and the wrong in society on certain principles which would be accepted by all as fair. He knows here how difficult it is to assess whether the motivations of a person's actions are just. In lieu of such yardsticks he assumes the opposite, namely, that the individuals in the original position are gathered together to promote their own interests as best as they can. In such a condition Rawls places the restriction that such self-motivated persons would be allowed to decide on the principles of justice to govern them only after they are denied of all possibility of knowing how these principles are going to affect each one of them. Hence although the motivations, to begin with, of these individuals are all self-centred the potency of their selfishness is immobilized by preventing them from anticipating the future of their desires under the regime of justice which they formulate. Rawls is, therefore, beginning from the 'bottom', from selfish individuals, and then working 'upwards' by trying to see how they can be got together to formulate bases of justice on which they would all roughly agree, that is, how principles of justice can be formulated. In other words he is giving Kant a better chance by adapting it to reality as he sees it. Instead of making the somewhat dodgy 'purity of heart' as the basis of formulating fair principles of justice, he assumes the more commonly perceived fact that people are selfish and proceeds to make these individuals agree to a couple of higher-order or universal justifications—*principles*. Far from not being a Kantian interpretation, Rawls can be read as a more pragmatic Kantian interpretation and therefore a Kantian interpretation which is likely to succeed.

The Kantian spirit is furthered by Rawls when he relates justice as fairness to the public sphere. The principles of justice are not principles of the inner recesses of one's emotions or morals but principles in the public realm. "For once we think of moral principles as a legislation for a kingdom of ends, it is clear that these principles must not only be acceptable to all but public as well" (Rawls 1972, 252). Justice as fairness and its principles are more political than moral. This is roughly the manner in which Kant discusses how the realm of politics constitutes only the outer shell of the metaphysics of morality. Rawls can thus be read as using Kant to state that metaphysical principles do form the foundation of justice as fairness but barely so. The conditions of freedom are minimally metaphysical. Freedom is political.

The spirit of Rawls' enterprise is to make justice universal but by keeping, as much as possible, one's feet on the ground as it were. This is apparent later on in the *TJ* when he discusses the categorical imperative and distinguishes it from hypothetical imperative.

"The principles of justice are also categorical imperatives in Kant's sense. For by a categorical imperative Kant understands a principle of conduct that applies to a person in virtue of his nature as a free and equal rational being. The validity of the principle does not presuppose that one has a particular desire or aim. Whereas a hypothetical imperative by contrast does assume this.... The argument for the two principles of justice does not assume that the parties have particular ends, but only that they desire certain primary goods. These are things that it is rational to want whatever else one wants.... The preference for primary goods is derived, then, from only the most general assumptions about rationality and the conditions of human life. To act from the principles of justice is to act from categorical imperatives in the sense that they apply to us whatever our aims are" (Rawls 1972, 253).

The desires of the individuals in the original position behind the veil of ignorance is in consonance with the categorical imperative because they represent what every one of these individual wants and not what this or that individual wants. Individual desires represent hypothetical imperatives. Freedom is there in following the commands of the categorical imperative rather than hypothetical imperative. Rawls contends that the thing desired by all the individuals—all rational beings—is considered to be certain primary goods. The universal here is not the entire universe of society which is so abstract that it is difficult to state. That which is wanted by all rational beings is considered to be the universal. These desires seem to be primary goods. Primary goods is not something which is desired and known only by the desiring and knowing individual in the original position but it is something which is desired and known by all the parties in the original position. The categorical imperative is thus limited to only the public. Primary goods become then more a part and parcel of the metaphysics of politics than of the metaphysics of morality. In arguing this way Rawls is, on the one hand, limiting the operation of the categorical imperative, as the foundation of principles of justice, by preventing the universal from being extended infinitely and being located in the depths of the moral sphere. On the other hand Rawls can be read as stating that although comprehensive doctrines do not subtend justice as fairness it is nevertheless grounded in metaphysical assumptions. Hence, unlike what Johnson has to say (Johnson 1974, 62-63), either way the Kantian spirit is very much there.

Rawls concludes this discussion by saying that "The original position may be viewed, then, as a procedural interpretation of Kant's conception of autonomy and the categorical imperative (Rawls 1972, 256). Recall that he wrote earlier to the *TJ*, in the 'Outline of a Decision Procedure for Ethics', that he is concerned with "...a reasonable decision procedure which is sufficiently strong, at least in some cases, to determine the manner in which competing interests should be adjudicated, and, in instances of conflict, one interest given preference over another..." (Rawls 1951, 1). In other words the procedure which is followed in order to arrive at the principles of justice is rational. That is, individuals in the original position behind the veil of ignorance follow a rational procedure to arrive at the principles of justice. These persons are then rational beings. Only such rational beings constitute the parties in the original position. Now there is no doubt that Rawls understands rationality as a process whereby individuals, in the furtherance of their ends or desires, weigh their options carefully before coming to a decision on the most effective option for each of them. In this sense, as Johnson says (Johnson 1974, 63-66), the rationality of the individuals is instrumental and geared towards their desire and far from being universal or moral in nature. Here Kant seems far away.

However, rational choice procedure seems to have two components: one, individuals weigh options carefully in order to select the most effective means to their ends and two, the choice is guided by their specific desires. Now Rawls takes care to limit this instrumentality by making it blind by dropping the veil of ignorance over the desires of individuals. Desiring individuals without knowing the consequences of their specific desires from the principles of justice to be formulated in effect formulate principles which do not have connection to their specific ends as motivations. They have to now take decisions on the principles on the basis of the most general information about society. In such a situation they have to weigh the options amongst this general information and choose the best possible course of action.

In doing this therefore the individuals in the original position are following the first component of a rational choice method. They are acting as rational agents because they are taking decisions on the basis of an instrumental and 'optimal-effectiveness' procedure. This instrumentality is nonetheless disconnected from the individuals' specific desires and connected only to the most general features or characteristics of society. In this sense the individuals do not satisfy the second component of a rational choice procedure. In other words it is only with the most general knowledge of society and not with the knowledge of the specific desires or ends of individuals that the rational choice process is followed.

This 'dialectical' procedure is followed by individuals who in the original position have been described as being autonomous and in consonance with the categorical imperative. The parties in the original position are autonomous and not heteronomous because they are made to mull over and act under a veil of ignorance, but this autonomy is not the autonomy of a pure universal spirit or something but the autonomy of a selfish person stretched to its limits. These limited autonomous persons act on the basis of the categorical imperative, but the categorical imperative is no comprehensive moral doctrine lying deep in our bosoms but universally wanted primary goods. Finally, the politically moral individuals follow the rational choice method but they disconnect it from their own specific desires.

Therefore everywhere in Rawls there appears to be a straining towards the universal, only to be checked by a limiting of the universal. Put another way, although a full-blown metaphysics do not form the foundation of justice as fairness it is nevertheless grounded in a "thin theory of the good". Apparently therefore Rawls is interpreting Kant in the *TJ* etc. to argue that justice as fairness and its principles can be justified on metaphysical grounds although these grounds are barely philosophical.

Now after the *TJ* Rawls apparently changes course towards a non-universal or non-metaphysical political justification for the principles of justice as fairness. Patrick Neal says that "The distinctive features of Rawls' later work can be explained in terms of three phases that were absent from *A Theory of Justice* but now figure centrally in his thinking. The theory of justice is to be understood (1) as "political, not metaphysical", (2) as "political, not comprehensive", and (3) as designed to pursue the "practical task of political philosophy in a constitutional democracy" (Neal 1994, 78). The uneasiness with metaphysical propositions is taken to be anticipated in the works of the middle period before all metaphysics is abandoned in favour of a political conception of justice in the later works. Hence there is a shift away from comprehensive universal doctrines and a commitment to argue out the case of justice as fairness in the context of existing social practices in liberal democratic societies only. This has attracted the critical attention of numerous commentators (Hampton 1989, Neal 1990, Alejandro 1996 and Raz 1999). Most of them have complained that a non-metaphysical conception does not provide adequate grounds for political principles of justice. Some have gone further to contend that a political conception of justice in that sense is not only inadequate but impossible (Steinberger 2000). Most of these critics agree however that Rawls did say in his later works a few important things about justice which he had not in his early writings. In short, Rawls did a *volte-face*. Is that really the case?

Roger Sullivan argues that Kant's discussion of the metaphysics of morality and politics is done keeping the conception of the state as a nodal point (Sullivan 1995, 239-45). Kant was, like Thomas Hobbes, at pains to point out the universal mutual antagonism of men. In the state of nature described by Hobbes, where people are in a constant state of war, it is difficult to formulate rights and principles of justice. Therefore, when people do enter into a social contract to form and be part of a state it is out of a realization that it is in their own interest to limit their freedom to some extent. Civil laws of the state would try to protect each of them and thus facilitate the achievement of their goals. Hobbes had thought that an authoritarian government or state is required to ensure the rights of people and their self-preservation.

Kant had however argued differently. He agreed with Hobbes that a state with coercive powers was very much necessary. As there is the forever danger of men regressing to violence, barbarism and power-play a higher mediating authority like the state is required.

"Thus the first decision the individual is obliged to make, if he does not wish to renounce all concepts of right, will be to adopt the principle that one must abandon the state of nature in which everyone follows his own desires, and unite with everyone else (with whom he cannot avoid having intercourse) in order to submit to external, public and lawful coercion. He must accordingly enter into a state wherein that which is to be recognised as belonging to each person is allotted to him by law and guaranteed to him by an adequate power (which is not his own, but external to him). In other words, he should at all costs enter into a state of civil society" (Kant 1991b, 137).

But he contended that the justification of the state cannot be based on the fear and instinct of self-preservation of men. The state has to be based on the positive ideal of freedom which is innate in each rational being which not only calls for the individual's self-preservation and gratification of desires but also the acceptance by the individual of his obligation to recognize and respect the freedom of others. "... [Kant's] claim [is] that the *justification* of the state ultimately must rest on *moral* grounds..." (Sullivan 1995, 240). The state therefore initiates and develops a juridical regime which is geared towards ensuring the exercise of external freedom of all. "It is the moral law that makes the formal structure of the state something more than a more peaceful state of nature" (Sullivan 1995, 240). The main instrument in the hand of such a state is the civil constitution. Kant was clear that there is no alternative society outside the state because then the law of chaotic nature reigns. "Clearly submission to the authority of a state and the usually imperfect rule of civil law is both prudentially and morally preferable to the lawless rule of mobs and the violent resolutions of conflict" (Sullivan 1995, 242). He was also clear that revolution is not an option. Revolution for Kant implies a return to the state of nature and not anything else. Paradoxically therefore the coercive powers of the state are necessary to autonomy and freedom by preventing obstacles to their external exercise.

Kant can thus be read as saying that it is only within the context of the state that the innate freedom of the individual is assured expression—at least in its external form. There is chaos outside the state, and the Hobbesian state is promotive of people's freedom only on prudential grounds which are inadequate for a person. Moreover, revolution is banned because it implies a return to the state of nature. This shows that the metaphysical principles subtending morality and justice convey meaning for the individual only when the Kantian state exists. The transition from the natural condition in which human beings finds themselves to a civil, juridical and political condition can be effected only within a specific structure which is called the state. Morality's and politics' metaphysics hold only if it assumes a state. Autonomy and right comes to naught outside the state.

This limiting of the metaphysics of morals and politics by the state imbues it with certain characteristics. First, the Kantian state is a liberal one. It conveys certain basic tenets of the liberal tradition:

> "It is *individualist*, in that it asserts the moral primacy of the person against the claims of any social collectivity; *egalitarian*, inasmuch as it confers on all men the same moral status...*universalist*, affirming the moral unity of the human species and according a secondary importance to specific historic associations and cultural forms; and *meliorist* in its affirmation of the corrigibility and improvability of all social institutions and political arrangements." (Gray 1995, 234)

The liberal state is also a competitive one:

> "Given Kant's view of the innate and unsociable drives in human nature, the rule of law apparently does not mean that people within a juridical society will live together in perfect harmony, nor does it seem that the state should try to do way with all competition between them, for that would mean the end of progress in the development of reason within the state.... Rather, the state should allow everyone the greatest amount of latitude for the competitive pursuit of morally permissible goals, but within a lawful common life...." (Sullivan 1995, 242)

Kant also argues that if peace among peoples of the world is to ensue then the liberal and competitive states cannot limit themselves to being virulent nationalistic entities but come together to form a confederation of republics (Kersting 1992, 361-64). In order to achieve complete freedom the international state of nature of lawlessness has to be given up. "An essential condition of an enduring condition of peace among states is that all states become republics" (Kersting 1992, 362). Hence the liberal and competitive Kantian state is also an international federation. The moral and rightful grounds of justice presume a republican state which is also international.

Kant is, therefore, plainly saying that the transition from the state of nature to the state of moral justice leads to at one and the same time the formation of, and is done on the terrain of, an entity called the state which acquires the characteristics of liberalism, competitiveness and internationalism. The liberal and competitive international state is immanent in the process of formation of metaphysical grounds of justice. In other words the state, being a liberal competitive and international state, forms the condition for the metaphysics of morality and politics. If that were so then the metaphysics of morality and justice is a metaphysics limited to the liberal and competitive international state. That is, there is no metaphysics irrespective of the state which is such. Therefore, the metaphysics of morality and politics is not metaphysical. The upshot of this is that Kant can be read as arguing that in the context of justice there are no metaphysical foundations after all.

In the *TJ* Rawls indicates how his conception of justice is not universal but largely applies to a certain type of society when he elaborates on "the circumstances of justice" in the discussion on the original position (Rawls 1972, 126-30). According to him the issue of justice arises in societies where people are born into arrangements of voluntary association which are in need of rules of fair play. "The circumstances of justice may be described as the normal conditions under which human cooperation is both possible and necessary" (Rawls 1972, 126). The society which Rawls has in mind whilst discussing justice is a society which is marked by "cooperative venture for mutual advantage" (Rawls 1972, 126) and which is characterised by conflict and identity of interests. People cooperate because they are aware of the benefits which cooperation accrue to them whilst, on the other hand, they vie with each other for a greater share of the pie. The objective circumstance which makes cooperation possible and necessary is that "...many individuals coexist together at the same time on a definite geographical territory" (Rawls 1972, 126). These individuals are roughly homogenous in physical, intellectual and social terms. They also live under conditions of scarcity of natural resource endowments. The subjective conditions which make cooperation between these people possible and necessary are the differences in their plans and strategies for the good life which leads to conflictual situations under circumstances of scarcity. This situation is complicated by people having limited knowledge of affairs of the world and by the "diversity of philosophical and religious belief, and of political and social doctrines" (Rawls 1972, 127). "Thus, one can say, in brief, that the circumstances of justice obtain whenever mutually disinterested persons put forward conflicting claims to the division of social advantages under conditions of moderate scarcity" (Rawls 1972, 128). Now in order to bring about a resolution of this situation certain principles of justice are necessary. "Thus principles are needed for choosing among the various social arrangements which determine this division of advantages and for underwriting an agreement on the proper distributive shares" (Rawls 1972, 126).

Rawls does say that this situation is "...simply a part of men's natural situation" (Rawls 1972, 127) that is, the conditions of cooperation and conflict are universal to human society and that "The account of these conditions involves no particular theory of human motivation" (Rawls 1972, 130). But he also says that the self-oriented plans of the good life are "rational long-term plans (Rawls 1972, 129). Rational individualistic strategies of behaviour are normally, I think, taken to be characteristic of modern liberal societies and in the absence of any discussion of rationality in non-modern societies it is possible to read Rawls as holding that the circumstances of justice pertain to modern liberal societies. Rawls bases much of his account on David Hume's works (Rawls 1972, 126) and it is a truism that Hume's radical scepticism has been one of the hallmark contributions to the development of a modern and liberal society.

Further the fact that life in modern liberal societies needs the principles of justice implies the requirement of some agency which shall adjudicate and administer the principles. This agency shall also have the consensual authority of all individuals in such modern liberal societies. Now the adjudicating authority of justice in modern liberal societies is the state. Rawls does not say it as much but the assumption is there all over his discussion—he does not assume otherwise. Hence the principles of justice in justice as fairness are confined or limited to the modern liberal state. Accordingly they are not universal or metaphysical principles. They are principles which are necessarily internal to or immanent in the state, which also happens to be characterized by modernity and liberalism.

The parties in the original position know these very general circumstances of justice. They also know that in their deliberations they are taken to be persons promoting their own conceptions of the good life. These conceptions are also of a global nature because although they derive from a person's selfhood they are contingent in the sense of being constricted only by "...wealth, position, and influence, and the accolades of social prestige..." (Rawls 1972, 126). In this promotion of conceptions of the good life, although the individuals "are not bound by prior moral ties to each other" (Rawls 1972, 128) the desires are all not narrowly selfish. They are larger, finer and in a sense moral—even if they are the morality within or of the individual. Hence although the parties in the original position know only this very general information about the circumstances of justice and their conceptions of the good life and although they detach themselves from knowledge of the consequences of their decisions and actions on their selfish desires, they nevertheless remain within the framework of the modern liberal state. In other words the universal conditions of arriving at the principles of justice in the original position are universal only till or up to the borders of a limiting entity called the state, which further happens to be imbued with the characteristics of modernity and liberalism. Rawls can thus be read as holding that the conditions of justice as fairness are not metaphysical after all.

The Kantian concepts of autonomy and categorical imperative brought in by Rawls to give a metaphysical basis to the principles of justice as fairness carry forward this way of looking at universals which are not universals because framed by the larger context of the state. Whilst discussing the "real force" of Kant's views he says:

> For one thing, he begins with the idea that moral principles are the object of rational choice. They define the moral law that men can rationally will to govern their conduct in an ethical commonwealth.... This idea has immediate consequences. For once we think of moral principles as legislation for a kingdom of ends, it is clear that these principles must not only be acceptable to all but public as well. Finally Kant supposes that this moral legislation is to be agreed to under conditions that characterize men as free and equal rational beings. The description of the original position is an attempt to interpret this conception. (Rawls 1972, 251-52)

The ethical commonwealth of Kant is, as we have seen above, actualized through the state in the context of justice. The principles of justice that are usually considered to be a part of the metaphysics of politics (the philosophy of right) which form the outer shell of the metaphysics of morality, actually reveal that they are contextualized by the entity called the state (which, in our case, also happens to be modern, liberal and competitive) and hence may not be universal after all. The principles form the public sphere wherein the external freedom of the citizen is exercised and thereby presumes the terrain of the state.

Further the way to morality is, for Rawls' Kant, through rational choice. The parties in the original position are assumed to be persons who would weigh pros and cons with a clear idea of their ends in the process of making decisions. What is needed to guide these rational persons is not any comprehensive moral doctrine but an appropriate methodology: "Does there exist a reasonable method for validating and invalidating given or proposed moral rules and those decisions made on the basis of them?" (Rawls 1951, 1). Justice becomes a matter of method or procedure. "The original position may be viewed, then, as a procedural interpretation of Kant's conception of autonomy and the categorical imperative" (Rawls 1972, 256). We have noticed above how the proceduralism in Rawls is shaped by the adherence to the exercise of choice between options by the parties in the original position without reference to their very specific, narrow and selfish desires. One of the chief assumptions in the procedural or Kantian account has been the circumstances of justice and the dynamics of conflict-resolution under conditions of scarcity which they entail (Rawls 1972, 257). This assumption presumes the limiting entity of the state which has the features of modernity and liberalism.

Therefore it can be argued that Rawls is saying in the *TJ* that justice as fairness is not metaphysical at all. Rawls can be read as saying that the Kantian conception of justice presuming autonomy and categorical imperative does not necessarily mean that justice as fairness is subtended by metaphysical assumptions but that these Kantian notions are operational or expressible only within the terrain of the state, which happens to be modern liberal one. In other words although the induction of Kant in the argument of the *TJ* gives the impression that the effort is to seek for metaphysical or universal bases of the proposed principles of justice, Rawls is clear that these bases are themselves defined by another phenomenon called the state which is itself of a certain hue and shape.

Rawls continues his main argument—the foundations of justice as fairness are not metaphysical—in his writings of the middle and later periods but he turns, respectively, more inward from the state which is liberal to constitutional democracies like America (in 'Kantian Constructivism in Moral Theory') to existing intuitive social practices in modern liberal democracies (in 'Justice as Fairness: Political not Metaphysical' and in the *PL*). Rawls confides that "One thing I failed to say in *A Theory of Justice*, *or failed to stress sufficiently*, is that justice as fairness is intended as a political conception of justice.... In particular, justice as fairness is framed to apply to what I have called the 'basic structure' of a modern constitutional democracy" (Rawls 1985, 389) (emphasis added). The political conception of justice in the middle and especially later writings is a pointer towards the existence of a non-metaphysical justice as fairness in his earlier writings. In 'The Priority of Right and Ideas of the Good' (1988) he lays down as to what he means by a political conception of justice.

"The distinguishing features of a political conception of justice are, first, that it is a moral conception worked out for a specific subject, namely the basic structure of a constitutional democratic regime; second, that accepting the political conception does not presuppose accepting any particular comprehensive religious, philosophical, or moral doctrine; rather, the political conception presents itself as a reasonable conception for the basic structure alone; and third, that it is formulated not in terms of any comprehensive doctrine but in terms of certain fundamental intuitive ideas viewed as latent in the public political culture of a democratic society" (Rawls 1988, 450).

The principles of justice are to be found in practices already existing covertly in liberal democratic states which are geared towards working out "overlapping consensus" between divergent beliefs systems. The meaning of justice is somehow linked to the way it is practised. It remains a moral doctrine because it does not represent a temporary or expedient cessation of war between natural enemies, but because it evolves out of how modern citizens negotiate their lives in the face of competing claims to the good in the public sphere and is, therefore, not universal or metaphysical at all. The principles of justice are moral because they aim at securing a consensus across a broad bandwidth of people who are holding on to their religious or cosmological beliefs but the principles are not metaphysical because they are not aimed at establishing any one comprehensive doctrine as the ground for justice as fairness.

Rawls carries out his task in the later works which he had initiated in the *TJ*. He did not, therefore, say something in the *TJ* and something else in his middle and later works, whilst formulating a moral conception of justice as fairness and its principles. His work in the later phase points towards what was already similarly there in his earlier phase. For him then to say that there was a metaphysical issue in the *TJ* which is not there in the *PL* etc. is not a correct question. It is rather a non-question. The effort has been to justify justice as fairness on procedural grounds as distinguished from utilitarian or universal grounds and so metaphysical concerns were never an issue. To read Rawls as discussing metaphysics in the context of justice only to indicate it as a bogey later is itself a wrong way to look at his enterprise. Discussing justice as fairness as a philosophical enterprise is a bogus enterprise. Justice as fairness is a practical issue. How do we then relate this quietism to the question of personhood?

We have seen earlier how Nussbaum has identified two gaps in justice as fairness in its treatment of personhood which creates conditions conducive to the exclusion of women and people with physical and mental disabilities from the portals of justice and equality. Interestingly both the gaps can be traced to Rawls' Kantian heritage. We confine ourselves here to the question of gender. In the case of the family and women Rawls is said to contend that the principles of justice apply to the basic structure of society which does include the family but in the same breath he qualifies this view by stating that much of the internal life of the family is not amenable to the principles. This arises from Rawls' effort to rest the principles on grounds which makes raising the issue of the metaphysical inheritance of the principles unnecessary to the task at hand. The result of this is that Rawls takes Kant's sense of justice as something which is in the public realm, as something which is political, seriously. This usage of Kant is going on, we must not forget, in the context of Rawls' appropriating Kant as part of the search for non-prudential bases of the social contract. Taking justice largely to the realm of the public and the political is to eschew a conception of personhood based on the somewhat demeaning Hobbesian state of perpetual war and at the same time to escape from the necessity of having to advocate comprehensive moral doctrines for principles of justice. It has been noted of course that the upshot of this for the machinations in the private sphere of the family, especially for its women members, is not something to write home about. This is a genuine concern which Rawls does not appear to have addressed. What I would be wary of though—in redressing the situation—are efforts which point out the gaps in Rawls with the help of casual or otherwise references to the other social contractarian traditions. Nussbaum, for instance, invokes John Stuart Mill to show us the subjection of women in the family. This is all right as far as it goes but invoking the other traditions does poses difficulties if Rawls' motivation and the consequent argument to link up with Kant in order to overcome the well accepted shortcomings of the Hobbesian social contract (without at the same time walking into any Rousseaunian position) is considered as legitimate. In other words Rawls' effort to maintain quiet with regard to metaphysics even in the company of Kant whilst engaged in the business of formulating principles of justice for liberal democratic societies which are shaped as nation states does not appear to enable him to address the question of gender adequately. However, alternatives need to be clear of the desirability of comprehensive moral doctrines or a violent state of affairs subtending whatever principles of justice in an increasingly multicultural world. Nonetheless it is important to listen to Rawls' quietism as, in our case, it has implications for the fate of "primary goods".

### *2.6 Quietism and Primary Goods*

The idea of primary goods or, more correctly, "primary social goods" is introduced by Rawls in § 11 of the *TJ*. Rights, opportunities, wealth and self-respect are the primary goods, of which self-respect is considered to be the most important one (Rawls 1972, 440). Rawls says that:

> ...the basic structure of society distributes certain primary goods, that is, things that every rational man is presumed to want. These goods normally have a use whatever a person's rational plan of life. For simplicity, assume that the chief primary goods at the disposition of society are rights and liberties, powers and opportunities, income and wealth. (Later on in Part Three the primary good of self-respect has a central place.) These are the social primary goods. Other primary goods such as health and vigor, intelligence and imagination, are natural goods; although their position is influenced by the basic structure, they are not so directly under its control. (Rawls 1972, 62)

The primary social goods are the bare minimum which forms the expectations for any person no matter what the exact plans of his life are. These goods are to be seen as contributive of furthering the ends of the person irrespective of the specific plan held by the person. That is, primary goods can contribute to any rational plan prepared by a person to achieve the ends of his life. In this sense the primary goods have great power in the satisfactions of people's desires. The more people have these primary goods the more success they are likely to have in meeting their ends. The parties in the original position are permitted knowledge of these primary goods as part of their knowledge of the circumstances of justice. "While the persons in the original position do not know their conception of the good, they do know, I assume, that they prefer more rather than less primary goods. And this information is sufficient for them to know how to advance their interests in the initial situation" (Rawls 1972, 93). Therefore, primary goods also become an excellent tool to operationalize the second part of the second principle of justice—more famously, the "Difference Principle". The difference principle requires some measure of interpersonal comparison in order to decide how we are to say who are the least disadvantaged and on what grounds. This measure is that of primary goods. We can assess levels of disadvantage on the basis of access to primary goods which all rational beings desire.

The primary goods of roughly rights, opportunities, wealth and self-respect are based on a larger conception of what is good for persons and society. This larger conception is called by Rawls as the "thin theory of the good". It states that "The main idea is that a person's good is determined by what is for him the most rational long-term plan of life given reasonably favourable circumstances" (Rawls 1972, 92-93). The connection here therefore is that what is rational for the person—what is promotive of the person's desires—is the good: "...once we establish that an object has the properties that it is rational for someone with a rational plan of life to want, then we have shown that it is good for him" (Rawls 1972, 399). Adina Schwartz summarizes Rawls here fairly well:

> The three parts of the thin theory's definition correspond to three senses of the term "good": (1) the sense in which we say that an object is good since it achieves what is commonly desired in objects of its kind; (2) the sense in which we say that an object is good for a person since it achieves what he desires in objects of that kind; and

> (3) the sense in which we say that an object serves a person's good since it achieves what he wants in objects of that kind, and his desire is a part of a system of desires and aims which correctly reflects what he wants in life. (Schwartz 1973, 299)

In other words those objects which appear good or desirable to the person who is following a rational procedure in his decision-making are the objects in a thin theory of good. That is, if a person follows the procedure of weighing pros and cons of the choices available and selects a choice which is likely to give him the greatest beneficial effect then that choice constitutes the good for him. In this process there is no need to presume comprehensive doctrines and thus the thin theory of the good becomes for Rawls a morally neutral theory. The thin theory of the good however is distinguishable from the "thick" theory of the good:

> And in fact I shall distinguish between two theories of the good. The reason for doing this is that in justice as fairness the concept of right is prior to that of the good. In contrast with teleological theories, something is good only if it fits into ways of life consistent with the principles of right already on hand. But to establish these principles it is necessary to rely on some notion of goodness, for we need assumptions about the parties' motives in the original position. Since these assumptions must not jeopardize the prior place of the concept of right, the theory of the good used in arguing for the principles of justice is restricted to the bare essentials. This account of the good I call the thin theory: its purpose is to secure the premises about primary goods required to arrive at the principles of justice. Once this theory is worked and the primary goods accounted for, we are free to use the principles of justice in the further development of what I shall call the full theory of the good. (Rawls 1972, 396)

The thin theory of the good then turns out to be a procedural notion and we are aware that the rational choice involved in it presumes or requires a person with individualistic and liberal orientation. Therefore, the goods which are notified as primary and which are taken to arise from the more fundamental understanding of the good are specific to cultures and societies which permit if not valorise individualism and liberalism. In other words basic liberties and rights, equal opportunities, income and wealth, and self-respect become primary goods which every person will want no matter what his goals in life are only in societies which are bounded by the larger context or framework of liberalism. That is, individuals will find that these goods would provide value-addition to their pursuits of an improvement in life-situations no matter what their exact strategies or plans for improvement are.

Adina Schwartz (Schwartz 1973) and Thomas Nagel (Nagel 1973) have also pointed out that the thin theory of the good does not make sense unless one is a liberal democrat and also that it is more likely to help a person with individualistic tendencies than a person who seeks wish-fulfilment in communal goals or in the enhancement of finer human capacities and suppression of baser ones, etc. Nagel thus concludes that "The original position seems to presuppose not just a neutral theory of the good, but a liberal, individualistic conception according to which the best that can be wished for someone is the unimpeded pursuit of his own path, provided it does not interfere with the rights of others" (Nagel 1973, 228). Schwartz and Nagel however seem to harbour the notion that since, on the one hand, Rawls is claiming a universal status for the principles and for the primary goods from which they are derived in the original position and, on the other, the thin theory of the good is turning out to be specific to liberal societies, Rawls' principles of justice cannot be arrived at. The point however is precisely that Rawls is not saying that the principles of justice, primary goods and the thin theory are universal for all societies or that they incorporate some metaphysical elements. Rawls is saying that all of these are being discussed by him only in the context of liberal societies. Hence the general good is the general good only for liberal societies. The general is particular.

The same contention is made more explicitly by Rawls in *JFR*. Rawls says that the idea of primary goods has been introduced in order to arrive at a working definition of the least advantaged class in a liberal democratic society when discussing the second principle of justice or the difference principle (Rawls 2003, 57).

"These are various social conditions and all-purpose means that are generally necessary to enable citizens adequately to develop and fully exercise their two moral powers, and to pursue their determinate conceptions of the good. Here we look to the social requirements and the normal circumstances of human life in a democratic society. Primary goods are things needed and required by persons seen in the light of the political conception of persons, as citizens who are fully cooperating members of society, and not merely as human beings apart from any normative conception. These goods are things citizens need as free and equal persons living a complete life; they are not things it is simply rational to want or desire, or to prefer or even to crave. We use the political conception, and not a comprehensive moral doctrine, in specifying those needs and requirements" (Rawls 2003, 58).

There is no metaphysics involved in primary goods. Secondly, since it is now assumed that primary goods are goods because they arise from the normal life of citizens in democratic societies there is no need to have a second assumption that they arise from rational or procedural situations. Democratic societies are already rational or procedural. Hence Rawls is not saying that earlier he had understood primary goods as being universal because rational and now he is holding that primary goods are particular to liberal democratic societies. Here Rawls can be read as saying that primary goods were always specific to liberal democratic societies. The main new thing here is that he calls this notion of primary goods "political". As liberalism presumes the entity called the state, primary goods express the good only in liberal democratic states. Put another way, the notion of primary goods can be used only in the context of justice in societies which are organized as states which also happen to be liberal. In other words, the notion of primary goods cannot be used in any account of justice in any society other than in a liberal one organized as a state. Primary goods are not intended to account for justice in all types of societies universally.

However it is advantageous to remember here, in consonance with the feminist critique, that primary goods as evaluative mechanisms of justice in liberal democratic societies remain confined to the public sphere. They do not necessarily form the best possible measure of justice and freedom for private spheres such as the family which is so much the site of the gender question. What then are the implications of all this for Sen's critique of Rawls in term of capability and for his conception of development as freedom which emerges from this critique?

### 3. Capability and Primary Goods

What is capability? Sen says that:

> A person's achieved living can be seen as a combination of 'functionings', or 'doings and beings'. Given *n* different types of functionings, an '*n*-tuple' of functionings represents the focal features of a person's living, with each of its *n* components reflecting the extent of the achievement of a particular functioning. A person's 'capability' is represented by the set of *n*-tuples of functionings from which the person can choose any one *n*-tuple. The 'capability set' thus stands for the actual freedom of choice a person has over alternative lives that he or she can lead. (Sen 1990, 113-14)

A person values several things which he would like to do or be. These values which may vary from basic and elementary ones to more complex ones are called as "functionings". A person is said therefore to have a combination of functionings. One way of deciding whether the extent of freedom enjoyed by the person is enhanced is to investigate the amount or extent of realization of each functioning in the combination held by the person. Another way of assessing the extent of freedom is to see the availability of different combinations of these functionings from which a person is free to choose. Freedom then is assessed by the number and extent of alternatives available to a person to achieve what he values. These combinations available to the person at a point in time constitute his "capability set". "A person's 'capability' refers to the alternative combinations of functionings that are feasible for her to achieve. Capability is thus a kind of freedom to achieve alternative functioning combinations (or, less formally put, the freedom to achieve various lifestyles)" (Sen 2006a, 75). Hence freedom can be assessed by the degree of achievement of functionings in a combination and by the availability of alternative combinations of functionings from which a person can realistically hope to choose. Sen takes the choice between alternatives as indicative of a greater sense of freedom although both the measures have often been combined in development practice.

Here it is clear that a person's functionings and his capability are closely related but distinct: "A functioning is an achievement, whereas a capability is the ability to achieve. Functionings are, in a sense, more directly related to living conditions, since they are different aspects of living conditions. Capabilities, in contrast, are notions of freedom, in the positive sense: what real opportunities you have regarding the life you may lead" (Sen 1987, 36). Capability sets incorporate functionings but whereas functionings give us an idea of what a person actually has achieved at a point in time capability offers clues about sets of these achievements which appear as options to people. This is important because in their daily living people do make combinations of the achievements of their well-being and try to order and prioritise them. In this sense, with capability sets, one has a clear picture of the actual options at hand for a person and the leverage he gets to choose from these alternative options. Capability sets therefore point towards and offer a greater purchase on understanding something larger than specific achievements of well-being by a person: it indicates the freedom enjoyed by the person. Sen holds that this is a wider and better indicator of evaluation of the informational basis of justice than functionings (Sen 1995, 38-40).

Robert Sugden puts the whole argument rather nicely:

> A person's state of being is understood as a vector of functionings. In choosing what kind of life to live, a person chooses among such vectors. The set of feasible vectors for any person is that person's capability set. A capability set represents a person's opportunities to achieve well-being. We may also say that it represents a

> person's freedom, with "freedom" being understood in the positive rather than the negative sense—that is, in terms of "freedom to...", rather than "freedom from...". Sen proposes that, when we evaluate a person's good, we should focus on her functionings or on her capabilities, or on both. (Sudgen 1993, 1951)

Sen holds further that capability sets are a more appropriate informational measure for a theory of justice than utilities enjoyed by a person or the resources at his disposal. In this sense Sen claims that the capability approach is better than not only utilitarianism but also Rawls' justice as fairness. Sen agrees that Rawls has done a valuable service by shifting the attention of justice away from utility to freedom but it is inadequate because Rawls' resources—primary goods—by themselves do not have value (Sen 2002, 79-87). Their value is derived from the opportunities they offer to the person to pursue a life according to his own goals. Sen asks, why do we not then directly go to the opportunities which the resources offer and value them (instead of valuing primary goods)? Capabilities measure the extent of freedom or the actual freedom enjoyed whereas primary goods are merely the means to freedom:

> Since the conversion of these primary goods and resources into freedom to select a particular life and to achieve may vary from person to person, equality in holdings of primary goods or resources can go hand in hand with serious inequalities in actual freedoms enjoyed by different persons.
>
> In the capability-based assessment of justice, individual claims are not to be assessed in terms of the resources or primary goods the persons respectively hold, but in terms of the freedoms they actually enjoy to choose between different ways of living that they can have reason to value. It is this actual freedom that is represented by the person's 'capability' to achieve various alternative combinations of functionings, that is, doings and beings. (Sen 1990, 115)

The thrust of Sen's argument against Rawls is that it is not enough to survey the extent of primary goods held by a person in order to assess the degree of freedom enjoyed by him. It also becomes incumbent to investigate under what conditions and to what extent the person is able to channel or actualize these primary goods towards the goals which he values. "If the object is to concentrate on the individual's real opportunity to pursue her objectives (as Rawls explicitly recommends), then account would have to be taken not only of the primary goods the persons respectively hold, but also of the relevant personal characteristics that govern the *conversion* of primary goods into the person's ability to promote her ends" (Sen 2006a, 74). Therefore, the degree of freedom can be evaluated not only by the primary goods held by a person but also by the alternatives available to him to live the life which he wants to live.

Now, when Sen makes his critique of Rawls by stating that the notion of primary goods is inadequate compared to the capabilities which persons have to convert these primary goods into feasible or viable choices he appears to miss Rawls' point that these goods are primary for democratic societies with a liberal framework. Sen agrees with Rawls that the access to primary goods is important for any notion of a just society. However, he stresses that it is the range of opportunities or capabilities to use these goods which is more important than mere access. This means that Sen can be taken as saying that although equality of opportunity to access the primary goods of liberal democratic societies is important what is of greater importance is the enhancement of capabilities of persons to use these primary goods to meet their goals. Therefore, this major qualification apart, Sen can be safely taken to be saying that his capability theory of justice is largely for liberal democratic societies.

This impression is reinforced by the nature of the first debate between Sen and Rawls which ensued after Sen had made a preliminary critique of Rawls in 'Equality of What?' (1980) (Sen 1982, 365-66) and Rawls had written a rejoinder in 'The Priority of Right and Ideas of the Good' (1988) (Rawls 1988, 456), to which Sen further gave an elaborate reply in *Inequality Reexamined* (1995) (Sen 2002, 82-87). To Rawls' charge that Sen assumes "shared objectives" or "a particular comprehensive doctrine" (of the good) (Rawls 1988, 456) Sen replies that his notion of capability does not necessarily assume a monolithic conception of the good because capability sets are about opportunities for alternative lives and secondly, a notion of the comprehensive good is irrelevant because a disadvantaged person may accrue less benefit from primary goods than others irrespective of the comprehensive doctrine held by him (Sen 2002, 83). In this context therefore we would not be too far off the mark to say, amongst other things, that Sen is stressing that he is in agreement with Rawls about one the basic assumption—the liberal ideal of each individual having their own goals, ends and metaphysical or moral worldviews.

However, in fact, Sen presents his theory throughout his corpus as applicable to all societies. Sen's capability approach is meant to be universal and for all types of societies. If therefore Sen's formulation of capability as an advanced incorporation and improvisation of primary goods is to be admitted, as he is claiming that it be, then Sen has to recommend that all societies become liberal democratic in nature—that is, those societies which are not liberal democratic yet better become one. The problem thus is that whereas Rawls is building a model of justice for which a society already exits the operationalization of Sen's model becomes contingent on hitherto non-liberal democratic societies becoming as much.

Now this could degenerate into a hope or wish unless, of course, Sen's capability approach has also the requisite apparatus to deal with the process of engendering liberal democracies in societies which are not only not liberal democratic but also extremely diverse. What then does Sen do? He postulates development as freedom. He says that freedom is both an ends and means to development. That is, it is not only that the goal of development is freedom. The means to development is also freedom. In other words, it is not only that the goal of liberal democracy or the characteristic feature of liberal democracy is freedom but also that the means to liberal democracy is freedom. That is, the "instrumental freedoms" (viz. economic opportunities, political freedoms, social facilities, transparency guarantees, and protective security) are not only the features marking a liberal democracy (i.e. they are the ends of a liberal democracy) but also the means to attain it. Now how do ends become means? Or means become ends? Could we, for instance, achieve the end of political freedom through political freedom? That is, to "have freedom of political expression and an uncensored press" through "freedom of political expression and an uncensored press"? Or, could we acquire social facilities through social facilities? This is, "arrangements for education, health care and so on" through "arrangements for education, health care and so on"? The situation appears perplexing; especially when our discussion of freedom as development is not in a 'Hegelian' mode (it may be worth our while though to conduct such an exercise elsewhere). Looked at in this way therefore Sen, in all probability, has not given us feasible procedures of engendering liberal democracies in other different and diverse societies. This lack of specificity in public policy and politics has been noticed also by Stuart Corbridge (Corbridge 2002, 204-08) who claims that most of Sen's idealistic prescriptions would not be effective unless supplemented by a politics of confrontation and cooperation.

This lack of specificity has been noticed also in another sphere. To begin with Nussbaum and other feminist economists have been unabashed in their praise for Sen's capability approach as overcoming the problems associated with Rawlsian primary goods. For the shift from being a mere recipient of certain primary goods to a focus on one's ability to use them well certainly enables us to move from the public realm, penetrate the private wall of the family and address the concerns of women more specifically. Assessing what a woman can do or be is likely to be a more accurate estimate of justice and freedom than the mere possession of goods which are considered to be primary in society for the good and just life. However, the feminists have also pointed out a certain hesitation in the specification of the capabilities by Sen. This has political implications for policy, just as Corbridge has mentioned above. Sen seems to strongly recommend certain capabilities as universally basic but he stops short of enumerating them overtly, perhaps because of his respect for democratic deliberation (Nussbaum 2006, 50-51). This has the consequence further of prioritizing the notion of freedom at such a level of generalization that one is quite liable to forget how some freedoms could be inimical for certain basic capabilities and entitlements (Nussbaum 2006, 51-54; Gasper and Staveren 2006, 153-79). The contention then is that the edge of the capability approach and of development as freedom gets blunted if no effort is made to specify the capabilities at least to some extent (Nussbaum 2006, 39-69; Robeyns 2006, 70-105). Specified capabilities become more gender sensitive.

There is much to say for this argument but as is the case with Sen the way out has to be a mention at least of the some ways of transforming societies into liberal democratic nation states. That is, enumerated capabilities would be able to do a great deal for women and the other marginalized if an effort is made to till the soil of liberalism in societies where these specified capabilities are to be used for the informational evaluation of justice. Nussbaum feels and argues clearly for universal values and universal lists of capabilities (Nussbaum 2000, 34-110). However, this is done without an in-depth interrogation of the complexity of the interaction between the modern and the traditional, especially in societies which are not really liberal democracies. This comes out rather clearly, for instance, in her analysis of the rise of the Hindu right in India—the source of conflicts, it seems, are not so much in the clash of cultures or in the tensions between modernity and tradition but between universal opposing psychological and moral forces within an individual (Nussbaum 2007b). Hence although the capability approach as revised by the feminists appears more gender sensitive it remains uncertain in the face of a rather inadequate discussion of the process of engendering liberalism and democracies in societies which are not yet that.

The contingent nature of Sen's approach arises, I think, because somehow the main philosophical enterprise of Rawls appears to elide him. Rawls is able to speak of the centrality of primary goods in a scheme of justice and specify them in the same breath mainly because of his adoption of a Wittgenteinian quietist approach to the debate on metaphysics. Rawls' primary goods which are specific to liberal democratic societies are tied to the quietist recognition that raising the question of the metaphysical basis of principles of justice is a false one. Hence

Rawls works on principles of justice on the basis of the matter available to him from the society in which he lives. He, therefore, arrives at those specific goods which can be considered primary to his own liberal democratic society in the context of equality of opportunity in a discussion of a just society.

Had Sen read Rawls in a quietist fashion and thereby sensed the correct philosophical pulse two things perhaps could have happened. Either he would have agreed with Rawls, confined himself to speaking of a model of justice only for presently existing liberal democratic societies, and not have tried to build a new and different approach called the capability approach, claiming that it is more appropriate than the one offered by Rawls. This would perhaps have been more feasible to do, if we are to admit Rawls' elaboration of his relationship with Sen later in *JFR* (Rawls 2003, 168-76). Here Rawls makes the contention that primary goods have a basic link with capability.

"In reply, it should be stressed that the account of primary goods does take into account, and does not abstract from, basic capabilities: namely, the capabilities of citizens as free and equal persons in virtue of their two moral powers [i.e. sense of justice and conception of good]. It is these powers that enable them to be normal and fully cooperating members of society over a complete life and to maintain their status as free and equal citizens. We rely on a conception of citizens' capabilities and basic needs, and the equal rights and liberties are specified with these moral powers in mind" (Rawls 2003, 169).

Secondly, many of the instances picked up by Sen to exemplify the pivotal role of capability (e.g. illness, physical handicap, pregnancy) can be accommodated by primary goods and specified at the legislative and juridical stages instead at the original position. In addition primary goods are the expectations of individuals over the complete course of their lives and thus include periodic bouts of illnesses or other handicaps. Moreover, primary goods include public income and wealth besides personal income and wealth—such expenditure thus takes care of periodic handicaps which are normal in society.

On the other hand, if Sen did not take this path he would have recognized the Wittgenstein quietism in Rawls and differed with it. He would have then adopted a different philosophical stance, which would have allowed him to build a model of justice—with or without a consideration of capabilities—for all societies or for societies which are not liberal democratic in nature, without any need to incorporate primary goods as an essential part of capabilities or of the model generally.

In Sen as we have him, none of these positions are taken. He does not limit himself to existing liberal democratic societies nor does he construct an approach without primary goods based on a different philosophical understanding. The result is that, first, his argument requires him to specify public policy and political measures to engender the liberalism his theory would universally have and, second, he is somewhat indeterminate and vague in his recommendations. A similar difficulty dogs the feminist revision of Sen's theory. An emergent powerful voice on alternative thinking in the development sector from within the liberal paradigm thus gets diffused.

## REFERENCES

Alejandro, R. 1996. 'What is Political about Rawls's Political Liberalism?. *The Journal of Politics* 58(1): 1-24.

Bagchi, A. 1999. 'Capabilities, Freedom and Human Development—Amartya Sen's Human Science of Development: Part III'. *Frontline* 16(14): 88-93.

Baker, G.P. and P.M.S. Hacker 2000. *An Analytical Commentary on the Philosophical Investigations, Vol. 2: Wittgenstein—Rules, Grammar and Necessity*. Oxford: Blackwell.

Barry, B. 1975. 'The Liberal Theory of Justice: A Critical Examination of the Principal Doctrines' in *A Theory of Justice by John Rawls*. Oxford: Clarendon.

Coffa, J.A. 1998. *The Semantic Tradition from Kant to Carnap: To the Vienna Station*. Cambridge: CUP.

Corbridge, S. 2002. 'Development as Freedom: The Spaces of Amartya Sen'. *Progress in Development Studies* 2(3): 183-217.

Diamond, C. 1996a. 'Introduction II: Wittgenstein and Metaphysics'. In C. Diamond, *The Realistic Spirit: Wittgenstein, Philosophy, and the Mind*. Cambridge, MA: The MIT Press.

Diamond, C. 1996b. 'Throwing Away the Ladder: How to Read the *Tractatus*'. In C. Diamond. *The Realistic Spirit: Wittgenstein, Philosophy, and the Mind*. Cambridge, MA: The MIT Press.

Gasper, D. and I.V. Staveren. 2006. 'Development as Freedom—And as What Else?'. In B. Agarwal et al., ed., *Capabilities, Freedom, and Equality: Amartya Sen's Work from a Gender Perspective*. New Delhi: OUP.

Grayling, A.C. 1988. *Wittgenstein*. Oxford: OUP.

Gutman, A. 1999. 'The Central Role of Rawls's Theory'. In H.S. Richardson, ed., *Development and Main Outlines of Rawls's Theory of Justice*. New York: Garland.

Hacker, P.M.S. 2000. 'Was He Trying to Whistle It?'. In A. Crary and R. Read, eds., *The New Wittgenstein*. London: Routledge.

Hampton, J. 1989. 'Should Political Philosophy be Done Without Metaphysics?'. *Ethics* 99(4): 791-814.

Harman, G. 2003. 'Three Trends in Moral and Political Philosophy'. *Journal of Value Inquiry* 37(3): 415-25. [online version:1-19; url: www.princeton.edu/~harman/Papers/Published.html]

Hylton, P. 1992. *Russell, Idealism and the Emergence of Analytic Philosophy*. Oxford: Oxford University Press.

Johnson, O.A. 1974. 'The Kantian Interpretation'. *Ethics* 85(1): 58-66.

John Gray cited in R.J. Sullivan. 1995. *Immanuel Kant's Moral Theory*. Cambridge: CUP.

John Wisdom cited in G. Pitcher. 1972. *The Philosophy of Wittgenstein*. New Delhi: Prentice-Hall of India.

Kant, I. 1956. *Critique of Practical Reason*. Trans. L.W. Beck. New York: Macmillan.

Kant, I. 1964. *Groundwork of the Metaphysic of Morals*. Trans. H.J. Paton. New York: Harper Torchbooks.

Kant, I. 1990. *Prolegomena to Any Future Metaphysics That Can Qualify as a Science*. Trans. P. Carus. La Salle: Open Court.

Kant, I. 1991a. 'The Metaphysics of Morals: Introduction to the Theory of Right'. In H. Reiss, ed., *Kant: Political Writings*. Cambridge: CUP.

Kant, I. 1991b. 'The Metaphysics of Morals: The Theory of Right, Part II—Public Right". In H. Reiss, ed., *Kant: Political Writings*. Cambridge: CUP.

Kersting, W. 1992. 'Politics, Freedom, and Order: Kant's Political Philosophy'. In P. Guyer, ed., *The Cambridge Companion to Kant*. Cambridge: CUP.

Kukathas, C. and P. Pettit. 1998. *A Theory of Justice and its Critics*. Cambridge: Polity.

McGinn, M. 1999. 'Between Metaphysics and Nonsense: Elucidation in Wittgenstein's *Tractatus*'. *The Philosophical Quarterly* 49(197): 419-513.

Monk, R. 1991. *Ludwig Wittgenstein: The Duty of Genius*. London: Vintage.

Nagel, T. 1973. 'Rawls on Justice'. *The Philosophical Review* 82(2): 220-34.

Neal, P. 1990. 'Justice as Fairness: Political or Metaphysical?'. *Political Theory* 18(1): 24-50.

Neal, P. 1994. 'Does He Mean What He Says? (Mis)Understanding Rawls's Practical Turn'. *Polity* 27(1): 77-111.

Nussbaum, M. 2000. *Women and Human Development*. New Delhi: Kali for Women.

Nussbaum, M. 2006. 'Capabilities as Fundamental Entitlements: Sen and Social Justice'. In B. Agarwal et al., ed. *Capabilities, Freedom, and Equality: Amartya Sen's Work from a Gender Perspective*. New Delhi: OUP.

Nussbaum, M. 2007a. *Frontiers of Justice: Disability, Nationality, Species Membership*. New Delhi: OUP.

Nussbaum, M. 2007b. *The Clash Within: Democracy, Religious Violence, and India's Future*. Ranikhet: Permanent Black.

Pitcher, G. 1972. *The Philosophy of Wittgenstein*. New Delhi: Prentice-Hall of India.

Pogge, T.W. 1989. *Realizing Rawls*. Ithaca: Cornell University Press.

Pogge, T. 1999. 'A Brief Sketch of Rawls's Life'. In H.S. Richardson, ed. *Development and Main Outlines of Rawls's Theory of Justice*. New York: Garland.

Pohlhaus, G. and J.R. Wright. 2002. 'Using Wittgenstein Critically: A Political Approach to Philosophy'. *Political Theory* 30(6): 800-27.

Proops, I. 2001. 'The New Wittgenstein: A Critique'. *European Journal of Philosophy* 9(3): 106-26.

Rawls, J. (1951) 1999. 'Outline of a Decision Procedure for Ethics'. In S. Freeman, ed., *Collected Papers: John Rawls*. New Delhi: OUP.

Rawls, J. (1958) 1999. 'Justice as Fairness'. In S. Freeman, ed., *Collected Papers: John Rawls*. New Delhi: OUP.

Rawls, J.A. 1972. *A Theory of Justice*. Oxford: Clarendon.

Rawls, J. (1975a) 1999. 'A Kantian Conception of Equality'. In S. Freeman, ed., *Collected Papers: John Rawls*. New Delhi: OUP.

Rawls, J. (1975b) 1999. 'Fairness to Goodness'. In S. Freeman, ed., *Collected Papers: John Rawls*. New Delhi: OUP.

Rawls, J. (1975c) 1999. 'The Independence of Moral Theory'. In S. Freeman, ed., *Collected Papers: John Rawls*. New Delhi: OUP.

Rawls, J. 1977. 'The Basic Structure as Subject'. *American Philosophical Quarterly* 14: 159-65.

Rawls, J. (1980) 1999. 'Kantian Constructivism in Moral Theory'. In S. Freeman, ed., *Collected Papers: John Rawls*. New Delhi: OUP.

Rawls, J. 1982. 'The Basic Liberties and Their Priority'. In S. MacMurrin, ed., *The Tanner Lectures on Human Values, Vol. 3*. Cambridge: CUP.

Rawls, J. (1985) 1999. 'Justice as Fairness: Political not Metaphysical'. In S. Freeman, ed., *Collected Papers: John Rawls*. New Delhi: OUP.

Rawls, J. (1987) 1999. 'The Idea of an Overlapping Consensus'. In S. Freeman, ed., *Collected Papers: John Rawls*. New Delhi: OUP.

Rawls, J. (1988) 1999. 'The Priority of Right and Ideas of the Good'. In S. Freeman, ed., *Collected Papers: John Rawls*. New Delhi: OUP.

Rawls, J. (1989) 1999. 'The Domain of the Political and Overlapping Consensus'. In S. Freeman, ed. *Collected Papers: John Rawls*. New Delhi: OUP.

Rawls, J. 1993. *Political Liberalism*. New York: Columbia University Press.

Rawls, J. 1999. *A Theory of Justice*. Revised Edition. New York: Oxford University Press.

Rawls, J. 2003. *Justice as Fairness: A Restatement*. Cambridge, MA.: Harvard University Press.

Raz, J. 1999. 'Facing Diversity: The Case of Epistemic Abstinence'. In P.J. Weithman, ed., *Reasonable Pluralism*. New York: Garland.

Reiss, H. 1991. 'Introduction'. In H. Reiss, ed., *Kant: Political Writings*. Cambridge: CUP.

Richardson, H.S. 1999. 'Volume Introduction'. In H.S. Richardson, ed., *Development and Main Outlines of Rawls's Theory of Justice*. New York: Garland.

Robeyns, I. 2006. 'Sen's Capability Approach and Gender Inequality'. In B. Agarwal et al., ed., *Capabilities, Freedom, and Equality: Amartya Sen's Work from a Gender Perspective*. New Delhi: OUP.

Sen, A. 1982. 'Equality of What?'. In A. Sen, *Choice, Welfare and Measurement*. Oxford: Blackwell.

Sen, A. 1983. 'Development: Which Way Now?'. *The Economic Journal* 93(372): 745-53.

Sen, A. 1987. 'The Standard of Living'. In G. Hawthorn, ed., *The Standard of Living*. Cambridge: CUP.

Sen, A. 1990. 'Justice: Means Versus Freedoms'. *Philosophy and Public Affairs* 19(2): 111-21.

Sen, A. 1995. 'Capability and Well-Being'. In M.C. Nussbaum and A. Sen, eds., *The Quality of Life*. Oxford: Clarendon.

Sen, A. 2002. *Inequality Reexamined*. New Delhi: OUP.

Sen, A. 2003. 'Sraffa, Wittgenstein, and Gramsci'. *Journal of Economic Literature* 41(4): 1240-55.

Sen, A. 2006a. *Development as Freedom*. New Delhi: OUP.

Sen, A. 2006b. 'Foreword to *Pathologies of Power*'. Reprinted in *Maitreyee* 6: 2-17. [internet version]

Schuurman, F.J. 2002. 'The Impasse in Development Studies'. In V. Desai and R.B. Potter, eds., *The Companion to Development Studies*. London: Arnold.

Schwartz, A. 1973. 'Moral Neutrality and Primary Goods.' *Ethics* 83(4): 294-307.

Steinberger, P.J. 2000. 'The Impossibility of a "Political" Conception'. *The Journal of Politics* 62(1): 147-65.

Sugden, R. 1993. 'Welfare, Resources, and Capabilities: A Review of Inequality Reexamined by Amartya Sen'. *Journal of Economic Literature* 31(4): 1947-62.

Sullivan, R.J. 1995. *Immanuel Kant's Moral Theory*. Cambridge: CUP.

Wittgenstein, L. 1987. *The Blue and Brown Books*. Oxford: Blackwell.

Wittgenstein, L. 1988a. *Tractatus Logico-Philosophicus*. London: Routledge.

Wittgenstein, L. 1988b. *Philosophical Investigations*. Oxford: Blackwell.

Wright, C. 2001. *Rails to Infinity: Essays on Themes from Wittgenstein's Philosophical Investigations*. Cambridge, MA: Harvard University Press.

# Cities, Gender Budgeting and Civic Governance*

6

*Vibhuti Patel*

## Introduction

Elected Women Representatives (EWRs) in Urban Self-government Bodies have made their presence felt after the 74th amendments in the Indian constitution in 1994. Now, we have 33 per cent women in municipal bodies. But when we do gender audit of municipal budgets, we realize that not much has been contributed for urban poor women.

The Ninth Five Year Plan onwards provision of women component plan ensures that not less than 30 per cent of development sectors funds and benefits flow to women. Currently, 56 ministries and departments have set up Gender Budget Cell and as per GR of Ministry of Finance, they are expected to submit gender audit of allocation and actual expenditure on women.

Right to information has proved to be an important tool in the hands of civil society for transparency in public expenditure.

## Municipal Budgets

In municipality, the Accounts Superintendent tables statement for income and expenditure in December. Also he/she gives estimates of income and expenditure for the financial year end and seeks responses from Municipal Commissioner, President of Municipality and standing committee. Portion for committed fund can't be changed by councillors at the time of final approval. Revision of property tax takes place once in 4 years.

* http://www.europe-solidaire.org

There are three Sources of Income for Municipal councils/ corporations:

1. State and Central governments' Allocation, State and Centrally sponsored schemes
2. Revenues obtained through local taxes—water, electricity, road, etc.
3. Funds obtained from the Finance Commissions.

### *Gender Concerns*

For past 15 years, gender economists and women's groups are making efforts to answer the following questions:

- How to enable women to direct economy through designing and constructing fiscal policy?
- How to link economic governance to political governance?
- How to enable EWRs to participate in the budget-making efforts?

They have used methods of Participatory Appraisal (PA) and Focus Group Discussion (FGD) to identify gender concerns.

### *Macro-economic Policies and Gender Audit of Municipal Budgets*

Trend analysis of allocation to social sector in the pre (before 1991) and post (after 1991) Structural Adjustment Programme (SAP) phase has revealed that poor women have suffered the most due to drastic budgetary cuts in PDS and public health, safe public transport and child care facilities, food security, drinking water and sanitation.

Gender sensitive budget demands re-prioritisation of financial allocations by municipal bodies in favour of:

- Working women's hostels, crèches, cheap eating facilities, public toilets.
- Housing—subsidized for single/deserted/divorced/ widowed women.
- Nutrition—strengthening PDS, mid-day meals.
- Health—Abolition of user fees for BPL population, one stop crisis centre in public hospital for women/girls survivors of violence linked with shelter homes.

- Skill training centres for women and tailor made courses.
- Safe, efficient and cheap public Transport—bus, train, metro.
- Water—Safe drinking water in the community centres.
- Waste Management—Technological upgradation—Occupational health and safety of recycling workers/ rag pickers.
- Proper electrification in the communities.
- Multipurpose Community centres, halfway homes for elderly and mentally disturbed women.

**Method of Revenue Generation**

Government of Maharashtra has sent GR regarding allocation of 5 per cent of total revenues for women and children. Moreover, urban local self-government (LSGs) bodies can raise revenues by heavy taxes on Tobacco, alcohol, private vehicles and entertainment industry. Portion of fine collected for causing damage to environment (introduction of Green Tax), high speed driving, wrong parking and breaking rules can be used for welfare of women and children.

Surcharge, earmarked charge for specific purpose such as Education Cess—2 per cent of salary, income tax for disaster management has raised revenues for urban LSG. In Maharashtra, transport cess at the time of Bangladesh war in 1971, later on was diverted to EGS kitty.

**Meetings with the Stakeholders**

Urban LSGs should organize discussion on needs identified by EWRs with GOs, NGOs and SHGs. They should be made aware of Socio-economic Profile of the Municipality. The ward officers should ensure scrutiny of needs and perceived problems by impartial experts who can also suggest methods to fulfil needs (Labour, land, services). Financial aspects of programmes and projects should be discussed in a transparent manner.

**Tasks of Citizens Association**

Civil society groups must be allowed to give their opinions on suitable budgetary allocations and generation of revenues from local sources. They can verify/cross check collected data and results of the surveys/interactive workshops and prepare a vision document. Sub-committees can work out details of different budget heads and it must have all stake groups of the ward. Presentation of reports of these sub-committees should be made through EWRs to the municipal authorities. Currently women's groups are lobbying for reprioritisation of allocation to reflect women's interests. E.g. Financial allocation for implementation of DV act, PCPNDT Act, utilisation of funds earmarked for Swadhar scheme for women in difficult circumstances and working women's hostels in urban centers.

### Activity Mapping

Women's groups are discussing of micro-economics involved in dealing with problems faced by women at ward levels such as drinking water, health centers, garbage-disposal and are moving beyond grievance redressal. Women's groups such as Anandi (Ahmedabad), Alochana (Pune), Stree Mukti Sangathana (Mumbai), National alliance of women's Organisations (Bhubaneshwar), Sagamma Srinivas Foundation (Bangalore), Action India (Delhi) are organizing workshops for awareness about technicalities of budget, building knowledge about programmes, schemes, projects under different departments, gathering procedural information about critical issues/felt needs, skills of proposal writing. Stack groups in support of EWRs are Self-Help Groups, gender sensitive administrators, corporators/ councilors, individuals within political parties, NGOs and Women in the communities. They make efforts to seek allocation under appropriate budget heads to identify streams of revenue, available revenue and the required expenditure.

### *Some Unresolved Issues*

Decision-makers in the urban LSG bodies need to address the following issues demanding urgent attention:

- How to bridge the gap between notional allocation and actual allocation?
- Accounting, auditing and record keeping of gender disaggregated data and allocation.

- How to achieve physical and performance/achievement targets?
- Implementation of maternity benefits, Tribal Sub Plan, Scheduled Caste Plan for the urban poor.
- Major departments claiming indivisibilities of allocation of resources.
- Notional allocation projected as real allocation.
- Absence of uniform guidelines and procedures.

## Gender Budgeting in Urban LSG Bodies

Process of gender budgeting demands special programmes targeting women based on enumeration of differential impact of expenditures across all sectors and services—gender disaggregated impact on literacy, school drop outs, mortality, morbidity, malnutrition, illnesses, safety and security. Hence, they need to ensure the review of equal opportunity policies and opportunities in the public sector-jobs, school education, wages, health care, skills, technical training, and computer education.

## Allocation and Expenses of Resources for Women in Panchayat Budgets

NIPFP has recommended the following classification of financial allocation on schemes and programmes for gender audit as well as gender budgeting:

- Women specific schemes where 100 per cent of the allocation is required to be spent on women, targeted 100 per cent to women by Ministry of Women and Child Development (MWCD).
- Pro-women schemes where at least 30 per cent of allocation and benefits flow to women. E.g. All anti-poverty programmes.
- Gender Neutral Schemes meant for community as a whole (Employment generation programmes, Jawaharlal Nehru National Urban Renewal Mission [JNNURM]).
- Residual schemes for disaster management.

All India Institute of Local Self-Government, AIILSG gives details of all schemes under these 4 categories through its publications, workshops and training programmes. Moreover, it also teaches the elected representatives the efficient ways of programme implementation through budgeting from below (Virmani, 2002).

**Budgetary Allocation for Protective and Welfare Services**

These are the schemes directly benefiting women for crisis management of situations arising out of economic and socio-cultural subordination and dehumanisation of women such as shelter homes, short stay homes, rehabilitation schemes for women survivors of violence, pensions for widows and destitute women.

Budgetary allocation for Social Services Expenditure for capacity building, reduction of domestic drudgery and better quality of life for girls and women:

- Education
- Health
- Crèche
- Working women's hostels
- Housing
- Nutrition
- Water supply
- Sanitation—toilets, drainage
- Fuel
- Waste management
- Transport

Budgetary allocation for Economic Services to provide economic opportunities to women:

- SHGs—credit, loans to self-employed women.
- Training programmes—Vocational training in Sunrise sectors, e.g. Biotechnology, IT, etc.
- Physical infrastructure—transport, energy.
- Urban housing—10 per cent reserved flats/tenements for single women.

- Marketing facilities for women entrepreneurs and self-employed women—10 per cent of shops reserved for businesswomen, women vendors/traders in municipal markets, women's *haats/bazars*.
- Public toilets for women without userfees.
- Safe and efficient transport for working women and women vendors.

Budgetary allocation for Regulatory Services to put in place institutional structures and mechanisms:

- State Commission for Women/Municipal Commission for Women.
- Women Development Cell in municipal bodies.
- Budgetary allocation and space for ward-wise WDC for prevention of sexual harassment of women in the organised and unorganised sectors.
- Women's cell at the police stations, LSG bodies' offices, municipal hospital and schools.
- Awareness generation programmes.

## Need of an Hour

State governments must devolve substantive powers, funds, functions and functionaries upon LSG bodies. The central government should strive for simplifications of programme guidelines by central ministries and departments regarding women specific schemes—Swadhar, working women's hostels, maternity benefits for BPL, etc. Moreover, centrally sponsored Schemes must be recast to empower municipal bodies. PRIs must get untied funds to formulate plans according to their needs and priorities. Structures and mechanisms for RTI Act must be put in place to sort out problems concerning utilisation of funds allocated for area development. To avoid urban unrest and guarantee socio-economic justice, at least 100 days of employment at minimum wages must be provided under EGS in all urban centres.

## Financial Matters and PRIs

Elected representatives, ward officials and NGOs working in the area should act as facilitators in preparation of the plan for area development and social justice. The UN system has supported allocation of resources for women in PRIs, right from the beginning. "The evidence on gender and decentralisation in India thus suggests that while women have played a positive role in addressing, or attempting to address, a range of practical gender needs[1], their impact on strategic gender needs[2] is not remarkable" (UNDP, 2002). Hence, WERs deserve to be empowered to address the strategic gender needs.

There is a need for provisions in the composite programmes under education, health and skill development to target them specifically at girls/women as the principal beneficiaries and disaggregated within the total allocation. It may also be necessary to place restrictions on their re-appropriation for other purposes.

## Conclusion

Budgets garner resources through the taxation policies and allocate resources to different sections of the economy. Budget is an important tool in the hands of state for affirmative action for improvement of gender relations through reduction of gender gap in the development process. It can help to reduce economic inequalities, between men and women as well as between the rich and the poor (NCAS, 2003). Hence, the budgetary policies need to keep into considerations the gender dynamics operating in the economy and in the civil society. There is a need to highlight participatory approaches to pro-poor budgeting, bottom up budget, child budget, SC budget, ST budget, green budgeting, budgeting for differently abled people, local and global implications of pro-poor and pro-women budgeting, alternative macro scenarios emerging out of alternative budgets and inter-linkages between gender-sensitive budgeting and women's empowerment. Serious examining of budgets calls for greater transparency at the level of international economics to local processes of empowerment. There is a need to provide training and capacity building workshops for decision-makers in the government structures, municipal bodies, parliamentarians and audio-visual media (Patel, 2004).

Gender Commitments must be translated into Budgetary Commitment. By using our Right to Information (2005), transparency/accountability for revenue generation and public expenditure can be ensured. For Reprioritisation in public spending we must prepare our 'bottom up budgets' and lobby for its realisation in collaboration with the elected representatives. Gender economists must lift the veil of statistical invisibility of the unpaid 'care economy' managed by poor women and highlight its equality and efficiency dimension and transform macro-policies so that they become women friendly.

## NOTES

1. Strategic Gender Needs are different in different economic contexts and are determined by statutory provisions, affirmative action by the state, pro-active role of the employers to enhance women's position in the economy and social movements.
2. Practical Gender Needs are identified keeping into consideration, gender based division of labour or women's subordinate position in the economy. They are a response to immediate perceived necessity, identified within a specific context. They are practical in nature and often are concerned with inadequacies in living conditions such as provision of fuel, water, healthcare and employment. For details see, Moser, 1993.

## REFERENCES

Patel, V. (2002). "Gendering the Budget at State and National Level and Gender Audit of the Union Budget—A Critical Approach", *Urdhva Mula,* Mumbai, Vol. 1, No. 1, pp. 30-57.

Patel, V. (2002). Women's Challenges of the New Millennium, Gyan Books, Delhi, p. 70. websites: www. cehat.org and www.humanscapeindia.net

Patel, V. (2003). "Gender Budget Initiatives in India", paper presented at Workshop on "Gender Budget Initiatives in Orissa" organised by School of Women's Studies, Utkal University, Bhubaneshwar, Orissa on 22nd to 24th September 2003.

Patel, V. (2003). "Gender Budget—A Case Study of India", Centre for Advanced Study in Economics, Department of Economics, University of Mumbai, Working Paper UDE (CAS) 7(7)/2003, also published in *Vikalpa*, Vol. XI, No. 1, 2003 published by Vikas Adhyayan Kendra, Mumbai.

Patel, V. (2004). "Gender Budget: Media Concerns and Policy for India" in Kiran Prasad (Ed), *Communication and Empowerment of Women: Strategies and Policy Insights from India*, The Women Press, Delhi.

Patel, V. (2005). "India's Economic Reform and Women" in Susheela Subramanya, Meera Chakravorty and N.S. Viswanath (Eds.) (2005) *Women in Nation Building—Perspectives, Issues and Implications*, A Southern Economist Publication, Bangalore.

UNDP (2001). *Decentralisation in India—Challenges and Opportunities*, United Nations Development Programme, New Delhi.

Virmani, S. (1999). "Social Mapping, Modelling and Other Participatory Methods", *All India Institute of Local Self-Government*, Mumbai.

# *Fasting, Feasting:* Foods, Consumption and Politics of Power

7

*Arpana Nath*

## INTRODUCTION

This paper will look at some of the cultural practices around food and eating rituals based on a reading of Anita Desai's *Fasting, Feasting*. Food-related practices have an intrinsic association with women as homemakers, and play a crucial role in the formation of gendered identities. It is important to examine patterns of everyday behaviour because what is normally accepted as naturally ordered is not without its share of contradictions, paradoxes, and ambiguities. The significance of food is socially constructed and is multi-layered. Food being a part of our everyday life and practice, the taken-for-granted attitude to eating as an activity essential for bodily well-being obscures the complex set of relationships and assumptions around food-related practices. It is an important means of self-definition. The transmission and perpetuation of cultural values also takes place through food since eating and food conventions reflect the cultural system. Food and eating practices have wider social and cultural implications. Gender ideology in relation to food occurs invisibly and the particular patterns of behaviour that link food with women and are reproduced through the family and social structure. Gender being an important component of the social structure, the culture of food and eating provides an entry point in the negotiation of social relationships and gender roles. These practices demand some attention as they play a vital role in naturalizing gender norms since in most cultures, women have the primary responsibility of looking after the family. I shall offer here a reading of Anita Desai's *Fasting, Feasting* to show the role food plays in maintaining gender stereotypes. Food as one of the areas and practices of everyday life needs to be scrutinized, as it is a fundamental signifier of the way human subjects are produced by culture and discourse.

*Fasting, Feasting* is divided into two parts. The first part deals with an Indian family: the parents who are called MamaPapa and their three children, Uma, Aruna and Arun. Uma, who is the eldest daughter, has to stay at home to look after her younger brother Arun. Aruna has a successful marriage and has almost forgotten her filial connections. Arun is the youngest in the family. Uma has to give up her education to take care of Arun. The second part of the book deals with the Patton family in America. Arun is the connecting thread between these two sections. He goes there for higher studies and spends his summer break with this family. The Patton family comprises of Mr. and Mrs. Patton who offer implicit comparison to Arun's parents MamaPapa. They have a daughter Melanie who suffers from an eating disorder; their son Rod is anxious to have a well-built physique. When Arun first lands in America, he is bewildered by the contrasts in culture. The two sets of families are the twin focal points of Desai's novel.

## Food, Gender and Eating

The domestic sphere has been traditionally characterized as the space presided over by women. Women have been assigned the roles of both social and biological reproduction and a good part of the responsibility of producing social relations also rests with women ("Food, Gender and the Body", *The Canada Food Guide*). These practices are characteristically represented as female-specific whereas men occupy the dominant position of providing for the family. Since the cultural values of patriarchy structure most social institutions and relationships, including domestic relations, the conflicting nature of its demands results in a situation of unequal distribution of power and control even within family relationships. Food becomes a way of expressing cultural attitudes of gendered behaviour in the way it is coded as 'feminine': a woman's work is to prepare meals and cook for her family. Men only eat the food that women have prepared. This gives rise to gender hierarchy where men are constructed as active dominant agents and women serve and satisfy others through domestic cooking. Of course food-centred practices are never static and are context bound. But this responsibility of feeding, whether in a family situation or at a community level, invariably falls on the woman thus reinforcing gender hierarchy. In the context of Desai's novel even though the parents, MamaPapa, are presented as a single entity, it is the father who exerts authority in the family. The mother plays a supportive role where her only concern is to look after the comfort of her husband and the upbringing of their son Arun. Indeed the excess concern and obsequious respect that the mother puts on at meal times ironically plays out the superficiality of such arrangements. Gendering of food-related practices and eating are reflected in the way men and women are associated with different types of food:

> In my day, girls in the family were not given sweets, nuts, good things to eat. If something special had been bought in the market, like sweets or nuts, it was given to the boys in the family. But ours was not such an orthodox home that our mother and aunts did not slip us something on the sly. (6)

This passage from the novel is a good example of how the serving and provisioning of food indicate gender differences. It also points to a common occurrence where scarce food resources are kept aside for the male members of the family. In contrast girls and women are seen as not having the need for such food in a similar way. It is paradoxical that women who have the main responsibility for food provisioning and taking care of family nutrition tend to be ignored when it comes to their own nutritional requirements. It speaks of cultural prejudice against women where only males have access to scarce food resources in the family. Ironically the mother who faced discrimination as a young girl does no better when it comes to her daughters thus perpetuating the gender discrimination by giving greater importance to the food needs of Arun. Food rationing, preparation and serving of meals are also related to issues of power sharing between women members of the household. The opening chapter of the novel has Uma receiving instructions on evening tea preparation:

> We are having fritters for tea today, Will that be enough? Or do you want sweets as well? Yes, yes, Yes—there must be sweets—must be sweets, too...Uma must tell cook. (4-5)

While Uma's duty is to manage the kitchen, she is not entitled to choose the items on the family menu. It has to have the approval of her mother who takes it upon herself to defer to her husband's wishes to order the day's ration of foodstuff. Even though women hold responsibility over domestic food requirements, this responsibility does not translate into any real control, which in many cases resides with men. The interlinking of food and desire shows how the eating of food and its denial can become a metaphor of control (Sharma 2002). Uma's subservience in meeting the food needs of her parents at the cost of her own desires is a marker of her lack of agency. Uma is denied access to the fulfillment of her appetite for good food. The only time she eats food outside the house is with her cousin Ramu who treats her in a restaurant. Happy and excited at the novelty of eating out Uma returns home tipsy with drink. She is severely reprimanded by her parents for acting like a "hussy": "You, you disgrace to the family—nothing but disgrace ever" (53). Clearly the enjoyment of food is viewed as having the potential to act as a sexual catalyst, which can lead to the transgression of social mores. Thus Uma's "hunger for food becomes a tool of control—in *Fasting, Feasting* it symbolizes the subjection of Uma's desires to her parents. Eating, that is Uma's enjoyment of food with people other than her parents is thus strictly prohibited because it would allow Uma a license, a sensual experience that feeding the parents keeps firmly in check" (Sharma 2002: 154).

The correlation between food and concepts of masculinity and femininity are conceptualized through gender role relations within the family and through the different consumption patterns of food. The preferential treatment given to sons in traditional Indian culture is indicated by the amount of food consumed by Arun:

> As for his meals, she watched over him like a dragon, determined that a fixed quantity of milk was poured down his gullet whether he wanted it or not and, later, the prescribed boiled egg and meat broth. Then, when Papa returned home from office, he would demand to know how much his son had consumed and an answer had to be given: it had to be precise and it had to be one that pleased. (30)

If the consumption of meat is a signifier of male dominance and physical prowess, its denial to widowed members of the family link the control of female sexuality and power to men. Restricted access to food symbolizes male control of female sexuality. It is how "class, caste, race and gender hierarchies are maintained, in part, through differential control over and access to food" (Goody as quoted in Counihan 1998: 2). It also brings out the ambivalent relationship between mothering and food; the good mother is a good cook who nourishes, sustains and services the child's physical and emotional needs while remaining herself an invisible figure existing only to serve others. This makes the maternal role ambiguous; as mothers women are "powerful providers of food" but they are also "socially and domestically disempowered by their nurturing, serving role" (Sceats 2000: 11). While women may express their affection and appreciation for the partner by preparing and serving food, it may also be viewed as a strategic gesture to retain some measure of control over the husband. But this sort of an emotional hold is exercised through the acceptance of a disempowered role. By aligning herself with Papa's concern over Arun, Mama tries to position herself in a situation of strength where she has some influence over the other members of the family. But this position entails a tacit acceptance of a subordinate status and she can never assume to be on an equal footing with the husband. Women's food provisioning thus acts both as a "potential source of influence on husbands and children through the ability to give them a valued substance-food-but one that is also linked with female subordination through women's need to serve, satisfy, and defer to others..." (Sceats 2000: 3). The preparation and serving of meals has a symbolic function where the woman accepts a subordinate status in exchange for a degree of imagined power. Since gender is a matter of doing, an act, a performance (Butler 2001: 2497), it is socially constructed and the assumptions around food and eating practices reflect the imbalance of power that are inherent to gender role-playing. While they are not irreversible, the patriarchal family structure makes it difficult to dislodge traditionally received assumptions and they are reinforced through having to repeatedly perform them in domestic set up. In fact, traditional Indian culture encourages the observance of ritual fasts on certain days of the year, both by married women for the well-being and prosperity of their husbands, and by unmarried girls to get a good husband. Neera Desai and Maithreyi Krishnaraj argue that "...the subtle expression of patriarchy is through symbolism giving messages of inferiority of women through legends highlighting the self-sacrificing, self-effacing pure image of women that through the ritual practices which day in and day out emphasized the dominant role of a woman as a faithful wife and devout mother" (Desai and Krishnaraj 2004: 299). It does so by privileging men and giving women a secondary status. But these norms about gender duties are not all-inclusive. They are defined differently for different cultures. It is the manner in which women experience such norms and the influence it has in constituting woman's self-identity that defines such socio-psychological processes.

Arun is the connecting link to the second part of *Fasting, Feasting* which unfolds in a suburban American middle class family. Arun is the focal point in the novel through whose consciousness the East-West encounter is dramatized. He is sent to America for higher studies and he spends his summer break with the Patton family. Arun finds the casual and easy ways of this family a contrast to his own family ruled by his father. The metaphor of feasting represents the abundance of material wealth in American society and is characterized by the food habits of the Patton family. Mrs. Patton is a compulsive visitor to the local supermarket and enjoys buying convenience food for her family. Melanie, the teenaged daughter, has an aloof and distant manner. She treats Arun as an intruder. She suffers from bulimia nervosa, a condition characterized by unrestrained eating while her brother

Rod is anxious about the fitness of his body. Mr. Patton presumes his authority as the head of the family.

## Gender, Consumption and the Body

The nature of food consumption in the Patton family and their lifestyle reflect the changes taking place within middle-class family life in American society. They eat canned and frozen foods and have labour saving gadgets to do their work for them. Instead of the entire family gathering at the dinner table to have their meals together they eat it watching television or in their own rooms, especially the children. When they have their meals together, it is a source of great anxiety to Mrs. Patton. It is at such times that squabble about food and tensions among the family members surface. Mrs. Patton's mannerism and attitude clearly show her emotional and economic dependence on her husband. Her desire to please her husband prompts her to act in a way that reminds Arun of the helplessness of his own mother during meal times. Alan Beardsworth and Teresa Keil's discussion of M.L. DeVault's book *Feeding the Family: The Social Organization of Caring as Gendered Work* brings out the fact that the food-related roles women perform is itself a way of creating and maintaining the family (Beardsworth and Keil 2004: 82). The preparation and serving of meals by women means "non-compliance may be regarded as a serious dereliction of female 'duty'.... Within the family women are seen as essentially subordinate to men and are required to assume responsibility for preparing and serving food while actually exercising relatively little control over the underlying patterns of provisioning and food selection, in which areas men's tastes and preferences are the authoritative ones" (85). However, this labour remains largely invisible and there is little appreciation for women's work in the kitchen. Women themselves find it difficult to explain as to why they accept such roles as natural and given. Such work by women is crucial to the organization of family routine. Men, on the other hand, are consumers of women's labour at home. It conceals the fact that women essentially make "choices to please and accommodate others" (82) and more often than not, such unequal division of domestic labour only entrenches them in their gender roles. Gendered discourses of food and motherhood intrinsically link good cooks as good mothers (Rai 2005: 134). Her understanding of this tenuous association fuels Melanie's resentment towards her mother.

For the Patton family members, eating is a way of asserting their distinctive identities. It is by consuming certain kinds of food and excluding others that they try to establish their individual as well as class position in society. Mrs. Patton decides to become a vegetarian because for her it is something strange, different, and exotic. It is this taste for new and the innovative that becomes a synonym of individuality and difference. Mr. Patton reminds Arun of his own father's partiality for meat. Curiously, Mr. Patton's fondness for barbecuing can be interpreted as part of a popular American perception that Harvey Levenstein associates with male cooking: "outdoor cooking is a man's job" (Levenstein, qtd. in Hollows 2000: 1). According to Levenstein, although outdoor cooking may have been the first significant challenge to gender norms, it does little to dislodge the traditional perception that domestic cooking is a feminine occupation. Commenting on the role of cookbooks in propagating kitchen culture as a feminine activity in 1950's America, Jessamyn Neuhaus argues that gender discourse tried to establish a link between food and gender norms in two ways. One was by "sexualizing the process of cooking" and the other was by "gendering particular cooking processes or types of food, in particular linking masculine behaviour to meat preparation and barbecuing" (Neuhaus 1999: 7). It presented women as responsible for the preparation of everyday meals while men only cooked special meals. The idea behind it does not assume a sharing of everyday cooking duties, only that men were doing what was their natural role as meat consumers—displaying their skill with meat preparation. Women may be adept cooks, but when it comes to the cooking of meat men know the best way of doing it. Meat thus signifies male desire and privilege and feminine acquiescence (Neuhaus 1999: 11). Neuhaus's remark makes a subtle distinction between routine cooking by women in the kitchen and masculine cooking in which male cooking becomes a creative, leisurely pastime and assumes a desirable social value and is removed from the drudgery of everyday cooking which is typically associated with women's work in the kitchen. In his work "The Body in Consumer Culture" Mike Featherstone has argued that this phenomenon may be attributed to the rise of the new professional classes and consumer culture in postwar suburban American society that invested in the art of lifestyle (Featherstone 1991). The middle classes in this way single themselves out through their conspicuous consumption. As men started participating in what was traditionally considered a feminine occupation it gained more social acceptability until it developed into "'an acceptable male pursuit: As more males mastered home cooking, its status rose; as its status rose, it became more acceptable for males to do it'" (Levenstein, qtd. in Hollows 2000: 6).

In fact the way the Pattons eat demonstrates the effect of mass-consumption food industries on the concept of a traditional meal by the fast-food culture and the manner in which instances of isolated and private eating seriously interferes with family socialization. Having a meal suggests a degree of sociality because meals have to be taken by everyone with other people who are also present for the same purpose, whether they are family members or social acquaintances with a good measure of "communication, give and take, a search for consensus, some common sense about individual needs, compromise through attending to the needs of others" (Mintz 1986: 201-02). The modern-day concept of fast food or take-away meals is the very opposite of social eating. In place of it is a new economy of time and money, a replacement of the old eating structure of meals with a diet of processed and refined foods and an obliteration of the meaning of "social eating" to more "individualized and noninteractive" forms of consumption which transforms the earlier ritual of eating together to one of "desocialized eating" where choices about food and eating are dictated less by "reference to fellow eaters, and within ranges predetermined, on the one hand, by food technology and, on the other, by what are perceived as time constraint" (Mintz 1986: 201-02). This influence of this new food culture is to be seen in the eating habits of the Pattons who eat as and when they want to eat without having to stick to the restricting demands of a meal schedule. They hardly ever sit down for a meal together. While it frees the individual from the constraints of having to stick to a meal schedule and be able to choose the content of consumption without having to consult the preference of other eaters, the self-sufficiency and freedom it ensures leads to alienation as more and more people eat outside their homes, often alone, and in impersonal surroundings. Melanie's problem is a problem of loneliness and excess of consumption that is characteristic of an impersonal urban culture that thrives on alienation:

> We don't sit down to meals like we used to. Everyone eats at different times and wants different meals. We just don't get to eating together much now that they are grown. So I just fill the freezer and let them take down what they like, when they like. Keeping the freezer full—that's my job. (197)

Arun's first contact with suburban modernity in America reinforces this impression of dissociation or separateness from familiar surroundings where people live isolated lives in enclosed spaces, with only television sets for amusement and company:

> There are so many objects, so rarely any people. Only occasionally a woman crosses one of these illuminated rooms, withdraws. There seems to be more happening in the darkened rooms where the uncertain light of television sets flicker. Here he might see undefined shapes huddled upon a couch, sprawled on the floor.... The windows are shut, he cannot hear a sound. (160)

Arun's feelings of release and liberation at the anonymity of life in America disappear soon when he comes to live with the family of the Pattons. He finds himself reluctantly drawn into the difficult position of being witness to family conflicts, which are played out at the dinner table during meal times. Food becomes a metaphor to address a wide range of feelings: feelings of anger, guilt, and resentment and of dominance and power within the family unit. There is a certain paradox to Mr. Patton's cooking that needs attention. For one thing, the time and labour that the effort of cooking for the family demands makes the ritual even more important because it is Mr. Patton, the male head of the family, who is preparing the meal. This is accompanied by a sense of the other alternative that of consuming prepared food from the market as not having the same respect as a cooked meal at home. Packaged food is an efficient alternative to cooked food and it functions precisely for the sake of convenience and economy: whether it is also nutritious and agreeable to health is another matter. As Mrs. Patton remarks:

> now if more Americans ate that food, we shouldn't be making ourselves so sick—with heart disease and cancer and—and dreadful diseases all due to a terrible, terrible diet. (193)

Arun is struck by the preoccupation with food and the resulting anxiety about the body and its appearance and starts to seriously wonder at the obsession with fitness and body image that he sees in the Patton household. Rod's obsession with fitness, Mrs. Patton's efforts to lose weight and Melanie's conscious restriction of diet calls attention to the "contemporary cult of slimness" (Beardsworth and Keil 2004: 175) found in most western societies. Melanie's self-imposed illness critiques the media portrayal of women with unattainably thin body types that adversely affects women's psychological well-being and influence their perceptions, attitude and behaviours. At a more serious level, images that show women as glamorous and alluring attempt to script women's minds by asking them to conform to a set of prescriptions that is subtly but surely patriarchal in outlook. Melanie's condition is as much an outcome of emotional malnourishment as it can be said to be the outcome of the media stereotyping of girls and women that affect body image and is a contributing factor of many food-related eating disorders in young women and teenaged girls.

Desai's text thus provides a cross-cultural context for reading gender ideology in relation to food practices within domestic cultures. The use of irony to articulate the gap between the expression of reality and our understanding of the nature of that reality enacts the political import of Desai's novel. What *Fasting, Feasting* does for us is to make us look at some cultural attitudes related to food and eating, and their association with women's relationship to food, both in traditional and non-traditional contexts, to reveal to us the ritualization of women's subordination through the task of domestic feeding. In fact the attribution of neutrality to women's food-related work in the domestic domain is a way to disguise the ideological bias of this ritualization. The ritualized aspect of gendered attitudes helps to keep intact the gender arrangements and the underlying power structures that inhere in social relations and family situations that are maintained by the process of domination through consent. At the same time it is also an oversimplification to say that women's relationship with food is merely an imposition by patriarchy to keep them in a subordinate status. In fact women's association with food can play a crucial role in maintaining positive social relationships and meaningful exchange between members of social groups and within the family. However, such exchanges can only happen in contexts of equal reciprocal relationships. The positive affirmation of women's role in socialization and in the keeping up of the smooth rhythm of social relations seems suspect for the very reason that these associations are based on the assumption that it is solely the woman's responsibility to keep social relations within the family and in the community running smoothly. The problem with the assumption lies in its association of the private or the domestic with the feminine. Ritualized attitudes such as these create the problem of role fixity for women. It is the given inevitability and acceptability of such unequal transactions in gender relations that poses a problem because of the highly nuanced, circumstantial and never-easy-to-define nature of the provisions. Attitudinal changes do not happen uniformly and at the same frequency. While it may be safely assumed that the man as the sole provider model may have been modified to a great extent to suit the changing realities of women, it has not been dismantled altogether (Kemmer 2000: 327-30). In the circumstances following a globalized world, cultural and personal identities are largely shaped by market forces and are a result of complex social, biological and economic influences that are a direct response to social-psychological shifts taking place. Whether these influences will be beneficial and permanent remains open to speculation. While it is important to locate the sites of oppression within the post-colonial space it is useful to take note of the number of changes that have already taken place over the past decades. Greater access to education and employment opportunities has improved women's overall position in society. But such studies will need to be contextualized in their proper historical setting with reference to the social, cultural and economic factors in evaluating their effects on the subject *vis-à-vis* the social structure. That however falls outside the scope of this paper. The proposed aim of this paper has been to give visibility to our programmed understanding of gender and its related associations with food and consumption so as to have a sense of how cultural assumptions of food and gender arrangements work in interpersonal interactions and social relationships.

## WORKS CITED

Ashley, Bob et al. *Food and Cultural Studies.* London and New York: Routledge, 1997.

Beardsworth, Alan and Keil, Teresa. *Sociology on the Menu. An Invitation to the Study of Food and Society.* London and New York: Routledge, 2004, pp. 82, 85, 175.

Butler, Judith. "Gender Trouble" in The *Norton Anthology of Theory and Criticism.* Ed. Vincent B. Leitch. New York: Norton and Company. 2001, pp. 2488-2501.

Counihan, Carole M. and Kaplan, Steven L. *Food and Gender: Identity and Power.* Amsterdam: Harvard Academic Publishers, 1998, p. 2.

Desai, Anita. *Fasting, Feasting.* London: Chatto & Windus, 1999.

Desai, Neera and Krishnaraj Maithreyi. "An Overview of the Status of Women in India" in *Class, Caste, Gender.* Ed. by Monoranjan Mohanty. New Delhi: Sage Publication, 2004, pp. 299.

DeVault, M.L. *Feeding the Family: The Social Organization of Caring as Gendered Work.* University of Chicago Press, 1991.

Featherstone, M. "The Body in Consumer Culture", in M. Featherstone, D. Hepworth and B. Tumer, eds., *The Body: Social Process and Cultural Theory.* London: Sage, 1991, pp. 187.

"Food, Gender and the Body", *The Canada Food Guide.* Accessed April 20, 2008.

classes.uleth.ca/200501/anth1000a/Gender,%20Food%20and%20the%20Body.ppt—date unknown.

Goody, Jack. *Cooking, Cuisine and Class: A Study in Comparative Sociology.* New York: Cambridge, 1982.

Hollows, Joanne. "The Bachelor Dinner: Masculinity, Domesticity and Food Practices in Playboy, 1953-63", pp. 6, Accessed September 2, 2006.
<http:// food.oregonstate.edu/ref/culture/hollows.html>. Updated and copyrighted Oregon State University, 2000.

Kemmer, Debbie. "Tradition and Change in Domestic Roles and Food Preparation". *Sociology* Vol. 34, No. 2, 2000, pp. 323-33, Accessed January 30, 2007
<http://www.journals.cambridge.org/article>

Leavinstein, Harvey. *Paradox of Plenty: A Social History of Eating in Modern America.* University of California Press, 2003.

Mintz, W. Sidney. *Sweetness and Power: The Place of Sugar in Modern History.* New Delhi: Penguin, 1985, pp. 201-02.

Neuhaus, Jessamyn. "The Way to a Man's Heart: Gender Roles, Domestic Ideology, and Cookbooks in the 1950s". *Journal of Social History.* Spring 1999 issue, pp. 7, 11, Accessed September 5, 2006 <http:// www.findarticles.com/p/articles/>

Rai, Sudha. "The Discourse of Food and Matrilineages in Contemporary Women's Writing", in *Rethinking Modernity.* Ed. Santosh Gupta, Prafulla C. Kar, Parul Dave Mukherjee. New Delhi: Pencraft International, 2005. pp. 133-43.

Sceats, Sarah. *Food, Consumption and the Body in Contemporary Women's Fiction.* Cambridge University Press, 2000, pp. 3, 11. Accessed April 20, 2008 http://www.questia.com/library/book/food-consumption-and-the-body-in-contemporary-womens-fiction-by-sarah-sceats.jsp

Sharma, Anjana. "Food Transfigured: Writing the Body in Indian Women's Fiction in English", in *Translating Desire: The Politics of Gender and Culture in India.* (ed.) Brinda Bose. New Delhi: Katha, 2002, pp. 154.

# Problem of Gender Inequality and Expansion of Education of Women in West Bengal

8

*Pallav Mukhopadhyay*

West Bengal is an unusual, unique state in the country. It is the only one of the states in our country to have been ruled continuously (since 1977) by a progressive, coalition government for about three decades. This government in turn has been motivated by a different vision of political, social, economic cultural change. The pace of social changes in West Bengal has accelerated in recent years but the problem of gender inequality in the state has revealed as a new dimension. Despite the land of various political, social, economic and cultural movements, the state has failed to organize a movement for development and upliftment of women as an entire class. Even after entering the new millennium the popular saying frequently heard from the men and even the women "Sonar Aantir Abar Banka Na Soja" (The golden ring is free from crooked or straight) upholding their male counterparts. The little example clearly explains the degree of prevailing gender inequality in once renaissance enlightened Bengal.

Women in West Bengal are commonly portrayed as among the most oppressed and majority of them are grounded in both poverty and patriarchy. Patriarchy limits women's ownership and control over property and other economic resources including the products of their own labour. Women's mobility in West Bengal is constrained and their access to education and information hindered. The clearest examples of gender inequality are the various forms of violence systematically meted out against women. They are practically excluded from decision-making.

Preventable diseases and unequal access to health care still affect women and girls, especially those in rural sector. HIV infection among women continues to increase. Incidents of physical violence against women in West Bengal are increasingly mentioned in the media but rarely within the context of longer processes of gender discrimination.

## Objective of the Study

The project has tried to evaluate how much gender inequalities have been created and reproduced in the households, markets and societies in the state. The factors that underlie gender inequality have been tried to examine. The research project has tried to investigate the opportunities and constraints that women face in and outside the home. This work has tried to study how far the problem of gender inequality has been solved by the expansion of education of women in West Bengal. The rate of infancy marriage in Kerala is only 7 per cent. In comparison in this state the rate is higher. 53.3 per cent women are illiterate among the women secretly removed. The age of 40 per cent of them is less than 18 years. The secretly removal of women has increased 45 per cent in last few years. 65 per cent of the women less than 18 years have attained early marriage. Oppression on women, dowry system, still exist in the society. Early motherhood, ill health due to malnutrition, concept of male and female child in obtaining higher education have worried the government, administration and social scientists. According to census, 2001 the gender development index in West Bengal is 0.549. Districts like Howrah, North 24 Parganas, Burdwan and Cooch-Behar obtain gender inequality as an alarming situation. The reservation for women has already been put in place in Panchayats and local bodies and experience of its working can only be described as encouraging.

## Research Methodology

### *Observation, documentation and analytical research*

The research work has followed the guideline with the help of discussions, seminars, symposia, sharing views, exchanges dialogue with common mass, rural and urban women, reports of Women Commission, Administration, Human Development, conversation with Women Activists, Social Workers and also with the help of opinion surveys. The project has interacted with different groups of people including students, housewives and non-government organizations.

## Case Study

The method has provided a host of observations, ideas, insights to and several aspects of a single case.

Gender discrimination has been an important feature of economic and social processes in the state. It has declined in some respects in the areas of the State. But it is more evident in economic variables and in literacy rate that indicate improving health position of women in comparison with their male counterparts. This comes out very clearly in the calculations of the Gender Development Index (G.D.I.) which are presented in Table 8.1.

**Table 8.1:** Gender Development Indices by District

| District | Health Index | Income Index | Education Index | GDI | Rank |
|---|---|---|---|---|---|
| Darjeeling | 0.731 | 0.356 | 0.714 | 0.600 | 2 |
| Jalpaiguri | 0.614 | 0.281 | 0.581 | 0.492 | 11 |
| Cooch-Behar | 0.497 | 0.287 | 0.628 | 0.471 | 13 |
| Dinajpur | 0.616 | 0.291 | 0.527 | 0.478 | 12 |
| Malda | 0.491 | 0.291 | 0.465 | 0.416 | 17 |
| Murshidabad | 0.566 | 0.176 | 0.527 | 0.423 | 16 |
| Birbhum | 0.533 | 0.178 | 0.595 | 0.435 | 14 |
| Bardhman | 0.740 | 0.270 | 0.669 | 0.560 | 7 |
| Nadia | 0.649 | 0.215 | 0.653 | 0.506 | 9 |
| North 24 Parganas | 0.721 | 0.219 | 0.752 | 0.564 | 6 |
| Hooghly | 0.764 | 0.259 | 0.720 | 0.581 | 3 |
| Bankura | 0.662 | 0.215 | 0.605 | 0.494 | 10 |
| Purulia | 0.606 | 0.161 | 0.506 | 0.424 | 15 |
| Midnapore | 0.683 | 0.323 | 0.728 | 0.578 | 4 |
| Howrah | 0.773 | 0.194 | 0.742 | 0.570 | 5 |
| Kolkata | 0.824 | 0.320 | 0.783 | 0.642 | 1 |
| South 24 Parganas | 0.705 | 0.192 | 0.666 | 0.521 | 8 |
| West Bengal | 0.697 | 0.270 | 0.681 | 0.549 | |

*Source*: West Bengal Human Development Report, 2004.

From Table 1 it is observed that the rankings of the GDI broadly follow the same pattern as the HDI rankings. The districts having low HDI also tend to have low GDI. Some districts like Howrah, North 24 Parganas, Bardhaman and Cooch-Behar tend to have worse ranking in term of GDI than HDI indicating especially acute gender discrimination. The very low "Income Index" component of the GDI essentially reflect the low workforce participation of women in West Bengal, which in turn suggests a combination of greater restrictions on women's economic agency as well as social look of recognition of women's unpaid work. Both of these striking features suggest a considerable undercurrent of gender inequality and discrimination in the society.

The problem of gender inequality and discrimination is interlinked with the differential rates of literacy of a particular locality, access to primary and basic education, health and nutrition indicators. The policy interventions of the West Bengal Government have had mixed effects in this regard. The beneficiaries of policy of land reform tended to aggravate gender discrimination. Women's participation in Panchayat, has been greater and much significant effect than in many other states and there are some regions within the state where this has had very striking positive social impact. It upholds the very notion empowerment of women in more diverse form. With respect to human security issues, women in West Bengal are in relatively better position than in other states of the country. Economic exclusion appears as one of the most significant problems for women in the state, which tends to have spill-over effects in other aspects of life. However, the trends in all of these variables are broadly in a positive direction, although the pace of change is not as rapid as could be desired.

## Gender Inequality and Discrimination in Education Sector

There is a perception in society even in urban also that girls are more homely and are better at taking care of things. That is why arts, fashion, designing and drama are generally fields reserved for women. Engineering and other related fields are considered hardcore; so more men than women enroll in these programmes. This perception is however, gradually changing. Women students have family affairs to attend to. Some students say they are better at attending to these jobs. Studying social sciences gives them this kind of freedom and flexibility. For instance, the teaching profession, which appears to have been completely taken over by women. Even today, we find more women than men in this profession both at the school and college level, as they find it relatively easy to juggle home and career. A majority of women are still being "pushed" into disciplines, which have traditionally been called "soft". It is just the reverse for male students. The so-called "soft" disciplines are Education and Social Sciences, while the "core male" disciplines are Engineering and IT. A few women's college do offer science course, the majority do not and this pushes more women into taking "softer" options. That is how we have scores of all women's colleges running Social Sciences, Humanities and Mass Media programmes. Again, while Business/Commerce and Science disciplines are (to an extend) skewed in favour of men, Medicine and Social Sciences are singularly dominated by women.

## Gender Issues and Mainstream Media

Perception about women seem to be one of the few things constant in this fast changing world. Or so it appears from a study conducted by researchers at the School of Women's Studies (SWS), Jadavpur University, which analyzed the representation of women in the media and how it is changing with time. The Director, SWS Samita Sen said "We discovered that although there is an apparent change, the basic roles and presumptions about women's worlds remain the same." According to Prof. Sen, the depiction of women in television serials showed a distinct binary between the good woman and the vamp. The regional channels and the Bengali serials, however, had greater diversity while the so-called K-soaps mainly concentrated on interiorized, Hindu upper caste women. A narrowing down of diversity in women's representation has also noticed in some of the newspapers analyzed during the information gathering process. It is evident that though some of the newspapers have done away with pages devoted exclusively for women. There is a tendency of increasing preoccupation with celebrities and glamorous women.

**Expansion of Education and Women in Local Governance**

In West Bengal, in the decades of fifties, sixties and mid-seventies the question emerged gradually was why women should join the mahila mandal or attend the functional literacy session. Almost three decades later, concrete and tangible achievements have paved the path of women's participation, giving them their right to association and opportunity to exercise their choices due to expansion of education in West Bengal. The articulate presentations by women on their real life experiences as elected representatives in Panchayat and other local bodies or forums are really encouraging. In the light of education the shyness of a woman gradually disappears and there is a tendency of pervasive boldness and enthusiasm in 'queuing up' to speak from the podium. The directness of communication is astounding. It is equally amazing that the spontaneous interventions from the floor from women without distinction of class, location, religion, caste or literacy.

In the rural Bengal a woman is able to identify the levels and locus of her needs and objectives. She clearly explains why girls' schools should have lavatories. Is that not women empowerment? The women representatives plead for direct dispensation of funds to the gram panchayat without intermediaries. Is that not a visible milestone for devolution of power? Due to the gradual expansion of basic or primary education, women representatives express their desired role in rural development planning and agree to assume responsibility for pure water facilities, set up village school and the anganwadi. So, there is no scope of disillusionment about the capacity of rural women to assert their rights for equal participation in local governance. When and how did this change happen? The women's political activism, the strength of their intellectual analysis and discourse, their boldness to break barriers of male-dominated institutions and the solidarity of their network made irreversible dents in the policy and administrative fabric of the state. The openness of the few but influential male allies to join the struggle and steer the change from within the system is a major support and cannot go unrecognized. The facilitating factors have been the increasing participation of women in public and private spheres, the equalizing of salary for equal work, targeted credit and economic assistance and incentive linked girls' education.

## Stereotype Representation of Women in Media

There is no better metaphor for how tragically trapped in polarizations the modern gender debate has become. If we go through the mainstream media apparently we see there only two kinds of women in India. Type A is draped in gold and gaudiness, she is devoted to duty. She is selfless and servile. And she is usually fat. Type B is draped in barely anything. She has a perfectly toned body and slithers like a snake to the beat of her own sensuality. And she usually does not eat.

## Violence Against Women and Legal Provisions

Violence against women remains a constant practice across societies. Crawling under the umbrella of violence is an array of horrifying acts—female foeticide, trafficking, workplace harassment, domestic torture and rape. When women defy societal norms and prejudices to report criminal action they are confronted by unequal laws that refuse to give them redressal. The UN says that violence against women is a major cause of death and disability for women 16 to 44 years of age. Crimes against women are committed with impunity in the absence of any meaningful punishment or deterrent for their perpetrators legal luminaries and citizens' groups engage in lofty debates on the merits of current punishment patterns, yet verdicts that may qualify as justice done are few and far between. Whether it is female foeticide or trafficking of girl children, domestic rape or harassment at workplace, there seems to be an unhappy acceptance that these 'wrongs' will continue. Little progress can be made if the roots of such violence are not needed out. Expressions of violence against women reflect a society's values, law and order responses act only as deterrents. Yet, the scale of the challenge should not deter us from pressing on in this battle, on all fronts—community education, better law enforcement and deterrent punishment.

## Equality and Efficiency Dimensions of Gender Budgeting

Gender budgeting means the entire budge via a gender lens to identity differential gender impacts and translate gender commitments into budgetary ones. The real challenge lies in the analysis of mainstream, 'non-rival', public expenditure whose benefits all get to enjoy, irrespective of caste, creed or sex. Gender budgeting enhance the transparency of and accountability for public expenditure and revenue and examines the gender disaggregated incidence of benefits of budgetary policies for effective public expenditure targeting. It stresses reprioritization. A key thrust is to lift the veil of statistical invisibility of the unpaid 'care economy' and incorporate it in fiscal policy. It is also a people-centred initiative can redress capability deprivation across genders and accords with the last decade's UN conferences. It has yet to percolate to state and local governments. Tax benefits extended to women workers are expected to reduce the double burden that they face at home and the work place—the gains, for example, can be utilized to appoint domestic help. But can't the working husbands of working women pay for them too? If the husbands are dependents, this move would be seen as a positive one for women's welfare. Women continue to bear the double burden and the state ends up paying for the domestic help. Isn't that a subsidy to the married working male? Gender sensitive budget is a gender sensitive approach if a chunk of development outlay is specifically spent on women's health, education and employment generation. This can help them overcome household inequalities and negative development outcomer (like environmental degradation) that affect women more.

An important and better way of empowering the women in West Bengal would be to upgrade their skills and spread education inexpensively; that can yield them better access to earning opportunities. That holds also for the enforcement of equal wages in the unorganized sector; that is urgently needed and the requisite incentive structures should be speedily devised. Finally, the nutritional status, education and overall well-being of the girl child depends largely on her mother's earning and particularly so within low-income households. Despite that, a gender differential in wages in the unorganized sector cannot be treated as an excuse to artificially like women's net incomes in the organized sector.

Real legal reform in West Bengal can only follow vital social reform. The idea of gender equality needs to be implemented first within the deep recesses of our society through liberal education, increased cultural socialization between the minority and the majority communities. It is only when the basic power relationships in our society—between men and women are also debated, analyzed and critiqued within the civil society will it be possible to translate the new law against domestic violence into practice.

## Role of Media in Gender Discrimination in West Bengal

Politics apart, there are other sectors where women allege gender bias. Media studies, time and again, emphasize that men restrict women. At a recent round table conference on the role of the media in projecting development needs of women, male editors were blamed for keeping women reporters out. In a government sponsored study, media were criticized for not reporting on women's issues. Women journalists are invited to discuss the report expressed helplessness at the apathy of news managers in projecting women's issues. If a good story deals with women, it is not spiked. It finds space in the media not because it deals with women but because it is a good story. By the same standard, an average story will not command attention, even it is gender based.

## Gender Discrimination and The Protection of Women from Domestic Violence Act, 2005

No one speaks of its women suffer it in silence. They are schooled to believe that ultimately it is their fault. Women are abused physically, emotionally, verbally. But these stories rarely make it to the public domain because the victims themselves will not speak. Women think there is no option but keep quiet and accept. Domestic violence is a violation of the human right of women. The Protection of Women from Domestic Violence Act, 2005 which was notified on October 25, 2006. Accordingly to this Act, all forms of physical, sexual, verbal, emotional or economic abuse are defined as "domestic violence". It offers women victims of such violence civil remedies of a kind not available to them earlier. Some critics argue that a poor uneducated woman would be unaware of her rights or would not know how to turn to the Law. The paper raises a question why do so many educated middle class women also tolerate abuse? Women have to be made aware that such an act exists. The research paper expresses its concern at the lack of knowledge on women's legal rights even amongst educated young women studying in some of our renowned educational Institutions. These are the very same middle class women. Despite their education, these women act also like the women of lower class believing that they have to tolerate abuse because they have no option. So, public information and education of the kind that has taken on the Right to Information Act is essential on this. The Protection of Women from Domestic Violence Act, 2005 came into force from October 26. State Government officials are now formulating the government's charter of demands to the center including more funds and recruitment of additional hands for implementation of the Act. Government orders are being issued for appointment of District Social Welfare Officers as Protection Officers (POs) with immediate effect. The POs would have to investigate each case of domestic violence reported in the areas under his/her jurisdiction. To educate the POs about the aspects of the Act and their duties, a brainstorming session has been organized in Kolkata on November 11. The Additional District Magistrates overseeing various programmes and schemes for women and child development attended the session. The POs and other district officials have been asked to involve NGOs and voluntary agencies in acting as "service providers" in compliance with the provisions of the new Act. The opinion that men and women are not equal is derived from the view that gender follows naturally from sex. In other words, a man is biologically masculine by birth and a woman is feminine. There is need for much greater gender equality and sexual liberalization. Every person should have equal rights to education regardless of whether they are male or female or for that matter, rich or poor, Dalit or Brahmin. Similarly, every person should have equal freedom to pursue a career or hold a job. In West Bengal the rate of women is higher than the national rate but the situation of Kolkata is not so good. The number of women is 828 in per thousand man. The statistics and information say that female foeticide is increasing in well to do families than downtrodden.

## Real Condition of Women in Rural Bengal

Some critics advocate that all women are terminal in the male dominating society. Women are the worst sufferer of destruction and sexual harassment. Women of lower class are compelled to accept it. They do not know how to protect it. 25th November and 10th December are observed each year as "International Women Oppression Day" and "International Human Rights Day". But the morning newspapers cover the incidents of sexual harassment, rape, wife oppression, female foeticide, removal of women secretly on a daily basis. Effect of gender biasness directly fall on the women. Imbalance deprives women from education, health, physical and economic resources, etc. They are deprived in the field of politics, economics, social and culture even. Rural women do not work by laptop but in the cropfield. They have to be understood about their rights. Urban women know the language of protest. They have achieved freedom in a considerable degree. But the rural women are still in the climate of darkness. Child marriage, dowry system and female foeticide are still happening even in the progressive state like West Bengal are treated since their childhood as "You are a woman" not "You are a human being". Boys are still at the top of the priority list than girls. They are fed by nutritious food. The village women do not know about women freedom, women liberty, women emancipation, etc. Light of education can only provide the necessary awareness amongst the victimized poor women.

## Combat Against Oppression

Combat against oppression of women will be initiated from all corners of the society. Domestic violence will be closed if the male members of the home become careful. Women are verbally, emotionally, psychologically abused since the teen age. Women face sexual harassment at their work place. Many of them have been forced to enter the business of flesh trade. Widows, unmarried or lonely women are oppressed physically, psychologically or sexually. Oppression free life is the fundamental right of women. Eradication of the gender biasness can only save the right of women. We have to implement such value system oriented education that will provide a boy and a girl equal benefits and opportunities.

### Come Forward Men

An ideal family always exhibit the equal dignity of men and women. Men should not take upper hand in the family due to their masculinity. Men have to protest in streets, markets, work places, shopping malls, tramcars, buses, trains or hotels, restaurants against any sort of abuse of women. It is essential to treat the matter as a social issue. Men should forward their hands towards oppressed women as a real friend. Protest against dowry system should be initiated from the corner of men. Women deserve equal share and status in a family and men have to accept it.

Virginia Woolf once commented that there were two wants in woman's life—self-income and self-residence. Women now uphold their voices. They form associations. They unitedly try to change the existing situation.

### Case Studies

Namita Das is a member of a downtrodden family. Her husband is a rickshaw puller. Namita's son Mukai fell ill one day. Namita had no money to bring her son to a medical practitioner. Namita borrowed Rs. 200 from a self-dependent group and made necessary arrangements for her son's treatment.

Chhabi Kundu and her husband are rice dealers. But the majority share of their profit was consumed to meet the interest of the moneylender. The want of the family went on. Chhabi became the member of "Surabhi"—a self-dependent group. Now, she has achieved the provision of loan. Now their profit increased. Her economic stability and social establishment have enhanced.

Arati Mandal lives in Bankura. Majority of her land was sterile. Her husband was daily wage worker. One day he passed away. There was no option infront of Arati than went to city for searching a new job. But the other members of self-dependent group helped her to stay in village.

The villages of West Bengal have gradually changed. Village does not mean the story of grief and failure. Namita, Chhabi, Arati are identified with their stories of success. They form self-help and self-dependent group to stand firm on their own feet. Distant villages of West Bengal exhibit two features. Self-dependent groups and deposit loan and insurance. These groups being changes in the life of backward women especially in the remote villages in the state. In fact, self-dependent group means association of 10-15 socially and economically backward women having equal status. This association is area based. Deposit of money and loan help them to form the group. As the group strengthens, the women become self-confident.

The expansion of primary and basic education help them to give more attention on the education of their children, nurturing of the little girls. The exploitation of women, oppression on women become decreased. Women are now eager to know the functions and activities of Panchayats. They are participating in the session of Gram Sansad. Group formation, financial management, group based organization formation, relation with bank-these are some developments in the rural sector of this state. The role of self-dependent group may be important in the Gram Unnayan Samity in West Bengal.

At present, there are about 3 lakh groups in the state. Thirty-six lakh families are involved with it. One crore eighty lakh people are attached with these activities.

Besides NGOs, the State Government has extended its hands for the development of rural women. Swarnajayanti Gram Swarojgar Yojana (1 lakh 40 thousand groups) of Deptt. of Panchayat and Rural Development, Swayangsiddha Project (6,000 groups) of West Bengal Women Development Corporation. NABARD, Co-operative banks, Samabaya Krishi Unnayan Samity have helped a lot. SIDBI and Rashtriya Mahila Kosh have worked well. Cash project of care and its associated organization (11,000 groups) have done well in this sector. Self-

Help Group Promotional Forum has arranged with the association of State Panchayat and Rural Development Organization. They have arranged Annual Conferences every year. Women participated in this conference coming from Kalchini to Kakdwip, Basirhat to Bandoan and from all districts of the state. They attend, participate in the discussion and ultimately frame the future plan of action. The fifth Conference was held at Bagnan in Howrah district during 10-12 February 2006. As a consequence, gender discrimination, educational discrimination have decreased. Though in a slow rate but decreasing.

### Survey

A questionnaire based survey was conducted by the Researcher during August 2006 to October 2006 on the urban, sub-urban, rural women of the state. 600 women participated in this survey. A replica of the questionnaire is given here.

## QUESTIONNAIRE

*Region of the State where opinion maker belongs to

(a) North (b) East (c) West (d) South

*Area (a) Urban (b) Sub-Urban (c) Rural

*Name of City/Town/Village: Range Ward:

*Name:

*Present & Permanent Address:

*Sex: (a) Male (b) Female.

*Age: *Marital Status:

*Education:

*Occupation:

*Family income per month:

*Religion: *Caste:

*Whether belong to SC/ST/OBC:

*Mother Tongue:

1. How do you label gender discrimination in our state?

   (a) Alarming, (b) Moderate, (c) A little bit of, (d) No discrimination.

2. The worst cases of gender discrimination takes place in (a) Urban, (b) Sub-Urban, (c) Rural areas.
3. What is the status of women in the family/society in West Bengal?

   (a) Very good, (b) Good, (c) Satisfactory, (d) Not so good, (e) Dissatisfactory.
4. Problem of gender inequality may be eradicated by (a) Expansion of education,

   (b) Enhancement of social awareness of people,

   (c) Giving them equal share and status in family/society,

   (d) All of the above.
5. What is the role of State Government in this regard (per cent wise)?

   (a) 81-100%, (b) 61-80%, (c) 41-60%, (d) 21-40%, (e) 0-20%.
6. How do you rate the mass media of this state to uphold this problem and cite solutions?

   (a) 81-100%, (b) 61-80%, (c) 41-60%, (d) 21-40%, (e) 0-20%.
7. What form of gender inequality/biasness/discrimination is dominant in West Bengal?

   (a) Female foeticide, (b) Rape, (c) Sexual harassment and assault, (d) Illegal removal of girls and women, (e) Abduction of women, (f) Murder of bride for dowry, (g) Oppression of wife, (h) Suicide of women due to intolerable situation, (i) All of the above.
8. Do you think expansion of women education in this state is satisfactory?

   (a) Yes, (b) No, (c) No comment.
9. Do you have any personal experience of gender discrimination?

   (a) Yes, (b) No, (c) No comment.
10. According to your opinion (a) 0-25%, (b) 26-50%, (c) 51-75%, (d) 76-100% of the women in our state are aware and conscious of gender discrimination.

## Result and Analysis of the Survey

Seventy per cent of the opinion maker have expressed their view about moderate gender discrimination in our state while 20 per cent have marked the situation as a little bit of worry.

Eighty per cent of the women have identified rural areas being the place of worst cases of gender discrimination.

Urban women expressed their status good but the position of sub-urban and rural women are not so good.

Majority of the women prescribed the eradication of this problem by means of political social economic cultural, educational awareness.

Seventy-five per cent of women marked 61-80 per cent role of State government in this regard where 20 per cent indicated 41-60 per cent role of the Government.

Majority of the women especially in urban areas are of opinion that mass media play a moderate role (41-60 per cent) in this regard.

Different forms of gender inequality have been identified by the opinion maker of which 40 per cent urban and sub-urban women indicated female foeticide, rape sexual assault, murder for dowry, oppression of wife whereas the 30 per cent rural women labelled illegal removal of girls and women, abduction of women as most striking forms besides others.

Majority of the women (60%) expressed their satisfaction in expansion of education in this state. But their demand is to enhance the level of education among women which will make them aware and conscious.

Sixty per cent of the women in the survey have first-hand personal experience of gender discrimination.

Seventy per cent of the women think that 26-50 per cent of women in our state are aware and consciousness of gender discrimination.

## Central Government's Stand Regarding this Issue

National Common Minimum Programme (NCMP) of United Progressive Alliance (UPA) was a commitment to empower

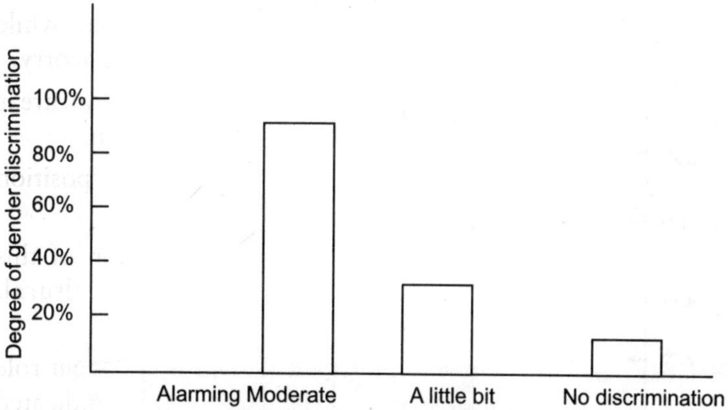


**Graph 1:** Bar graph showing degree of gender discrimination in our state.

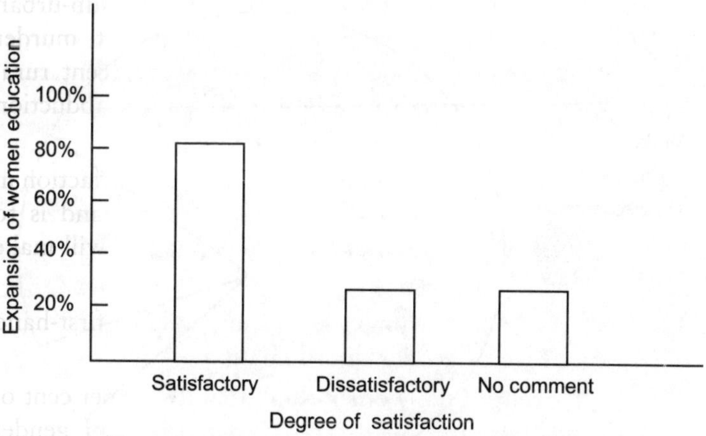


**Graph 2:** Bar graph showing degree of satisfaction regarding expansion of common education in the state

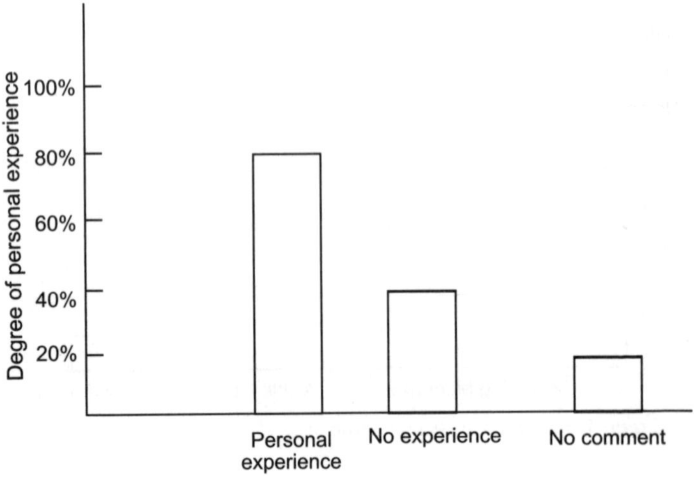


Graph 3: Bar graph showing personal experience of gender discrimination

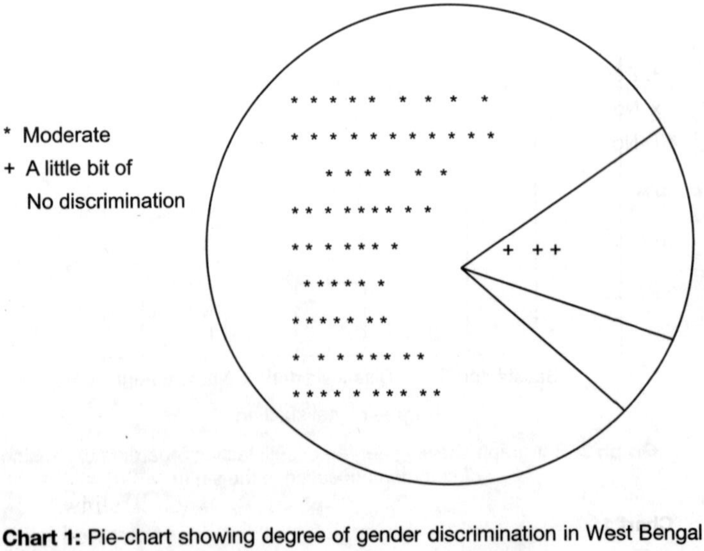


**Chart 1:** Pie-chart showing degree of gender discrimination in West Bengal

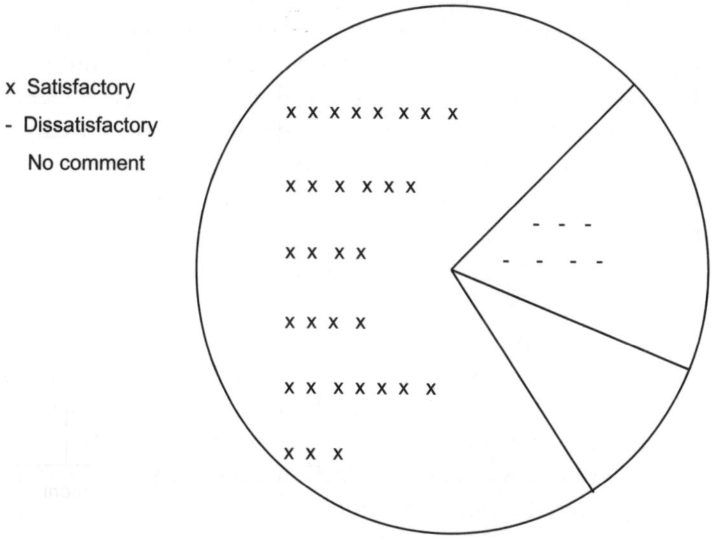


**Chart 1:** Pie chart showing expansion of women education in West Bengal

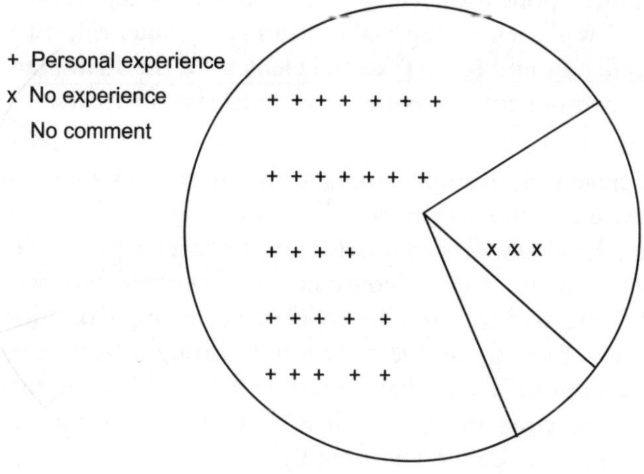


**Chart 1:** Pie chart showing degree of personal experience of gender discrimination of women in West Bengal

women politically, educationally and legally. Further, the NCMP promised to take the lead in introducing legislation to reserve for women one-third of the seats in the State Assemblies and in the Lok Sabha and address the issues of domestic violence, gender discrimination and discriminatory legislation. While many of these promises have remained on paper, the overall intent of the government on women's issues presented in the draft approach paper (DAP) to the Eleventh Five Year Plan (2007-12) has installed new fears among women's organizations.

In the DAP, titled "Towards Faster and More Inclusive Growth: An Approach to the 11th Five Year Plan", gender discrimination is confined to a few paragraphs under the sub-heading "Gender Balancing" in Chapter 5, "Bridging Divides: Including the Excluded". Even if the restricted nature of the content can be overlooked, the lack of perspective and strategy has disappointed women activities.

The paper states: "The 11th Plan strategy for gender balancing must take care of the special needs of women such as clean cooking fuels, care for pregnant and nursing women, etc.... Gender balancing would require appropriate provisions in government policies/schemes across Ministries/departments and sectors." While it says "Special measures for gender empowerment and equity should be an essential element of the 11th Plan", the gender component is missing in all the other chapters.

The link between patriarchy, caste and religion, all three of which have serious implications for the status of women. It says that "while women's needs will be specially tackled across all sectors, the Plan will particularly focus on three aspects—violence against women (VAW), economic empowerment and women's health" and will seek to check violence, ranging from domestic violence to foeticide and sexual assault, through effective policies and legislation. It says that "effect will be made to ensure that towns and cities under the NURM (National Urban Renewal Mission) are made women friendly".

Women's groups see VAW occurring in a socio-economic and political context and as such feel the need to change this particular context. Indira Hirway, Professor of Economics and

Director of the Ahmedabad-based Centre for Development Alternatives said that with the onset of globalization, there had been a declaration of employment in general and a decline in the quality and extent of employment of women in particular. A qualitative shift in the nature of women's work, a shift from regular to irregular forms of work, had taken place.

Vina Mazumdar, national research professor in social sciences, said, admitted that a "nation cannot be healthy unless its women are healthy". But as a remedy it suggests steps to reduce anemia and malnutrition but only among "adolescent girls" to eliminate "maternal and infant mortality". A huge chunk of women in the reproductive age group has been left out. According to the National Sample Survey 55th Round, July 1999-June 2000, of the around 106 million women in the workforce 40-45 per cent were in the reproductive age group.

The Mid-Term Appraisal (MTA) had underscored issues such an adverse sex ratios, high infant and maternal mortality, wide gaps in the rates of literacy and wages of men and women, feminization of poverty and the exploitation of women in the unorganized sector and in the export processing or special economic zones.

It recognized that women were both productive workers contributing to the economy and mothers and home-makers.

C.P. Sujaya, vesting Fellow at the Centre for Women's Development Studies, said: "Women's productive and non-productive roles and functions are both equally important and this should be a non-negotiable premise to the Eleventh Plan."

## Women's Participation in Decision-Making Process and Empowerment of Women

There has been substantial representation of the rural women who are social deprived in the elected bodies. This has helped to change the power equations in rural society and encourage the social and political empowerment of women. West Bengal has a history of substantial representation of women in Panchayats well before the 73rd and 74th amendments passed by Parliament. In 1980s and 1990s more than one-third of Panchayat members were women. Even Zilla Parishads exhibited women representation. The Panchayat Elections in 2003 have created even more gender balance because of the active policy of the ruling party and its partners in terms of fielding more women candidates, and now the Sabhadhipatis of several districts are women. Active women's participation due to expansion of education improves the local enforcement of the requirement of people. Special meals for girl students, nutrition programme for pregnant and lactating mothers, public health campaigns have been implemented more effectively due to greater participation of women workers. The significant increase in the proportion of girls in education, the better performance of girls in school and strong motivation of schooling even among girls in low income or socially deprived groups can be partly attributed to the influence of women Panchayats members in raising consciousness and gender awareness in the local communities. Even in the backward district like Purulia, young women Panchayat members from poor and socially disadvantaged backgrounds are increasingly more articulate and empowerable to express the concerns of women in public forums and conscious of the need to influence policy-making.

**Table 8.2:** Social composition of panchayat members elected in 1993 (per cent of total members in 8 districts)

| | Gram Panchayats | Panchayat Samitis | Zilla Parishads |
|---|---|---|---|
| Scheduled Caste women | 14.4 | 14.5 | 13.3 |
| Scheduled Caste men | 24.1 | 25.3 | 24.5 |
| Total Scheduled caste | 38.5 | 39.8 | 37.8 |
| Scheduled Tribe women | 3.0 | 3.2 | 3.2 |
| Scheduled Tribe men | 4.4 | 3.9 | 3.8 |
| Total Scheduled Tribes | 7.4 | 7.1 | 7.0 |
| Total Women | 35.5 | 34.6 | 36.1 |

*Source*: Charvak 2003, based on District Panchayat Profiles published by SIPRD.

## Expansion of Education of Women in West Bengal

The literacy rate is generally considered as one of the important indicators of the development of a population, and the educational level of a population is seen as an important determinant of its quality of life. In addition, of course, education interacts with other human development variables in crucial ways. For example, universal education and special attention to the education of women are critical in improving the health practices of a community. Universal education is also likely to be necessary for meaningful and effective decentralization, especially in the coming phase when panchayats are being given greater responsibility for a very wide range of activities.

The literacy rate in West Bengal has always been higher than the all-India average, and West Bengal ranks sixth among the major states in this regard. But until the last decade, the improvement in literacy has been relatively slow in the state, especially for women. However, in the past decade, the state government has been making concentrated efforts through various special schemes such as 'total literacy campaigns', 'non-formal education', etc. apart from formal schooling for children to achieve the goal of 'education for all' as soon as possible. As a result, according to the Census, the literacy rate in West Bengal has increased from 48.6 per cent in 1981 to 57.7 per cent in 1991 and to 69.2 per cent in 2001. While rural literacy is predictably lower than in urban areas, it has improved more rapidly in the recent past. Literacy among rural females is still low compared to other groups, it has increased more rapidly in the recent past, going up by nearly 16 percentage points in the last decade.

It is encouraging that the largest improvements in literacy in the past decade have been in some of what were the most "backward" districts, and especially among females. Increases in the female literacy rate have been in excess of 20 percentage points in Dakshin Dinajpur and Cooch-Behar, and more than 15 percentage points in Jalpaiguri, Murshidabad, Malda, Darjeeling, Nadia and Birbhum, in the period between 1991 and 2001. So there is substantial improvement in literacy—and especially female literacy—in the recent period.

By 1998-99, 48 per cent of rural males and 27 per cent of rural females in the age group 15 years and above were estimated to have completed at least primary education, and around one-third of these had completed secondary education or above. In the urban areas, 79 per cent of adult males and 62 per cent of adult females were found by the NFHS-2 to be literate at least up to primary level or above.

There are variations in literacy rates across occupational groups in rural West Bengal for all the population above 7 years, and separately for females above 7 years. The relatively most deprived occupation group appears to be that of agricultural labour households, of whom more than half of all such population, and nearly two-thirds of the females, are non-literate. Households consisting of the self-employed in agriculture show the highest rates of literacy, for men and women in rural parts of the state. Gender gaps remain substantial, and women of rural labour households (both in agriculture and non-agriculture) are the worst off among the rural population in terms of illiteracy.

Interestingly, gender gaps in literacy appear to be slightly less marked in urban parts of the state. Casual labour households are the worst off, and nearly half the women in such households are illiterate. In urban areas, those households where the main source of income is from regular wages, as well as "other" households, show the lowest rates of illiteracy.

Quite obviously, females in the ST households in the rural areas of West Bengal need special attention to improve the education levels in the rural West Bengal. Next come SC households, where more than half of the women are illiterate. The gender gap seems to be approximately equal across caste category, indicating that gender discrimination is not more marked among any particular caste group, but is shared across all castes. Nor is the gender gap among Muslims higher than it is among Hindus, indicating that the general perception that Muslim women are less likely to be educated than their Hindu counterparts, is not borne out by the data. However, attendance rates for girls aged 6-10 years in rural West Bengal were generally better than the all-India average, although in urban areas the rate in West Bengal was slightly lower. For girls aged 11-13, attendance rates were higher or the same as the all-India average. Increasing the efforts for resource mobilization to enable more state government spending in necessary areas; and innovating and strengthening institutions and mechanisms to ensure the better delivery of public services. Such a strategy would help to generate a virtuous cycle of human development and economic growth positively reinforcing each other.

## Last Few Words

There are particular areas that require specific intervention which are mentioned very briefly here. The reversal of employment generation for urban women, and the large male-female wage-gap in urban work, both point to the need for focused intervention.

The low nutritional status of women and young children require urgent attention. Areas of public intervention that can be usefully pursued in this regard include the provision of sanitary facilities and campaigns to improve food consumption practices to ensure adequate nutrition. Targeted interventions in terms of provision, access and raising public consciousness about desirable food intake patterns are especially necessary, given the large production of vegetables, which do not appear to be consumed within the state.

In education, certain spatial and social pockets of illiteracy need to be addressed. In occupational terms, agricultural labour households (and especially females in such households) require special policy attention. Scheduled Tribe households (especially females) also require a focused drive to increase literacy.

The Constitutional provisions of social equality and justice need to be strengthened by the efforts of common people in our villages and cities. Efforts to end gender based discrimination should be implemented aggressively. Expansion of education of women in West Bengal should be aimed at ending injustice and enhancing the individual potential as well as social contribution of those member of society who have limited opportunities.

The year 2005 marks the 10th Anniversary of the Beijing Declaration and Platform for Action—the world's first truly comprehensive plan in the areas of critical concern to women's advancement. The Government of West Bengal should ratify the United Nations Convention on the Elimination of All Forms of Discrimination Against Women (1979). Gender equality can only be achieved truly if along with observation of International

Women's Day (8th March) people around the State rededicate themselves to provide women their due in social safety nets, in decision-making, development of the State and most importantly in the home.

## REFERENCES & BIBLIOGRAPHY

### *Background papers*

1. Basabi Bhattacharya, Survey of literature and assessment of human development indicators database in West Bengal.
2. V. Nagi Reddy, Spread and quality of primary education in West Bengal: Emerging issues.

### *Books and Articles consulted*

1. Bandopadhyay, Nripen (1995). Agrarian Reforms in West Bengal—An Enquiry into its Impact and Some Problems, Paper presented at Workshop on 'Agricultural Growth and Agrarian Structure in Contemporary West Bengal and Bangladesh', Calcutta, January, 1995.
2. Bose Buddhadeb (1981). Agrarian Programme of the Left Front Government in West Bengal, *Economic and Political Weekly*, XVI, 50, 2053-60.
3. Bureau of Applies Economics and Statistics (2002). Statistical Abstract, Kolkata.
4. Chatterjee, Biswajit and Dilip Kumar Ghosh (2001). In Search of a District Development Index, State Institute of Panchayats and Rural Development, Kalyani, West Bengal.
5. Chatterjee, Nandita, Bhattacharyya, Nikhilesh and Haldar, Animesh (1998). Socio-economic Profile of Households in Calcutta Metropolitan Area: 1996-97, CMDA.
6. Chattapadhyay, Raghabendra, and V. Nagi Reddy (2002). The status of elementary and technical education in West Bengal, Background Paper submitted for West Bengal State Development Report and Perspective 2007-08, Kolkata: May.
7. Chavan, Pallavi and Rajshree Bedamatta (2003). Trends in agricultural wages in India, 1964-65 to 1999-2000, Paper presented to All-India Conference on Agriculture and Rural Society in Contemporary India, Bardhaman, West Bengal December 17-20, 2003.
8. Gazdar, Haris, and Sunil Sengupta (1997). "Agrarian Politics and Rural Development in West Bengal" in *Indian Development: Selected Regional Perspectives* (eds.) Jean Dreze and Amartya Sen. Oxford University Press, Delhi.

9. Jack, J.C. (1916, 1975). *The Economic Life of a Bengal District*, Delhi: Agam Prakashan.
10. Lieten, G.K. (1992). *Continuity and Change in Rural West Bengal*, New: Sage Publications.
11. Listen, G.K. (1996). *Development, Devolution and Democracy: Village Discourse in West Bengal*, Sage Publications, New Delhi.
12. Mishra, Surjya Kanta (1991). *An Alternative Approach to Development: Land Reforms and Panchayats*, Information and Cultural Affairs Department, Government of West Bengal.
13. Mukherji, N. and D. Bandopadhyay (1993). New Horizons for West Bengal's Panchayats, report submitted to the Department of Panchayats, Government of West Bengal.
14. Mukhopadhyay, Rabindranath (2002). Tribal Education: The case of West Bengal, Background Paper submitted for West Bengal State Development Report and Perspective 2007-08, Kolkata: May.
15. Rana Kumar, Samantak Das with Amrita Sengupta and Abdur Rafique (2003). State of Primary Education in West Bengal, *Economic and Political Weekly*, May 31.
16. Sengupta, Sunil (1993). Land Reforms in West Bengal, Rural Poverty Performance and Perspectives, Paper presented at the National Workshop on the Socio-economic Impact of Land Reforms, organized by Visva-Bharati University and the Board of Revenue, West Bengal.
17. West Bengal Human Development Report 2004, Development and Planning Department, Government of West Bengal.

### Journals

1. *Diary of Political Events*
2. *Frontline*
3. *India Today*
4. *Outlook*
5. *Politics India*
6. *The Link.*

### Newspapers

1. *Free Press Journal*
2. *Hindustan Times*
3. *The Indian Express*
4. *M.P. Chronicle*
5. *National Herald*
6. *Patriot*

7. *The Hindu*
8. *The Pioneer*
9. *The Telegraph*
10. *The Times of India*
11. *The Statesman.*

# National Policy for the Empowerment of Women (2001)

9

## Introduction

The principle of gender equality is enshrined in the Indian Constitution in its Preamble, Fundamental Rights, Fundamental Duties and Directive Principles. The Constitution not only grants equality to women, but also empowers the State to adopt measures of positive discrimination in favour of women.

Within the framework of a democratic polity, our laws, development policies, Plans and programmes have aimed at women's advancement in different spheres. From the Fifth Five Year Plan (1974-78) onwards has been a marked shift in the approach to women's issues from welfare to development. In recent years, the empowerment of women has been recognized as the central issue in determining the status of women. The National Commission for Women was set up by an Act of Parliament in 1990 to safeguard the rights and legal entitlements of women. The 73rd and 74th Amendments (1993) to the Constitution of India have provided for reservation of seats in the local bodies of Panchayats and Municipalities for women, laying a strong foundation for their participation in decision-making at the local levels.

1.3 India has also ratified various international conventions and human rights instruments committing to secure equal rights of women. Key among them is the ratification of the Convention on Elimination of All Forms of Discrimination Against Women (CEDAW) in 1993.

1.4 The Mexico Plan of Action (1975), the Nairobi Forward Looking Strategies (1985), the Beijing Declaration as well as the Platform for Action (1995) and the Outcome Document adopted by the UNGA Session on Gender Equality and Development and Peace for the 21st century, titled "Further actions and initiatives to implement the Beijing Declaration and the Platform for Action" have been unreservedly endorsed by India for appropriate follow up.

1.5 The Policy also takes note of the commitments of the Ninth Five Year Plan and the other Sectoral Policies relating to empowerment of women.

1.6 The women's movement and a widespread network of non-Government Organizations which have strong grass-roots presence and deep insight into women's concerns have contributed in inspiring initiatives for the empowerment of women.

1.7 However, there still exists a wide gap between the goals enunciated in the Constitution, legislation, policies, plans, programmes, and related mechanisms on the one hand and the situational reality of the status of women in India, on the other. This has been analyzed extensively in the Report of the Committee on the Status of Women in India, "Towards Equality", 1974 and highlighted in the National Perspective Plan for Women, 1988-2000, the Shramshakti Report, 1988 and the Platform for Action, Five Years After—An Assessment.

1.8 Gender disparity manifests itself in various forms, the most obvious being the trend of continuously declining female ratio in the population in the last few decades. Social stereotyping and violence at the domestic and societal levels are some of the other manifestations. Discrimination against girl children, adolescent girls and women persists in parts of the country.

1.9 The underlying causes of gender inequality are related to social and economic structure, which is based on informal and formal norms, and practices.

1.10 Consequently, the access of women particularly those belonging to weaker sections including Scheduled Castes/ Scheduled Tribes/Other Backward Classes and minorities, majority of whom are in the rural areas and in the informal, unorganized sector—to education, health and productive resources, among others, is inadequate. Therefore, they remain largely marginalized, poor and socially excluded.

## Goal and Objectives

1.11 The goal of this Policy is to bring about the advancement, development and empowerment of women. The Policy will be widely disseminated so as to encourage active participation of all stakeholders for achieving its goals. Specifically, the objectives of this Policy include:

(i) Creating an environment through positive economic and social policies for full development of women to enable them to realize their full potential.

(ii) The *de jure* and *de facto* enjoyment of all human rights and fundamental freedom by women on equal basis with men in all spheres—political, economic, social, cultural and civil.

(iii) Equal access to participation and decision-making of women in social, political and economic life of the nation.

(iv) Equal access to women to health care, quality education at all levels, career and vocational guidance, employment, equal remuneration, occupational health and safety, social security and public office, etc.

(v) Strengthening legal systems aimed at elimination of all forms of discrimination against women.

(vi) Changing societal attitudes and community practices by active participation and involvement of both men and women.

(vii) Mainstreaming a gender perspective in the development process.

(viii) Elimination of discrimination and all forms of violence against women and the girl child; and

(ix) Building and strengthening partnerships with civil society, particularly women's organizations.

## Policy Prescriptions

### *Judicial Legal Systems*

Legal-judicial system will be made more responsive and gender sensitive to women's needs, especially in cases of domestic violence and personal assault. New laws will be enacted and existing laws reviewed to ensure that justice is quick and the punishment meted out to the culprits is commensurate with the severity of the offence.

2.2 At the initiative of and with the full participation of all stakeholders including community and religious leaders, the Policy would aim to encourage changes in personal laws such as those related to marriage, divorce, maintenance and guardianship so as to eliminate discrimination against women.

2.3 The evolution of property rights in a patriarchal system has contributed to the subordinate status of women. The Policy would aim to encourage changes in laws relating to ownership of property and inheritance by evolving consensus in order to make them gender just.

### *Decision-Making*

3.1 Women's equality in power sharing and active participation in decision-making, including decision-making in political process at all levels will be ensured for the achievement of the goals of empowerment. All measures will be taken to guarantee women equal access to and full participation in decision-making bodies at every level, including the legislative, executive, judicial, corporate, statutory bodies, as also the advisory Commissions, Committees, Boards, Trusts, etc. Affirmative action such as reservations/quotas, including in higher legislative bodies, will be considered whenever necessary on a time bound basis. Women-friendly personnel policies will also be drawn up to encourage women to participate effectively in the developmental process.

## Mainstreaming a Gender Perspective in the Development Process

4.1 Policies, programmes and systems will be established to ensure mainstreaming of women's perspectives in all developmental processes, as catalysts, participants and recipients. Wherever there are gaps in policies and programmes, women specific interventions would be undertaken to bridge these. Coordinating and monitoring mechanisms will also be devised to assess from time to time the progress of such mainstreaming mechanisms. Women's issues and concerns as a result will specially be addressed and reflected in all concerned laws, sectoral policies, plans and programmes of action.

## Economic Empowerment of Women

### *Poverty Eradication*

5.1 Since women comprise the majority of the population below the poverty line and are very often in situations of extreme poverty, given the harsh realities of intra-household and social discrimination, macro-economic policies and poverty eradication programmes will specifically address the needs and problems of such women. There will be improved implementation of programmes which are already women oriented with special targets for women. Steps will be taken for mobilization of poor women and convergence of services, by offering them a range of economic and social options, along with necessary support measures to enhance their capabilities.

### *Micro Credit*

5.2 In order to enhance women's access to credit for consumption and production, the establishment of new, and strengthening of existing micro-credit mechanisms and micro-finance institution will be undertaken so that the outreach of credit is enhanced. Other supportive measures would be taken to ensure adequate flow of credit through extant financial institutions and banks, so that all women below poverty line have easy access to credit.

### *Women and Economy*

5.3 Women's perspectives will be included in designing and implementing macro-economic and social policies by institutionalizing their participation in such processes. Their contribution to socio-economic development as producers and workers will be recognized in the formal and informal sectors (including home based workers) and appropriate policies relating to employment and to her working conditions will be drawn up. Such measures could include:

(i) Reinterpretation and redefinition of conventional concepts of work wherever necessary e.g. in the Census records, to reflect women's contribution as producers and workers.

(ii) Preparation of satellite and national accounts.

(iii) Development of appropriate methodologies for undertaking (i) and (ii) above.

***Globalization***

Globalization has presented new challenges for the realization of the goal of women's equality, the gender impact of which has not been systematically evaluated fully. However, from the micro-level studies that were commissioned by the Department of Women and Child Development, it is evident that there is a need for re-framing policies for access to employment and quality of employment. Benefits of the growing global economy have been unevenly distributed leading to wider economic disparities, the feminization of poverty, increased gender inequality through often deteriorating working conditions and unsafe working environment especially in the informal economy and rural areas. Strategies will be designed to enhance the capacity of women and empower them to meet the negative social and economic impacts, which may flow from the globalization process.

***Women and Agriculture***

5.5 In view of the critical role of women in the agriculture and allied sectors, as producers, concentrated efforts will be made to ensure that benefits of training, extension and various programmes will reach them in proportion to their numbers. The programmes for training women in soil conservation, social forestry, dairy development and other occupations allied to agriculture like horticulture, livestock including small animal husbandry, poultry, fisheries, etc. will be expanded to benefit women workers in the agriculture sector.

***Women and Industry***

5.6 The important role played by women in electronics, information technology and food processing and agro industry and textiles has been crucial to the development of these sectors. They would be given comprehensive support in terms of labour legislation, social security and other support services to participate in various industrial sectors.

5.7 Women at present cannot work in night shift in factories even if they wish to. Suitable measures will be taken to enable women to work on the night shift in factories. This will be accompanied with support services for security, transportation, etc.

***Support Services***

5.8 The provision of support services for women, like child care facilities, including crèches at work places and educational institutions, homes for the aged and the disabled will be expanded and improved to create an enabling environment and to ensure their full cooperation in social, political and economic life. Women-friendly personnel policies will also be drawn up to encourage women to participate effectively in the developmental process.

**Social Empowerment of Women**

***Education***

6.1 Equal access to education for women and girls will be ensured. Special measures will be taken to eliminate discrimination, universalize education, eradicate illiteracy, create a gender-sensitive educational system, increase enrolment and retention rates of girls and improve the quality of education to facilitate life-long learning as well as development of occupation/vocation/technical skills by women. Reducing the gender gap in secondary and higher education would be a focus area. Sectoral time targets in existing policies will be achieved, with a special focus on girls and women, particularly those belonging to weaker sections including the Scheduled Castes/Scheduled Tribes/Other Backward Classes/Minorities. Gender sensitive curricula would be developed at all levels of educational system in order to address sex stereotyping as one of the causes of gender discrimination.

### *Health*

6.2 A holistic approach to women's health which includes both nutrition and health services will be adopted and special attention will be given to the needs of women and the girl at all stages of the life cycle. The reduction of infant mortality and maternal mortality, which are sensitive indicators of human development, is a priority concern. This policy reiterates the national demographic goals for Infant Mortality Rate (IMR), Maternal Mortality Rate (MMR) set out in the National Population Policy 2000. Women should have access to comprehensive, affordable and quality health care. Measures will be adopted that take into account the reproductive rights of women to enable them to exercise informed choices, their vulnerability to sexual and health problems together with endemic, infectious and communicable diseases such as malaria, TB, and water borne diseases as well as hypertension and cardio-pulmonary diseases. The social, developmental and health consequences of HIV/AIDS and other sexually transmitted diseases will be tackled from a gender perspective.

6.3 To effectively meet problems of infant and maternal mortality, and early marriage the availability of good and accurate data at micro level on deaths, birth and marriages is required. Strict implementation of registration of births and deaths would be ensured and registration of marriages would be made compulsory.

6.4 In accordance with the commitment of the National Population Policy (2000) to population stabilization, this Policy recognizes the critical need of men and women to have access to safe, effective and affordable methods of family planning of their choice and the need to suitably address the issues of early marriages and spacing of children. Interventions such as spread of education, compulsory registration of marriage and special programmes like BSY should impact on delaying the age of marriage so that by 2010 child marriages are eliminated.

6.5 Women's traditional knowledge about health care and nutrition will be recognized through proper documentation and its use will be encouraged. The use of Indian and alternative systems of medicine will be enhanced within the framework of overall health infrastructure available for women.

### *Nutrition*

6.6 In view of the high risk of malnutrition and disease that women face at all the three critical stages viz., infancy and childhood, adolescent and reproductive phase, focused attention would be paid to meeting the nutritional needs of women at all stages of the life cycle. This is also important in view of the critical link between the health of adolescent girls, pregnant and lactating women with the health of infant and young children. Special efforts will be made to tackle the problem of macro and micro nutrient deficiencies especially amongst pregnant and lactating women as it leads to various diseases and disabilities.

6.7 Intra-household discrimination in nutritional matters *vis à vis* girls and women will be sought to be ended through appropriate strategies. Widespread use of nutrition education would be made to address the issues of intra-household imbalances in nutrition and the special needs of pregnant and lactating women. Women's participation will also be ensured in the planning, superintendence and delivery of the system.

### *Drinking Water and Sanitation*

6.8 Special attention will be given to the needs of women in the provision of safe drinking water, sewage disposal, toilet facilities and sanitation within accessible reach of households, especially in rural areas and urban slums. Women's participation will be ensured in the planning, delivery and maintenance of such services.

### *Housing and Shelter*

6.9 Women's perspectives will be included in housing policies, planning of housing colonies and provision of shelter both in rural and urban areas. Special attention will be given for providing adequate and safe housing and accommodation for women including single women, heads of households, working women, students, apprentices and trainees.

***Environment***

6.10 Women will be involved and their perspectives reflected in the policies and programmes for environment, conservation and restoration. Considering the impact of environmental factors on their livelihoods, women's participation will be ensured in the conservation of the environment and control of environmental degradation. The vast majority of rural women still depend on the locally available non-commercial sources of energy such as animal dung, crop waste and fuel wood. In order to ensure the efficient use of these energy resources in an environmental friendly manner, the Policy will aim at promoting the programmes of non-conventional energy resources. Women will be involved in spreading the use of solar energy, biogas, smokeless chulahs and other rural application so as to have a visible impact of these measures in influencing eco-system and in changing the lifestyles of rural women.

***Science and Technology***

6.11 Programmes will be strengthened to bring about a greater involvement of women in science and technology. These will include measures to motivate girls to take up science and technology for higher education and also ensure that development projects with scientific and technical inputs involve women fully. Efforts to develop a scientific temper and awareness will also be stepped up. Special measures would be taken for their training in areas where they have special skills like communication and information technology. Efforts to develop appropriate technologies suited to women's needs as well as to reduce their drudgery will be given a special focus too.

***Women in Difficult Circumstances***

6.12 In recognition of the diversity of women's situations and in acknowledgement of the needs of specially disadvantaged groups, measures and programmes will be undertaken to provide them with special assistance. These groups include women in extreme poverty, destitute women, women in conflict situations, women affected by natural calamities, women in less developed regions, the disabled widows, elderly women, single women in difficult circumstances, women heading households, those displaced from employment, migrants, women who are victims of marital violence, deserted women and prostitutes, etc.

**Violence Against Women**

7.1 All forms of violence against women, physical and mental, whether at domestic or societal levels, including those arising from customs, traditions or accepted practices shall be dealt with effectively with a view to eliminate its incidence. Institutions and mechanisms/schemes for assistance will be created and strengthened for prevention of such violence, including sexual harassment at work place and customs like dowry; for the rehabilitation of the victims of violence and for taking effective action against the perpetrators of such violence. A special emphasis will also be laid on programmes and measures to deal with trafficking in women and girls.

**Rights of the Girl Child**

8.1 All forms of discrimination against the girl child and violation of her rights shall be eliminated by undertaking strong measures both preventive and punitive within and outside the family. These would relate specifically to strict enforcement of laws against prenatal sex selection and the practices of female foeticide, female infanticide, child marriage, child abuse and child prostitution, etc. Removal of discrimination in the treatment of the girl child within the family and outside and projection of a positive image of the girl child will be actively fostered. There will be special emphasis on the needs of the girl child and earmarking of substantial investments in the areas relating to food and nutrition, health and education, and in vocational education. In implementing programmes for eliminating child labour, there will be a special focus on girl children.

**Mass Media**

9.1 Media will be used to portray images consistent with human dignity of girls and women. The Policy will specifically strive to remove demeaning, degrading and negative conventional stereotypical images of women and violence against women. Private sector partners and media networks will be involved at all levels to ensure equal access for women particularly in the area of information and communication technologies. The media would be encouraged to develop codes of conduct, professional guidelines and other self-regulatory mechanisms to remove gender stereotypes and promote balanced portrayals of women and men.

## Operational Strategies

### *Action Plans*

10.1 All Central and State Ministries will draw up time bound Action Plans for translating the Policy into a set of concrete actions, through a participatory process of consultation with Centre/State Departments of Women and Child Development and National/State Commissions for Women. The Plans will specifically including the following:

(i) Measurable goals to be achieved by 2010.

(ii) Identification and commitment of resources.

(iii) Responsibilities for implementation of action points.

(iv) Structures and mechanisms to ensure efficient monitoring, review and gender impact assessment of action points and policies.

(v) Introduction of a gender perspective in the budgeting process.

10.2 In order to support better planning and programme formulation and adequate allocation of resources, Gender Development Indices (GDI) will be developed by networking with specialized agencies. These could be analyzed and studied in depth. Gender auditing and development of evaluation mechanisms will also be undertaken alongside.

10.3 Collection of gender disaggregated data by all primary data collecting agencies of the Central and State Governments as well as Research and Academic Institutions in the Public and Private Sectors will be undertaken. Data and information gaps in vital areas reflecting the status of women will be sought to be filled in by these immediately. All Ministries/Corporations/Banks and financial institutions etc. will be advised to collect, collate, disseminate and maintain/publish data related to programmes and benefits on a gender disaggregated basis. This will help in meaningful planning and evaluation of policies.

**Institutional Mechanisms**

11.1 Institutional mechanisms, to promote the advancement of women, which exist at the Central and State levels, will be strengthened. These will be through interventions as may be appropriate and will relate to, among others, provision of adequate resources, training and advocacy skills to effectively influence macro-policies, legislation, programmes, etc. to achieve the empowerment of women.

11.2 National and State Councils will be formed to oversee the operationalisation of the Policy on a regular basis. The National Council will be headed by the Prime Minister and the State Councils by the Chief Ministers and be broad in composition having representatives from the concerned Departments/ Ministries, National and State Commissions for Women, Social Welfare Boards, representatives of Non-Government Organizations, Women's Organizations, Corporate Sector, Trade Unions, financing institutions, academics, experts and social activists, etc. These bodies will review the progress made in implementing the Policy twice a year. The National Development Council will also be informed of the progress of the programme undertaken under the policy from time to time for advice and comments.

11.3 National and State Resource Centres on women will be established with mandates for collection and dissemination of information, undertaking research work, conducting surveys, implementing training and awareness generation programmes, etc. These Centers will link up with Women's Studies Centers and other research and academic institutions through suitable information networking systems.

11.4 While institutions at the district level will be strengthened, at the grass-roots, women will be helped by Government through its programmes to organize and strengthen into Self-Help Groups (SHGs) at the Anganwadi/Village/Town level. The women's groups will be helped to institutionalize themselves into registered societies and to federate at the

Panchayat/Municipal level. These societies will bring about synergistic implementation of all the social and economic development programmes by drawing resources made available through Government and Non-Government channels, including banks and financial institutions and by establishing a close Interface with the Panchayats/Municipalities.

**Resource Management**

12.1 Availability of adequate financial, human and market resources to implement the Policy will be managed by concerned Departments, financial credit institutions and banks, private sector, civil society and other connected institutions. This process will include:

(a) Assessment of benefits flowing to women and resource allocation to the programmes relating to them through an exercise of gender budgeting. Appropriate changes in policies will be made to optimize benefits to women under these schemes.

(b) Adequate resource allocation to develop and promote the policy outlined earlier based on (a) above by concerned Departments.

(c) Developing synergy between personnel of Health, Rural Development, Education and Women and Child Development Department at field level and other village level functionaries.

(d) Meeting credit needs by banks and financial credit institutions through suitable policy initiatives and development of new institutions in coordination with the Department of Women and Child Development.

12.2 The strategy of Women's Component Plan adopted in the Ninth Plan of ensuring that not less than 30 per cent of benefits/funds flow to women from all Ministries and Departments will be implemented effectively so that the needs and interests of women and girls are addressed by all concerned sectors. The Department of Women and Child Development being the nodal Ministry will monitor and review the progress of the implementation of the Component Plan from time to time, in terms of both quality and quantity in collaboration with the Planning Commission.

12.3 Efforts will be made to channelize private sector investments too, to support programmes and projects for advancement of women.

## Legislation

13.1 The existing legislative structure will be reviewed and additional legislative measures taken by identified departments to implement the Policy. This will also involve a review of all existing laws including personal, customary and tribal laws, subordinate legislation, related rules as well as executive and administrative regulations to eliminate all gender discriminatory references. The process will be planned over a time period 2000-03. The specific measures required would be evolved through a consultation process involving civil society, National Commission for Women and Department of Women and Child Development. In appropriate cases the consultation process would be widened to include other stakeholders too.

13.2 Effective implementation of legislation would be promoted by involving civil society and community. Appropriate changes in legislation will be undertaken, if necessary.

13.3 In addition, following other specific measures will be taken to implement the legislation effectively:

(a) Strict enforcement of all relevant legal provisions and speedy redressal of grievances will be ensured, with a special focus on violence and gender related atrocities.

(b) Measures to prevent and punish sexual harassment at the place of work, protection for women workers in the organized/unorganized sector and strict enforcement of relevant laws such as Equal Remuneration Act and Minimum Wages Act will be undertaken.

(c) Crimes against women, their incidence, prevention, investigation, detection and prosecution will be regularly reviewed at all Crime Review fora and Conferences at the Central, State and District levels. Recognized, local, voluntary organizations will be authorized to lodge

Complaints and facilitate registration, investigations and legal proceedings related to violence and atrocities against girls and women.

(d) Women's Cells in Police Stations, Encourage Women Police Stations Family Courts, Mahila Courts, Counselling Centers, Legal Aid Centers and Nyaya Panchayats will be strengthened and expanded to eliminate violence and atrocities against women.

(e) Widespread dissemination of information on all aspects of legal rights, human rights and other entitlements of women, through specially designed legal literacy programmes and rights information programmes will be done.

**Gender Sensitization**

14.1 Training of personnel of executive, legislative and judicial wings of the State, with a special focus on policy and programme framers, implementation and development agencies, law enforcement machinery and the judiciary, as well as non-governmental organizations will be undertaken. Other measures will include:

(a) Promoting societal awareness to gender issues and women's human rights.

(b) Review of curriculum and educational materials to include gender education and human rights issues.

(c) Removal of all references derogatory to the dignity of women from all public documents and legal instruments.

(d) Use of different forms of mass media to communicate social messages relating to women's equality and empowerment.

**Panchayati Raj Institutions**

15.1 The 73rd and 74th Amendments (1993) to the Indian Constitution have served as a breakthrough towards ensuring equal access and increased participation in political power structure for women. The PRIs will play a central role in the process of enhancing women's participation in public life. The PRIs and the local self-Governments will be actively involved in the implementation and execution of the National Policy for Women at the grass-roots level.

## Partnership with the Voluntary Sector Organizations

16.1 The involvement of voluntary organizations, associations, federations, trade unions, non-governmental organizations, women's organizations, as well as institutions dealing with education, training and research will be ensured in the formulation, implementation, monitoring and review of all policies and programmes affecting women. Towards this end, they will be provided with appropriate support related to resources and capacity building and facilitated to participate actively in the process of the empowerment of women.

## International Cooperation

17.1 The Policy will aim at implementation of international obligations/commitments in all sectors on empowerment of women such as the Convention on All Forms of Discrimination Against Women (CEDAW), Convention on the Rights of the Child (CRC), International Conference on Population and Development (ICPD+5) and other such instruments. International, regional and sub-regional cooperation towards the empowerment of women will continue to be encouraged through sharing of experiences, exchange of ideas and technology, networking with institutions and organizations and through bilateral and multilateral partnerships.

# Ujjawala

10

*A Comprehensive Scheme for Prevention of Trafficking and Rescue, Rehabilitation and Re-Integration of Victims of Trafficking for Commercial Sexual Exploitation*

## Background

1. Trafficking of women and children for commercial sexual exploitation is an organized crime that violates basic human rights. India has emerged as a source, destination and transit for both in-country and cross border trafficking. The problem of trafficking of women and children for commercial sexual exploitation is especially challenging due to its myriad complexities and variation. Poverty, low status of women, lack of a protective environment, etc. are some of the causes for trafficking.
2. A multi sectoral approach is needed which will undertake preventive measures to arrest trafficking especially in vulnerable areas and sections of population; and to enable rescue, rehabilitation and reintegration of the trafficked victims.
3. Keeping the above issues and gaps in mind the Ministry has formulated a Central Scheme "Comprehensive Scheme for Prevention of Trafficking for Rescue, Rehabilitation and Re-Integration of Victims of Trafficking for Commercial Sexual Exploitation—Ujjawala". The new scheme has been conceived primarily for the purpose of preventing trafficking on the one hand and rescue and rehabilitation of victims on the other.

## Objectives of the Scheme

- To prevent trafficking of women and children for commercial sexual exploitation through social mobilization and involvement of local communities, awareness generation programmes, generate public discourse through workshops/seminars and such events and any other innovative activity.

- To facilitate rescue of victims from the place of their exploitation and place them in safe custody.
- To provide rehabilitation services both immediate and long-term to the victims by providing basic amenities/ needs such as shelter, food, clothing, medical treatment including counselling, legal aid and guidance and vocational training.
- To facilitate reintegration of the victims into the family and society at large.
- To facilitate repatriation of cross-border victims to their country of origin.

**Target Group/Beneficiaries**

- Women and children who are vulnerable to trafficking for commercial sexual exploitation.
- Women and children who are victims of trafficking for commercial sexual exploitation.

**Implementing Agencies**

The implementing agencies can be the Social Welfare/Women and Child Welfare Department of State Government, Women's Development Corporations, Women's Development Centres, Urban Local Bodies, reputed Public/Private Trust or Voluntary Organizations. The organization must have adequate experience in the field of trafficking, social defence, dealing with women and children in need of care and protection, children in conflict with law, etc.

**Eligibility Conditions**

The implementing organizations must fulfil the following eligibility conditions:

(a) The agency should be registered under law and must have a properly constituted Managing Body with its powers, duties and responsibilities clearly defined and laid down in its Constitution;

(b) The organization must not work for the profit of any individual or body of individuals;

(c) It should ordinarily have three years' experience after its registration;

(d) Its financial position should be sound;

(e) It should have facilities, resources, experience and personnel to initiate the scheme for which assistance is sought.

### The Components of Scheme and Pattern of Assistance

The Scheme shall have the following main components:

1. Prevention
2. Rescue
3. Rehabilitation
4. Re-integration
5. Repatriation

The implementing agencies may seek assistance for one or more the components as mentioned under the scheme. While applying for a particular component(s), the implementing agencies should provide justification for selecting the specific components and the location of projects.

*Note*: The implementing agency can leverage their sanctioned funds (upto 10%) within and between components.

### Description of the Components of Scheme

Assistance will be provided for the following:

### 1. Prevention

1.1 Formation and functioning of Community Vigilance Groups.

1.2 Formation and functioning of Balika (adolescent girls)/ Balala (adolescent children) Sanghas.

1.3 Sensitization Workshops/Seminars.

1.4 Awareness generation through mass media including kalajathas, street plays, pupettery or through any other art forms, preferably traditional.

1.5 Development and printing of awareness generation material such as pamphlets, leaflets and posters (in local language).

**Component-1 (Prevention)**

| | | Annual Budget (in Rs.) |
|---|---|---|
| 1.1 | Formation and functioning of Community Vigilance Group (Minimum 3 Community Vigilance Groups): | |
| | (a) Formation | 6,000 |
| | (b) Nurturing (monthly meeting, correspondence, transport, etc.) | 18,000 |
| 1.2 | Formation and functioning of Balika (adolescent girls)/ Balala (adolescent children) Sanghas (Minimum 3 Sanghas): | |
| | (a) Formation | 6,000 |
| | (b) Nurturing (monthly meeting, correspondence, transport, etc.) | 18,000 |
| 1.3 | Sensitization Workshops/Seminars (2 days): | |
| | (a) Hiring of Venue | 5,000 |
| | (b) Communication | 1,000 |
| | (c) Resource Persons | 2,500 |
| | (d) Lunch and Refreshment (at least 30 participants x Rs. 75 x 2 days) | 4,500 |
| | (e) Resource material | 2,000 |
| | (f) TA/DA for participants | 3,000 |
| 1.4 | Awareness generation through mass media including kalajathas, street plays, pupettery or through any other art forms, preferably traditional: | |
| | (a) Formation of Group | 10,000 |
| | (b) Performance of play (includes travel, lodging/ boarding, publicity @ Rs. 2,500 x 10 plays) | 25,000 |
| 1.5 | Development and printing of awareness generation material such as pamphlets, leaflets and posters hoardings, advertisements, etc. (in local language) | 65,500 |
| | Total | 1,66,500 |

**2. Rescue**

2.1 Information gathering: Through formation of network of Police, NGOs, Women's Groups, Youth Groups, Panchayats, Hotels and tour operators, etc., to gather information on traffickers, suspicious people and vulnerable families.

2.2 Rescue operations: The scheme would provide for—

(a) Incentives to decoy customers/informers;

(b) Transportation cost of victim(s) from place of rescue to shelter home;

(c) Initial documentation.

2.3 Immediate Relief on Rescue: The scheme will provide food, shelter, toiletries, clothing, trauma care/counselling, medical aid, etc. during the interim period between rescue and production before the concerned authorities.

**Component-2 (Rescue)**

| | | Annual Budget (in Rs.) |
|---|---|---|
| 2.1 | Information gathering—Communication | 6,000 |
| 2.2 | Rescue operation: | |
| | (a) Informers | 5,000 |
| | (b) Transport | 2,000 |
| | (c) Documentation, filing of reports, etc. | 500 |
| 2.3 | Immediate Relief on Rescue: | |
| | (a) Basic Amenities | 5,000 |
| | (b) Medical Aid | 5,000 |
| | Total | 23,500 |

**3. Rehabilitation**

3.1 Setting up of Protective and Rehabilitative (P&R) Homes: The P&R Homes would be set-up by the agency.

3.2 Basic amenities: To provide basic amenities such food, clothing and other items of personal use.

3.3 Medical care: This Scheme would provide Doctor's fee, cost of medicines, hospitalization, appropriate linkages to de-addiction centers.

Since the victims of trafficking undergo immense psychological trauma, professional counselling services would be provided through a qualified clinical psychologist and psychiatrist.

3.4 Legal aid: As victims are the main witnesses against the trafficker/pimp/perpetrator, or to claim their right to property, marital rights, divorce, maintenance and custody of children, they will need to be provided with legal aid which would include court work and documentation relating to the victims court case.

3.5 Administrative costs: To support small contingencies arising out of the project.

3.6 Education: As a large proportion of the rescued victims are children, they will need to be inducted into the formal or open school system, for which some expenditure on text-books, notebooks, stationery, school uniform and other incidental expenses may have to be incurred.

3.7 Vocational Training and Income generation activities: In order to completely rehabilitate the victim it is necessary to provide alternate livelihood options. Therefore, support for vocational training is provided.

**Component-3 (Rehabilitation)**

| | | Annual Budget (in Rs.) |
|---|---|---|
| 3.1 | Setting up of Protective Homes (50 victims) | |
| | (a) Rent* | |
| | 'A' Grade Cities (Delhi, Mumbai, Kolkata, Chennai, Bangalore and Hyderabad) (Rs. 25,000 x 12 months) | 3,00,000 |
| | 'B' Grade Cities (Rest of India) (Rs. 20,000 x 12 months) | 2,40,000 |
| | (b) Staff # | |
| | Project Director (Rs. 10,000 x 1 x 12 months) | 1,20,000 |
| | Social Worker (2) (Rs. 5,000 x 2 x 12 months) | 1,20,000 |

*(Contd...)*

| | | | Rs. |
|---|---|---|---|
| | | Clinical Psychologist (Rs. 5,000 x 1 x 12 months) | 60,000 |
| | | Clerk-cum-Accountant (Rs. 3,000 x 1 x 12 months) | 36,000 |
| | | Guard (2) [Rs. 2,500 x 2 x 12 months] | 60,000 |
| | | Doctor (Part time) [Rs. 3,000 x 12 months] | 36,000 |
| | | Psychiatrist (Part time) [Rs. 3,000 x 12 months] | 36,000 |
| | (c) | Furniture, utensils, linen beds, locker, etc. (non-recurring) | 1,50,000 |
| | (d) | Electricity and Water (Rs. 3,000 x 12 months) | 36,000 |
| 3.2 | Basic amenities | | |
| | (a) | Food (Rs. 700 x 50 girls x 12 months) | 4,20,000 |
| | (b) | Personal (Rs. 150 x 50 girls x 12 months) *such as clothes, toiletries, sanitary items, etc.* | 90,000 |
| 3.3 | Medical Care (Medicines includes emergency care) [Rs. 200 x 50 x 12 months] | | 1,20,000 |
| 3.4 | Legal Aid (court work and documentation) [Rs. 200 x 12 x 50] | | 1,20,000 |
| 3.5 | Administrative Support | | 10,500 |
| 3.6 | Education | | |
| | (a) | Formal School [support—Rs. 200 x 12 x 30 victims] | 72,000 |
| 3.7 | Vocational Training and Income generation activities [Support—Rs. 5,000 x 20 victims] | | 1,00,000 |
| | | Total 'A' Grade Cities | 18,86,500 |
| | | 'B' Grade Cities | 18,26,500 |

* Subject to Rent Assessment Certificate from State PWD.

# Wherever possible appointment of eligible SCs/STs/OBCs/Minorities may be undertaken.

## 4. Re-Integration

4.1 Setting of Half-Way Home: Half-Way Home is a Home within the community, where a group of victims, ready for reintegration, live and work out of this place. This is to facilitate smooth transition from the life in P&R Home to an independent living in the community. A Half-Way Home is for a group of victims who are gainfully employed and can live semi-independently with minimum supervision. This is a phased approach to re-integration into the community.

4.2 Restoration to Families: The scheme would cover travel of the victim and an escort from destination area to her home town/village, expenses incurred towards her food during her travel and incidental expenses.

**Component-4 (Re-Integration)**

| | | | Annual Budget (in Rs.) |
|---|---|---|---|
| 4.1 | Setting of Half-Way Home (for 10-15 victims)* | | |
| | (a) | Rent for Half-Way Home (Rs. 6,000 x 12) | 72,000 |
| | (b) | Furniture/Utensils, etc. (one time, Non-recurring) | 10,000 |
| 4.2 | Restoration to Families | | |
| | (a) | Seed Money (Rs. 5,000 x 5 victims) | 25,000 |
| | (b) | Transport for the victim and escort (Rs. 1,000 x 2 x 5 victims) | 10,000 |
| | (c) | Networking/Follow-up including two visits (Rs. 1,500 x 5 victims) | 7,500 |
| | | Total | 1,24,500 |

* Subject to Rent Assessment Certificate from State PWD.

## 5. Repatriation (Cross-border)

5.1 Facilitate repatriation procedures: The scheme would provide for expenses incurred in fulfilling various formalities for obtaining repatriation order for the victim.

5.2 Repatriation to country of origin: The scheme would cover travel of the cross-border victim and an escort from destination area to her country of origin or border, expenses incurred towards her food during her travel and incidental expenses.

5.3 Setting-up of Transit Centers: The funds will be provided for setting up of transit camp, food and other incidentals at the border-check points.

**Component-5 (Repatriation—Cross Border)**

**Applicable only to those agency who have victims of cross-border trafficking**

| | | Annual Budget (in Rs.) |
|---|---|---|
| 5.1 | Facilitate Repatriation procedures, Communication and Documentation | 5,000 |
| 5.2 | *Repatriation to country of origin* (Transport to the victim and escort, includes food and other incidentals) | 20,000 |
| 5.3 | Setting-up of Transit Centers | 10,000 |
| | Total | 35,000 |

**Summary Statement of Grant Under all Components of the Scheme**

| Com-ponent | Name of the Component | Total Budget for the Component (in Rs.) | | |
|---|---|---|---|---|
| | | Recurring | | Non-recurring |
| | | Grade 'A' Cities | Grade 'B' Cities | For 'A' & 'B' Grade Cities |
| 1. | Prevention | 1,66,500 | 1,66,500 | - |
| 2. | Rescue | 23,500 | 23,500 | - |
| 3. | Rehabilitation | 17,36,500 | 16,76,500 | 1,50,000 |
| 4. | Re-Integration | 1,14,500 | 1,14,500 | 10,000 |
| 5. | Repatriation—Cross border | 35,000 | 35,000 | - |
| | Total | 20,76,000 | 20,16,000 | 1,60,000 |
| | Total Budget for all Component for the Project (Recurring + Non-Recurring) | 22,36,000 | 21,76,000 | |

## Project Proposal

1. The project proposals under the scheme shall be received in prescribed format (Annexure - I) through the State Governments/UT Administration.
2. The State Govt./UT Administration shall submit its Appraisal Report and recommendations as per the format prescribed (Annexure - II). The State Governments will ensure that the agency has capabilities and credentials in undertaking activities while recommending their proposal. The State Government will ensure that the project area selected by the agency is justified and the proposed

intervention will help in preventing and combating trafficking.

3. The Utilization Certificate and Guidelines for Chartered Accountants/Government Auditors shall be submitted in formats prescribed in Annexure - III.
4. The application will be normally submitted through the State Governments/UT Administration. In the case of National Organizations the Government may entertain an application from the agency and where necessary obtain the recommendations of the State/UT where the agency proposes to have the activity. Applications of State Branches of well-known agencies and reputed State level agencies, already known to the Ministry of Women and Child Development, can be entertained directly.

The project proposal complete in all aspects as mentioned above shall be submitted to Joint Secretary, CP, Ministry of Women and Child Development, Shastri Bhavan, New Delhi-110001 through Registered Post/Speed Post/Courier.

### Sanctioning of the Scheme

Each proposal shall be sanctioned by a Project Sanctioning Committee comprising of the following members:

(a) Secretary, Ministry of Women and Child Development (Chairperson).
(b) Financial Adviser, Ministry of Human Resource Development (MWCD).
(c) Secretary in-charge of Women and Child Development of the concerned State Governments/UT Administration.
(d) Joint Secretary of the concerned bureau in the Ministry (Convener).

### Monitoring of the Scheme

I. The continuation of grant to the agency would be based on the satisfactory performance reported by the State Government/UT Administration. In addition, it is proposed that periodic inspection will be undertaken. Separately periodic evaluations of the project will also be undertaken by reputed institutions, Panchayati Raj Institutions, block level institutions, district level institutions.

II. *Monitoring at the State Level*

The Secretary in-charge of Social Welfare/Department of Women and Child Development in the State Government/UT Admn. shall be the chairperson of the State Level/UT Administration Monitoring Committee for the Scheme. The other members of the Committee would be nominated by the Secretary. The Committee at the State Level/UT Administration shall meet at least twice a year and monitor the project.

III. *Monitoring at the Central Level*

MWCD shall also review the functioning of the Centre once a year.

IV. *Mid-term Evaluation of the Scheme*

The project shall be evaluated in the middle of Eleventh Five-Year Plan.

**Conditions of Grants**

(i) The grant approved will be paid in two installments, the first installment being normally released with the sanction of the Project and the second and subsequent installment will be released when the agency has spent the previous installment along with its own proportionate share of cost. Requests for release of these installments will be accompanied by a certificate from a Chartered Accountant or a Government Auditor indicating the total expenditure incurred on the project. In case of the project implemented by the State Government/UT Administration or its agencies the second installments of the grant may be released on receipt of the requisite certificate duly signed by an officer of the State Government or Union Territory, as the case may be.

(ii) The voluntary agency/institution shall maintain record of all assets acquired wholly or substantially out of Government Grant. Such assets shall not be disposed of encumbered or utilized for purposes other than those for which grant was given without prior sanction of the Government of India should the organization/institution cease to exist at any time such properties shall revert to the Government of India.

(iii) If the Ministry require clarification of any point not contained in the Application the institution/agency shall supply it within the time specified by the Ministry failing which the Application will not be considered.

(iv) Any unspent portion of the grant shall be refunded to the Government of India immediately.

(v) The sanctioned project shall be reviewed after three years of implementation. Further continuation of the projects will be decided on the basis of the review.

(vi) Guidelines for activities have been formulated. The implementing agency may kindly follow these while implementing the scheme.

## ANNEXURE - I

## APPLICATION FORM

*Note*: The application should be routed through the State Government concerned or the Officer authorized by the State Government concerned.

**PART - A: For the Agency (Details)**

1. Name and full postal address of the head-office of the agency (IN BLOCK LETTERS):
   District (IN BLOCK LETTERS):
   State (IN BLOCK LETTERS):
   Pin Code:
2. Telephone No. with STD code:
3. Fax No:
4. E-mail:
5. Do the bye-laws of the agency permit it to receive Govt. grants and implement women's programme in the proposed project area?
6. Objectives of the Organization:
7. Brief History of the Organization: (in one paragraph)

8. Whether registered under Indian Societies Registration Act (Act XXI of 1860)/Trust Act. If so, give the number and date of registration:
9. Whether the agency is of all India character: If yes, give the address of its branches in different States including the state Branch, which will take up the activity with Phone No., Fax No., e-mail, etc.
10. Whether organization is located in its own/rented building:
11. Major activities of the agency in the last 3 years:

| Name of activity and year | Coverage | Expenditure | Men | Women | Children |
|---|---|---|---|---|---|
| | | | | | |

12. Summary of financial status of the agency in the last 3 years:

(Rs. in lakhs)

| Year | Income & Exp. Acctt. | Receipt & Payment Acctt. | Surplus | Deficit |
|---|---|---|---|---|
| | | | | |

13. Details of grant received from Central Govt./State Govt. and other Govt. agencies in the last 3 years:

(Rs. in lakhs)

| Year | Sanction Order No. | Date | Amount | Scheme | Address of funding agency |
|---|---|---|---|---|---|
| | | | | | |

14. Details of Foreign Contribution received during last 3 years*:

| Country | Agency | Purpose | Amount |
|---|---|---|---|
| | | | |

* Please indicate whether prior permission of the Government of India was obtained. Copy of approval letter to be attached.

15. Details of office bearers of the agency:

| Sl. No. | Name & Address | Male/ Female | Age | Post | Qualification | Profes-sion | Annual income |
|---|---|---|---|---|---|---|---|
| | | | | | | | |

16. Details of employees of the agency:

| Sl. No. | Name & Address | Male/ Female | Age | Part time/ Full time | Qualification | Profes-sion | Annual income |
|---|---|---|---|---|---|---|---|
| | | | | | | | |

17. Details of Managing Committee members of the agency:

| Sl. No. | Name & Address | Male/ Female | Age | Qualification | Profession | Monthly income |
|---|---|---|---|---|---|---|
| | | | | | | |

## PART - B: The Proposal

The project proposal may be submitted in the following format along with Budget (as per the provisions laid down in the Scheme) and their break-up:

### 1. Component—Prevention

The activities under the prevention component are for areas, which are vulnerable to trafficking of women and children. Please ensure that the activities proposed by you are innovative and will achieve the objective and intention underlined in the Scheme. Preference will be given to those agencies located in the source/transit areas.

The following information sought in the proposal is indicative and the agency may like to provide information over and above the following:

**1.1 *Formation and functioning of Community Vigilance Groups (Minimum three Community Vigilance Groups)***

(a) Name of the State

(b) Name of the District

(c) Names of Blocks/Villages where the activity is proposed to be undertaken. Provide justification for choosing the project area

(d) Total Number of Community Vigilance Groups proposed to be formed

(e) Methodology that would be adopted to form the Community Vigilance Groups

(f) Activities proposed to be undertaken with the Community Vigilance Groups. Provide justification on how these activities will prevent trafficking

**1.2 *Formation and functioning of Balika (adolescent girls)/ Balala (adolescent children) Sanghas (Minimum three Balika/Balala Sanghas)***

(a) Name of the State

(b) Name of the District

(c) Names of Blocks/Villages where the activity is proposed to be undertaken. Provide justification for choosing the project area

(d) Total Number of Balika/Balala Sanghas proposed to be formed

(e) Methodology that would be adopted to form the Balika/ Balala Sanghas

(f) Activities proposed to be undertaken with the Balika/ Balala Sanghas. Provide justification on how these activities will help the Balika/Balala Sanghas to become social change agents

**1.3 *Sensitization Workshops/Seminars***

(a) Name of the place where the activity is proposed

(b) Number of Sensitization workshops/seminars proposed

(c) Duration

(d) Objective of the proposed workshops/seminars

(e) Target group

(f) Number of participants

### 1.4 *Awareness generation through mass media including kalajathas, street plays, pupettery or through any other art forms, preferably traditional*

(a) Name of the place where the activity is proposed. Provide justification for choosing the place

(b) Number and type of awareness generation programme proposed

(c) Duration

(d) Objective of the proposed awareness generation programme

(e) Target group

(f) Detail description on the awareness generation programme and the methodology proposed

### 1.5 *Development and printing of awareness generation material such as pamphlets, leaflets and posters*

(a) Details of material proposed to be developed, including the need for the material and how the implementing agency going to develop the material

(b) Language(s) of the material (Local language)

(c) Number of copies

(d) Details of the topic

(e) Target group

(f) Usage and Dissemination Methodology

## 2. Component Rescue

The activities under the rescue component are applicable to only those implementing agencies that are involved in rescue of women and children from place of exploitation.

The following information sought in the proposal is indicative and the agency may like to provide information over and above the following:

2.1 Information gathering (methodology proposed for gathering information)

2.2 Rescue operations (details on the methodology, network and relationship of the implementing agency with the local authorities, police, etc.)

2.3 Immediate Relief (Basic Amenities and Medical Aid)

**3. Component Rehabilitation**

The following information sought in the proposal is indicative and the agency may like to provide information over and above the following:

***3.1 Setting up of Protective and Rehabilitative (P&R) Homes***

(a) The (P&R) Home which provides rehabilitative shelter for women and children, should ensure that they are housed separately, unless the children are accompanying their mother.

i. Full address of the location of the P&R Home:

District:

Block:

Pin Code:

Telephone No. with STD code:

ii. Whether the location is a District HQ, Block HQ, Tehsil HQ or village

iii. Accommodation available for the shelter:

- No. of rooms
- Total Area (Sq. feet)
- Kitchen
- No. of Toilet
- No. of Bathrooms
- Store
- Verandah
- Recreation Hall
- Open Space
- Training Hall
- Office space

iv. Is it rent-free accommodation:

v. If not, proposed rent of the accommodation (attach copy of rent deed):

vi. Number of Beneficiaries:

| Women | | Trafficked Children (Below 18 years) | |
|---|---|---|---|
| *Number of Women* | *Number of Women with Children* | *Male* | *Female* |
| | | | |

(b) Staff

- Project Director
- Social Worker
- Clinical Psychologist
- Clerk-cum-Accountant
- Guard (2)
- Doctor (Part time)
- Psychiatrist (Part time)

(c) Furniture, Utensils, Linen, etc. (Non-Recurring)

(d) Electricity and water

**3.2 *Basic amenities***

(a) Food

(b) Personal

**3.3 *Medical Care***

**3.4 *Legal Aid***

**3.5 *Administrative Support***

**3.6 *Education***

**3.7 *Vocational Training and Income Generation Activities (provide details such as the type of vocational training programme of the vocational training and income generation activity proposed)***

## 4. Component Re-Integration

The component will be applicable to only those implementing agencies carrying out rehabilitation of trafficked victims. The following information sought in the proposal is indicative and the agency may like to provide information over and above the following:

### 4.1 *Setting of Half-Way Home*

(a) The Half-way Home will be set-up by the implementing agency only when there are enough women victims ready to leave the P&R Home and are in employment/vocational activity and can financially sustain themselves. It will not be set-up to serve as a substitute for P&R Home.

i. Full address of the proposed location of the Half-Way Home:

District:

Block:

Pin Code:

Telephone No. with STD code:

ii. Whether the location is a District HQ, Block HQ, Tehsil HQ or village:

iii. Accommodation available for the Half-Way Home:

- No. of rooms
- Total Area (Sq. feet)
- Kitchen
- No. of Toilet/Bathrooms
- Verandah

iv. Is it rent-free accommodation:

v. If not, proposed rent of the Half-Way Home (attach copy of rent deed)

(b) Furniture/Utensils, etc. (Non-recurring)

### 4.2 *Restoration to Families*

(a) Details

- Proposed number of Beneficiaries to be restored

- How does the implementing agency plan to conduct follow-up of the well-being of the victim, once restored

(b) Seed Money

(c) Transport for victim and escort

(d) Networking/Follow-up

**5. Component Repatriation**

The above component is applicable to only those implementing agencies that are involved repatriation of victims of cross-border trafficking. At the time of submitting proposal, the implementing agency will provide in detail the repatriation activity being carried out by the agency.

**5.1 *Facilitate repatriation procedures (details to be provided by implementing agency)***

**5.2 *Repatriation to country of origin***

(a) Number of victims proposed to be repatriated

(b) Mode of transport

**5.3 *Setting-up of Transit Centers***

(a) Location of the Transit Center:

District:

Block:

Pin Code:

Telephone No. with STD code:

(b) Whether the location is a District HQ, Block HQ, Tehsil HQ or village:

(c) Type of Transit Centre Proposed.

Date: Signature of Secretary/President of the organization

**PART – C: List of Documents to be Enclosed**

1. Registration certificate. If in a Regional Language, authenticated English version to be attached. Also state if the certificate is to be renewed annually.
2. Constitution of the agency/Bye-laws and Memorandum of Association.

3. Constitution of the Board of Management with brief particulars of each member.
4. Annual Report for the last 3 years.
5. Audited accounts for the last 3 years.
6. Rent deed for rented accommodation.

## ANNEXURE - II

### PART – A: Proforma for Pre-sanction Appraisal Report

(Enclosed Guidelines may be referred to very carefully before Pre-sanction Appraisal. The pre-sanction appraisal should be made by the State Government concerned or the officer designated by the State Government.)

1. Name and Designation:
2. Full Address of the Inspecting Officer:
3. Date and time of visit:
4. Name and Full postal address of agency:
5. Is a name board prominently displayed by the agency?
6. Have you inspected the original Registration Certificate of the agency and is it satisfactory?
7. Are any managing Committee Members related to each other? If yes, names of members and their relationship.
8. Are the office bearers of the agency associated with any other agency? If yes, names of the agency(s).
9. Does the agency have staff as mentioned in the application form? If not, please indicate the shortfall.
10. Are copies of the audited accounts submitted by the agency true copies of the original?
11. What is the present bank balance of the agency.
12. Whether credit entries are available in the passbook for various income of the agency mentioned in the audited Accounts? If yes, what amount has been credited in the passbook for the following income?
    - Year:

- Donations:
- Members Contribution:
- Sale of goods:
- Income from activities:
- Grants:
- Loans from members:

13. Do you have reason to doubt that the entries in the Audited Accounts are not genuine? Please elaborate.
14. Name the activities taken up by the agency for which evidence was available.
15. Is there any ongoing activity of the agency? If yes, please visit some of and report on performance.
16. Name the activities included in the Audited accounts and annual report for which no evidence was available.
17. Name the assets included in the Balance Sheet but not available for physical verification.
18. Are the local people aware of the agency and its activities?
19. What is the opinion of local people about the agency?
20. Have you come across any instance of mis-utilisation of funds or complaint involving the agency? If yes, please give details.
21. In your opinion, is the agency capable of implementing the project applied for? Please give reasons.
22. In your opinion, is there genuine need for the project in the proposed project area? Please give reasons.
23. As the agency furnished details of beneficiaries proposed to be covered? If yes, please visit a few of them and furnish the following information:
    - Name of Beneficiary
    - Whether genuinely in need of assistance under the project
24. Any other information about the agency.

I have read the guidelines for pre-sanction appraisal. This report does not contain any mis-representation of facts.

(SIGNATURE)
NAME :
DATE :
(OFFICE SEAL)

**PART - B: Recommendation by State Government**

1. Name and full address of the agency:
2. Name of scheme for which application is made:
3. Name and designation of the officer who inspected the agency:
4. Do you agree with the report of the Inspecting Officer and if not, reasons thereof:
5. Does the agency fulfil all eligibility criteria for grants under the scheme?
6. Will the State Government recover sanctioned grants in the event of mis-utilisation of funds?
7. Is the agency capable of implementing the project applied for?
8. Is there any complaint of mis-utilisation of funds or other irregularities by the agency?
9. What is the justification for the project applied for?
10. Is the proposal recommended for sanction of grants?

(Signature)
Name:
Designation:
Date:
(OFFICE SEAL)

## ANNEXURE - III

### PART – A: Utilisation Certificate

I have verified the account of ................................ (Name of grantee agency) in respect of the grant of Rs. ......... released by the Government of India, Ministry of Women & Child Development vide sanction No..................... dated......... for the project for the period.............. with the help of the vouchers and certify that they are correct and that an amount of Rs. .................. has been utilised upto......... for the purpose for which it was sanctioned.

(CHARTERED ACCOUNTANT)

(SEAL)

### PART - B: Guidelines for Chartered Accountants/Government Auditors

The Auditors certifying the accounts and endorsing Utilisation Certificate in respect of Government grants should bear in mind the following points:

1. If the number of inmates in P&R Home and Half-Way Home is below/or above the prescribed norms, the expenditure on their maintenance will vary accordingly at the prescribed rate.
2. Non-recurring expenditure will be sanctioned only once for a P&R Home and Half-Way Home.
3. In case a particular post has been lying vacant for specified period the salaries against that should not be claimed.
4. Accounts are to be sent in original signed by the Chartered Accountant in the forms of Income & Expenditure, Receipts & Payment and Balance Sheet including the Utilisation Certificate in the prescribed format.
5. The Accounts for grants for Project should be prepared separately. If this is not possible, the expenditure towards this scheme should be shown separately under the Head 'Project'. The expenditure incurred for the admissible items should be reflected clearly under each sub-head incorporated in the schematic pattern.

# Convention on Elimination of Discrimination Against Women (CEDAW)

11

### Article 1

For the purposes of the present Convention, the term 'discrimination against women' shall mean any distinction, exclusion, or restriction made on the basis of sex which has the effect or purpose of impairing or nullifying the recognition, enjoyment or exercise by women, irrespective of their marital status, on a basis of equality of men and women, of human rights and fundamental freedoms to the political, economic, social, cultural, civil or any other field.

### Article 2

States Parties condemn discrimination against women in all its forms, agree to pursue by all appropriate means and without delay a policy of eliminating discrimination against women and to this end, undertake:

(a) To embody the principle of the equality of men and women in their national constitutions or other appropriate legislation if not yet incorporated herein and to ensure through laws and other appropriate means, the practical realization of this principle;

(b) To embody the principle of the equality of men and women in their national constitutions or other appropriate legislation if not yet incorporated herein and to ensure through laws and other appropriate means, the practical realization of this principle;

(c) To establish legal protection of the rights of women on an equal basis with men and to ensure through competent national tribunals and other public institutions the effective protection of women against any act of discrimination;

(d) To refrain from engaging in any act or practice of discrimination against women and to ensure that public authorities and institutions shall act in conformity with this obligation;

(e) To take all appropriate measures to eliminate discrimination against women by any person, organization or enterprise;

(f) To take all appropriate measures, including legislation, to modify or abolish existing laws, regulations, customs and practices which constitute discrimination against women;

(g) To repeal all national penal provisions which constitute discrimination against women.

**Article 3**

States Parties shall take in all fields, in particular in the political, social, economic and cultural fields all appropriate measures, including legislation to ensure the full development and advancement of women, for the purpose of guaranteeing them the exercise and enjoyment of human rights and fundamental freedoms on a basis of equality with men.

**Article 4**

1. Adoption by States Parties of temporary special measures aimed at accelerating *de facto* equality between men and women shall not be considered discrimination as defined in the present convention, but shall in no way entail as a consequence the maintenance of unequal or separate standards; these measures shall be discontinued when the objectives of equality of opportunity and treatment have been achieved.

2. Adoption by States Parties of special measures, including those measures contained in the present Convention, aimed at protecting maternity shall not be considered discriminatory.

**Article 5**

States Parties shall take all appropriate measures:

(a) To modify the social and cultural patterns of conduct of men and women, with a view to achieving the elimination of prejudices and customary and all other practices which are based on the idea of the inferiority or the superiority of either of the sexes or on stereotyped roles for men and women.

(b) To ensure that family education includes a proper understanding of maternity as a social function and the recognition of the common responsibility of men and women in the upbringing and development of their children, it being understood that the interest of the children is the primordial consideration in all cases.

**Article 6**

States Parties shall take all appropriate measures, including legislation, to suppress all forms of traffic in women and exploitation of prostitution of women.

**Article 7**

States Parties shall take all appropriate measures to eliminate discrimination against women in the political and public life of the country and, in particular, shall ensure to women on equal terms with men, the right:

(a) To vote in all elections and public referenda, and to be eligible for election to all publicly elected bodies;

(b) To participate in the formulation of government policy and the implementation thereof and to hold public office and perform all public functions at all levels of government;

(c) To participate in non-governmental organizations and associations concerned with the public and political life of the country.

**Article 8**

States Parties shall take all appropriate measures to ensure to women, on equal terms with men and without any discrimination, the opportunity to represent their Governments at the international level and to participate in the work of international organizations.

**Article 9**

1. States Parties shall grant women equal rights with men to acquire, change or retain their nationality. They shall ensure to particular that neither marriage to an alien nor change of nationality by the husband during marriage nor change of nationality; by the husband during marriage shall automatically change the nationality of the wife, render her stateless or force upon her the nationality of the husband.

2. States Parties shall grant women equal rights with men with respect to the nationality of their children.

**Article 10**

States Parties shall take all appropriate measures to eliminate discrimination against women in order to ensure to them equal rights with men in the field of education and in particular to ensure, on a basis of equality of men and women.

(a) The same conditions for career and vocational guidance for access to studies and for the achievement of diplomas in educational establishments of all categories in rural as well as in urban areas; this equality shall be ensure in pre-school, general, technical, professional and higher technical education, as well as in all types of vocational training;

(b) Access to the same curricula, the same examinations, teaching staff with qualifications of the same standard and school premises and equipment of the same quality;

(c) The elimination of any stereotyped concept of the roles of men and women at all levels and in all forms of education by encouraging coeducation and other types of education which will help to achieve this aim and, in particular, by the revision of textbooks and school programmes and adaptation of teaching methods.

(d) The same opportunities to benefit from scholarships and other study grants.

(e) The same opportunities for access to programmes of continuing education, including adult and functional literacy programmes, particularly those aimed at reducing at the earliest possible time, any gap in education existing between men and women.

(f) The reduction of female student drop-out rates and the organization of programmes for girls and women who have left school prematurely.

(g) The same opportunities to participate actively in sports and physical education.

(h) Access to specific educational information to help to ensure the health and well-being of families, including information and advice on family planning.

**Article 11**

1. States Parties shall take all appropriate measures to eliminate discrimination against women in the field of employment in order to ensure, on a basis of equality of women and women, the same rights, in particular:

(a) The right to work as an inalienable right of all human beings;

(b) The right to the same employment opportunities, including the application of the same criteria for selection in matters of employment;

(c) The right to free choice of profession and employment, the right to promotion, job security and all benefits and conditions of service and the right to receive vocational training and retraining, including apprenticeships, advanced vocational training and recurrent training;

(d) The right to equal remuneration, including benefits, and to equal treatment in respect of work of equal value, as well as equality of treatment in the evaluation of the quality of work;

(e) The right to social security, particularly in cases of retirement, unemployment, sickness, invalidity and old age and other incapacity to work, as well as the right to paid leave;

(f) The right to protection of health and to safety in working conditions, including the safeguarding of the function of reproduction.

2. In order to prevent discrimination against women on the grounds of marriage or maternity and to ensure their effective right to work, States Parties shall take appropriate measures:

(a) To prohibit, subject to the imposition of sanctions, dismissal on the grounds of marriage or of maternity leave and discriminate in dismissals on the basis of marital status;

(b) To introduce maternity leave with pay or with comparable social benefits without loss of former employment, seniority or social allowance;

(c) To encourage the provision of the necessary supporting social services to enable parents to combine family obligations with work responsibilities and participation in public life, in particular through promoting the establishment and development of a network of child care facilities;

(d) To provide special protection to women during pregnancy in types of work proved to be harmful to them.

3. Protective legislations relating to matters covered in this article shall be reviewed periodically in the light of scientific and technological knowledge and shall be revised, repeated or extended as necessary.

**Article 12**

1. States Parties shall take all appropriate measures to eliminate discrimination against women in the field of health care in order to ensure, on a basis of equality of men and women, access to health care services, including those related to family planning.

2. Notwithstanding the provisions of paragraph 1 of this article, States Parties shall ensure to women appropriate services in connection with pregnancy, confinement and the post natal

period, granting free services where necessary, as well as adequate nutrition during pregnancy and lactation.

**Article 13**

1. States Parties shall take all appropriate measure to eliminate discrimination against women in other areas of economic and social life in order to ensure on a basis of equality of men and women, the same rights, in particular:

(a) The right to family benefits;

(b) The right to bank loans, mortgages and other forms of financial credit;

(c) The right to participate in recreational activities, sports and all aspects of cultural life.

**Article 14**

1. States Parties shall take into account the particular problems faced by rural women and the significant roles which rural women play in the economic survival of their families, including their work in the non-monetized sectors of the economy and shall take all appropriate measures to ensure the application of the provisions of this Convention to women in rural areas.

2. States Parties shall take all appropriate measures to eliminate discrimination against women in rural areas in order to ensure, on a basis of equality of men and women, that they participate in and benefit from rural development and, in particular, shall ensure to such women the right:

(a) To participate in the elaboration and implementation of development planning at all levels.

(b) To have access to adequate health care facilities, including information, counselling and services in family planning.

(c) To benefit directly from social security programmes.

(d) To obtain all types of training and education, formal and non-formal, including that relating to functional literacy, as well as, *inter alia*, the benefit of all community and extension services, in order to increase their technical proficiency.

(e) To organize self-help groups and cooperatives in order to obtain equal access to economic opportunities through employment or self-employment.

(f) To participate in all community activities.

(g) To have access to agricultural credit and loans, marketing facilities, appropriate technology and equal treatment in land and agrarian reform as well as in land resettlement schemes.

(h) To enjoy adequate living conditions, particularly in relation to housing, sanitation, electricity and water supply, transport and communications.

**Article 15**

1. States Parties shall accord to women equality with men before the law.

2. States Parties shall accord to women, in civil matters, a legal capacity identical to that of men and the same opportunities to exercise that capacity. In particular, they shall given women equal rights to conclude contracts and to administer properly and shall treat them equally in all stages of procedure in courts and tribunals.

3. States Parties agree that all contracts and all other private instruments of any kind with a legal effect which is directed at restricting the legal capacity of women shall be deemed null and void.

4. States Parties shall accord to men and women the same rights with regard to the law relating to the movement of persons and the freedom to choose their residence and domicile.

**Article 16**

1. States Parties shall take all appropriate measures to eliminate discrimination against women in all matters relating to marriage and family relations and in particular shall ensure, on a basis of equality of men and women:

(a) The same right to enter into marriage;

(b) The same right freely to choose a spouse and to enter into marriage only with their free and full consent;

(c) The same rights and responsibilities during marriage and at its dissolution;

(d) The same rights and responsibilities as parents, irrespective of their marital status, in matters relating *to their children,* in all cases the interests of the children shall be paramount;

(e) The same rights to decide freely and responsibly on the number and spacing of their children and to have access to the information, education and means to enable them to exercise these rights;

(f) The same rights and responsibilities with regard to guardianship, wardship, trusteeship and adoption of children, or similar institutions where these concepts exist *in national legislation*; in all cases the interests of the children shall be paramount.

(g) The same personal rights as husband and wife, including the right to choose a family name, a profession and an occupation;

(h) The same rights for both spouses in respect of the ownership, acquisition, management, administration, enjoyment and disposition of property, whether free of charge or for a valuable consideration.

2. The betrothal and the marriage of a child shall have no legal effect, and all necessary action, including legislation, shall be taken to specify a minimum age for marriage and to make the registration of marriages in an official registry compulsory.

# The Sexual Harassment of Women at the Workplace (Prevention and Redressal) Bill, 2004

12

A Bill to provide for the prevention and redressal of sexual harassment of women at workplaces, or arising during or out of the course of their employment and matters connected thereto, in keeping with the principles of equality, freedom, life and liberty as enshrined in the Constitution of India and in pursuance of the Convention signed...for the elimination of all forms of discrimination against women.

## CHAPTER I

### *Preliminary*

**1. Short Title, Extent and Commencement—**

(1) This Act may be called the Sexual Harassment of Women at the Workplace (Prevention and Redressal) Act, 2004.

(2) It extends to the whole of India except the State of Jammu and Kashmir.

(3) It shall come into force with immediate effect.

**2. Definitions**—In this Act, unless the context otherwise requires,—

(a) "aggrieved woman" means any female person, whether major or minor and includes a woman employed or working or studying, who has been subjected to sexual harassment;

(b) "appropriate Government" means,—

(i) in relation to any department of the Central Government or any establishment or undertaking wholly or substantially financed by that Government, or such other bodies or corporations established by or under the control of the Central Government, the Central Government; and

(ii) in relation to any department of a State Government or any establishment or undertaking wholly or substantially financed by that Government, or any local authority, or any establishment or undertaking established by or under the control of the State Government, the State Government;

(c) "complainant" means,—

(i) an aggrieved woman herself;

(ii) an aggrieved woman for herself and on behalf of others, in the case of more than one aggrieved woman;

(iii) the legal heir or representative, in the case of death of an aggrieved woman; or

(iv) a registered trade union or a women's organisation or a non-governmental organisation, on behalf of aggrieved woman or women referred to in sub-clause (i) or sub-clause (ii) or sub-clause (iii),

who files a complaint of sexual harassment under this Act;

(d) "Complaints Committee" includes the Internal Complaints Committee constituted under section 5;

(e) "defendant" means a person against whom a complaint is filed by a complainant;

(f) "District Special Officer" or "Special Officer" means a person appointed under section 6 or section 7, as the case may be;

(g) "educational institution" means a university, college, school, private coaching centre or any other institution at which education or training is provided;

(h) "employee" means a person employed for any work directly, or by or through any agency (including a contractor), with or without the knowledge of the principal employer, whether for remuneration or not, or working on a voluntary basis, whether the terms of employment are express or implied, and includes any person employed as a temporary, casual, badli, probationer, trainee, apprentice or by whatever name called, and a domestic servant employed in a house or dwelling place or any other establishment;

(i) "employer" means,—

(a) in relation to a department of the Central Government or a State Government, the authority prescribed in this behalf, or where no authority is prescribed, the head of the department;

(b) in relation to an establishment or undertaking wholly or substantially by the Central Government or the State Government or any local authority of a State Government, as the case may be, the authority prescribed in this behalf, or, where no person is so prescribed, the Chief Executive Officer;

(c) in a workplace not covered under sub-clauses (a) and (b), the person who, or the authority which, whether called a manager, managing director, managing agent, mukadam, or by whatever name called, is responsible for the supervision and control of the workplace or house, in which the employee is employed, and in respect of a contract employee includes the principal employer of the workplace in which the employee is working, as well as the contractor;

(d) in any other case, the person who is in a position of authority whether evaluatory, pecuniary or fiduciary including the owner or trustee of an educational institution.

(j) "Internal Complaints Committee" means a committee constituted by the employer under section 4;

(k) "Local Complaints Committee" means a Committee constituted under section 9;

(l) "owner", in relation to an educational institution, means the person who establishes an educational institution, or a trustee or the person who is responsible to manage it as a principal, manager or by whatever name called;

(m) "panel of experts" means the list of experts prepared and maintained by the District Special Officer under section 8;

(n) "proceedings" means any proceedings carried out by any authority prescribed or persons authorised under this Act;

(o) "sexual harassment" means any unwelcome sexually determined conduct whether physical, verbal or non-verbal, including but not limited to, sexual advances, demands or requests for sexual favours, molestation, sexually nuanced gestures, comments, remarks or jokes either verbal, textual, graphic or electronic;

(p) "workplace", in relation to an employee, means any place where an aggrieved woman or defendant is employed or works, or visits in connection with work during the course of or arising out of employment, including, but not limited to the following, namely:

(i) a factory, mine, plantation or forest;

(ii) a place where any agricultural operation is carried out;

(iii) a place of sale of agricultural or other products;

(iv) a brick kiln or a construction site;

(v) a shop, business establishment, a corporation or a private office;

(vi) an office or establishments of a professional or consultants;

(vii) an industrial establishment;

(viii) a banking or financial institution;

(ix) a restaurant, club, hotel, resort or other hospitality establishment;

(x) a hospital, nursing home or a health centre;

(xi) a court premise, police station, remand home or any judicial or quasi-judicial establishment;

(xii) an establishment wherein a person is employed for exhibition or performance of sporting or any other form of entertainment or preparation thereof;

(xiii) a house, dwelling place whether permanent, temporary or in transit;

(xiv) any government, semi-government, establishment or department including telegraph office, post office, telephone exchange, railways, statutory board or any governmental scheme instituted for profit or otherwise;

(xv) a free trade zone or special economic zone;

(xvi) a non-governmental organisation, a public or charitable trust a religious body, trust or institutions, a co-operative housing society or an association;

(xvii) a street;

(xviii) any form of transportation whether by road, sea or air;

(xix) any other public place.

## CHAPTER II

### *Sexual Harassment of Women*

**3. Prohibition from sexual harassment**—(1) No employer, supervisor or co-employee shall, in any manner whatsoever, sexually harass a female,—

(a) employee at the workplace where she is working;

(b) who, for whatsoever reason, is present in or at the workplace; or

(c) who, comes into contact with the employer, supervisor or employee in connection with her work or with the work of these persons.

(2) No owner or employee, including the teaching staff, of an educational institution, shall in any manner whatsoever, sexually harass a woman student who attends class or training or visits the educational institution.

(3) Notwithstanding anything contained in any other law for the time being in force, sexual harassment shall,—

(i) amount to misconduct in any employment and the service rules or regulations relating to conduct and discipline at the workplace or educational institution and such rules or regulations shall include provision for prohibiting sexual harassment and provide for appropriate penalties against an offender;

(ii) amount to an unfair labour practice within the meaning of clause (ra) of section 2 of the Industrial Disputes Act, 1947.

## CHAPTER III

### *Complaints Committees*

**4. Duty of the employer or owner to constitute Internal Complaints Committees**—(1) Every employer who employs or has employed fifty or more employees or every owner who registers or has registered fifty or more students in the preceding twelve months in a calendar year shall constitute an Internal Complaints Committee:

Provided that an employer or owner who employs or has employed less than fifty employees or registers or has registered students in any preceding twelve months in a calendar year may constitute an Internal Complaints Committee:

Provided further that the employer who has more than one office or branch office or the owner who has more than one educational institution or branch thereof shall constitute an Internal Complaints Committee in each of them:

Provided also that where an employer or owner has at any time constituted an Internal Complaints Committee under this section, such a Committee shall continue to exist notwithstanding that the number of employees or students at any time thereafter falls below fifty.

**5. Constitution of Internal Complaints Committee and duties thereof**—(1) An Internal Complaints Committee shall consist of a woman President and not less than one half of its members should be women:

Provided that an Complaints Committee shall nominate a representative of a non-gvernmental organisation or any other body which is working for the cause of upliftment of women and is familiar with the issue of sexual harassment.

(2) Not less than one half of the members of the Internal Complaints Committee shall be women:

Provided that where it is not possible to constitute an Internal Complaints Committee with the one half of women members due to non-availability of suitable women, the Committee shall be constituted with as many women members as near to one half of the total membership, after recording reasons therefor.

(3) It shall be the duty of an Internal Complaints Committee to make preliminary investigations into a complaint made to it by a complainant, hold enquiries into such complaints, to resolve the matter by amicable settlement, if so requested by the complainant, and to issue orders pursuant to the findings of the cnquiry.

**6. Appointment of Special Officers**—(1) Every employer and owner shall designate a female employee to be a Special Officer in every department or educational institution or branch or office of such department or educational institutions under his or its control to receive complaints under this Act.

(2) Every employer or owner shall endeavour to publicise widely the name or designation and duties of the Special Officer in every department or educational institution under his or its control.

**7. Appointment of District Special Officer for every district and duties thereof**—(1) The appropriate Government shall appoint a District Special Officer for every district, as may be prescribed, to deal with complaints arising out of provisions of this Act.

(2) The District Special Officer, referred to in sub-section (1), shall be of the rank not lower than the Assistant Labour

Commissioner and shall have his or her office in the office of the Labour Commissioner.

(3) The District Special Officer shall be a female, wherever a female officer in the rank specified in sub-section (2) is available.

(4) It shall be the duty of the District Special Officer to:

(a) receive complaints from the district concerned;

(b) prepare and maintain a panel of the experts;

(c) constitute a Local Complaints Committee; and

(d) forward a copy of an Order passed by the Local Complaints Committee to the complainant, defendant and employer or owner for compliance and carry out any other functions assigned to her or him under this Act.

**8. Panel of experts in every district**—Every District Special Officer shall prepare and maintain a panel of Group of Experts consisting of eminent persons from various fields who are generally involved with women's issues, women's rights activists, social workers, counsellors, lawyers, doctors, psychiatrists, trade unionists, journalists, etc. as enumerated in section 2(1)(j) at each District.

**9. Constitution of Local Complaints Committee**—(1) When a complaint is received by a District Special Officer, the District Special Officer shall constitute a Local Complaints Committee consisting of not less than three persons from the panel of experts:

Provided that not less than one half of its members shall be women:

Provided further that in case of non-availability of a suitable woman, such Committee shall be constituted without one half of the women members after recording reasons in writing therefor.

(2) The Local Complaint Committee shall be headed by a woman, who shall be its chairperson.

## CHAPTER IV

### *Procedure for Lodging a Complaint*

**10. Before the Internal Complaints Committee**—(1) Where an Internal Complaints Committee has been set up in a workplace or an educational institution, a complaint under this Act may be lodged with any member of the Internal Complaints Committee:

Provided that if a complaint is made to the employer it shall be forwarded to the Internal Complaints Committee:

Provided further that in case where a complaint of sexual harassment is against the employer or owner, the aggrieved woman shall make the complaint to the Special Officer or to any member of the Internal Complaints Committee.

(2) If the aggrieved woman complaints that she has been subject to an act of sexual harassment at another branch or office to which she has been deputed or to which she has visited in connection with her work or studies, a complaint in this regard shall be made either to the Internal Complaints Committee relating to her regular branch or office or to the Internal Complaints Committee relating to the branch office where the act of sexual harassment has allegedly taken place.

**11. Complaints to Special Officer or Local Complaints Committee**—(1) Save and except for the cases specified in section 12, a complaint under this Act may be made to the District Special Officer.

(2) When a complaint is made to the Special Officer, he or she shall constitute the Local Complaints Committee from the panel of experts within fifteen days of the said complaint and designate a female member as its chairperson.

(3) The Local Complaint Committee shall operate from the local proximity of the complainant's workplace or educational institution.

**12. Oral complaints to be reduced in writing**—Where an oral complaint is made to the employer or owner, or Internal Complaints Committee or any of its members, or the Special Officer, it shall be the duty of the employer or owner, or the Internal Complaints Committee or its member, or the Special

Officer, as the case may be, to reduce the said complaint in writing and read out the complaint to the complainant and obtain the signature thereon of the complainant.

**13. Written consent required in certain circumstances—** (1) A complaint made under section 10 or section 11 by a complainant referred to in sub-clause (iii) or sub-clause (iv) of clause (c) of section 2 shall be made only after obtaining a written consent of the aggrieved woman or, in the case of her death, her heirs or legal representative, authorising the organisation or individual to file the complaint on her or their behalf.

(2) The consent given under sub-section (1) may be withdrawn at any stage of the proceedings by the aggrieved woman or her legal heir or representative, as the case may be.

**14. Where sexual harassment amounts to criminal offence—** (1) Without prejudice to any proceedings initiated or any action taken under this Act (45 of 1860) where the conduct of a sexual harassment amounts to an offence under the provisions of the Indian Penal Code or any other law for the time being in force, it shall be the duty, of the employer or owner, or the Internal Complaints Committee or its member, or the Special Officer, as the case may be, who receives such a complaint, to immediately inform the complainant of her right to initiate action in accordance with law before the appropriate authority.

(2) Notwithstanding that whether the complainant opts to initiate any criminal proceedings under the provisions of the Indian Penal Code or any other law for the time being in force, the employer or owner, or the Internal Complaints Committee or any of its members, or the Special Officer, as the case may be, shall be bound to initiate proceedings as provided by or under this Act.

**15. Confidentiality of complaints—**All the complaints made under this Chapter shall be confidential and it shall be the duty of the members of the Internal Complaints Committee or the Special Officer to ensure that its confidentiality is maintained for ever.

## CHAPTER V

### *Procedures before the Complaints Committee*

**16. Inquiry**—(1) On receiving a complaint of sexual harassment, the Internal Complaints Committee shall conduct an inquiry into the complaint by interviewing the complainant and defendant and any witnesses, determining if there are individuals with direct or indirect information regarding the complaint, and, if so, by interviewing them or by obtaining information from such other persons and making such inquiries as it thinks fit.

(2) The Internal Complaints Committee shall complete its inquiry within ninety days from the date of the complaint, record in writing its findings and take appropriate action on the basis of the findings.

(3) During the course of enquiry, the complainant and the defendant shall be called separately to ensure freedom of expression and an atmosphere free of intimidation:

Provided that the complainant shall be entitled to accompany one representative during the enquiry.

(4) An Internal Complaints Committee shall be free to adopt its own procedure for carrying out the inquiry having regard to the sensitive nature of the complaint and the respective power position of the parties.

**17. Power to Summons**—(1) The Internal Complaints Committee shall, for the purposes of an enquiry under this Chapter, have the power to summon witnesses or call for documents or any information.

(2) If it has reason to believe that a person is capable of furnishing such documents or information, it may direct that person to produce the documents or information by serving notice in writing on that person, summoning the person or calling for documents or information at such place and within such time as may be specified in the notice.

(3) Where an information is recorded or stored by means of a mechanical, electronic or other device, to produce the same or to produce a clear reproduction in writing of the information.

(4) Where the documents or information are produced before the Internal Complaints Committee in accordance with this section, the Committee may—

(i) take possession of the documents and make copies or take extracts therefrom;

(ii) retain the possession of the documents for such period as may be deemed necessary for the enquiry.

**18. Power to issue interim orders**—The Internal Complaints Committee shall have the power to issue appropriate interim orders directing the employer or owner, on the demand of either the complainant or any witness giving evidence in her support, to implement such measures as transferring, changing shift of either the complainant, witness or defendant to protect the complainant or witnesses against victimisation or discrimination or may issues such other interim orders as may be deemed necessary to ensure the safety of the complainant or supporter or witness.

**19.** The complainant and the defendant shall have the right to receive copies of the proceedings, documents or any other evidence produced during the course of enquiry.

## CHAPTER VI

### *Findings and Directions*

**20. Findings and Directions**—(1) On the completion of an enquiry by an Internal Complaints Committee or a Local Complaints Committee, it may by a reasoned order,—

(a) dismiss the complaint which was the subject-matter of the inquiry; or

(b) pass any one or more of the following directions, namely:

(i) that the defendant shall not repeat or continue such unlawful conduct; or

(ii) that the defendant shall perform any reasonable act or course of conduct to redress any loss or damage suffered by the complainant; or

(iii) that the defendant shall pay to the aggrieved woman or her legal heirs damages by way of compensation for any loss or damage suffered by her or her legal heirs by reason of the conduct of the defendant; or

(iv) that the defendant shall give a written apology to the aggrieved woman clearly undertaking that such behaviour will not be repeated and that no retaliatory steps will be taken by him or on his behalf; or

(v) that a punishment in addition to above be imposed upon the defendant, where the defendant is an employee, by the employer or owner, according to the gravity of the act of which he has been found guilty and in accordance with the service rules or standing orders applicable to the workplace or the educational institution:

Provided that where there is no service rules or standing orders, the Committee may direct that, any of the following punishments, having regard to the gravity of the act of which he has been found guilty, be imposed on the defendant—

minor penalties:

(a) give him a warning or censure in writing;

(b) fine him, subject to and in accordance with the provisions of the Payment of Wages Act, 1936;

(c) withhold an increment for a period not exceeding one year;

(d) suspend him for a period not exceeding four days;

major penalties:

(e) withhold an increment for more than a year;

(f) reduce his rank or grade;

(g) terminate his services, by discharging or dismissing him, after paying any dues to which he is entitled to in law:

Provided further that before any action is taken under this clause, the defendant shall be given an opportunity to show cause as to why the proposed action should not be taken against him.

*Explanation*: For the purpose of this sub-section, "damage" shall include the injury to the feelings of the aggrieved woman or the humiliation suffered by her.

(2) Where the defendant is the employer or owner, or is a co-employee involved in the sexual harassment, or a complaint, led to or resulted in any adverse change to the service conditions of the aggrieved woman or any witness or representative, or any prejudice being caused to the victim or any witness in terms of their service conditions and employment, the concerned Committee may, in addition to any of the above directions, direct that,—

(a) the employer restore the particular service condition of the aggrieved woman or witness or representative, with retrospective effect and full benefits from the date it was adversely changed, including where the aggrieved woman or witness of sexual harassment has been terminated from service, to reinstate her or him with full back wages and continuity of services;

(b) the employer grant to the aggrieved woman or witness the particular service condition to which she or he would have been entitled but for the act of sexual harassment or consequences of the same, with retrospective effect and full benefits from the date the said service condition would have been granted to her or him but for the act of sexual harassment or consequences of the same.

(3) The findings and directions of the Internal Complaints Committee or the Local Complaints Committee shall be binding on the employer or the owner.

**22. Copies of the order to be given to the complainant and the defendant**—(1) Where the order has been passed by an Internal Complaints Committee, the said Committee shall forward a copy of the order each to the complainant, defendant and the employer or owner.

(2) Where the order has been passed by a Local Complaints Committee, it shall submit its order to the concerned Special

Officer, who shall forward a copy of the same to the complainant, defendant and the employer or owner.

## CHAPTER VII

### *Duties and Liabilities of an Employer*

**23. Duties of an employer**—(1) Every employer or owner shall,—

(a) ensure a safe work or study environment free from sexual harassment including prevention and deterrence;

(b) maintain a proactive programme to educate all employees or students as to the definition of sexual harassment and procedure for redressal;

(c) facilitate initiation of proceedings under this Act if an act of sexual harassment has been brought to his or her notice;

(d) ensure that the complainant or supporter or witness is not victimised, harassed or discriminated against for initiating or supporting or giving evidence in proceedings under this Act;

(e) not alter to the prejudice of the aggrieved woman or witness or representative concerned, the conditions of service prevailing immediately prior to the complaint being lodged as a consequence to the making and prosecuting of a complaint under this Act;

(f) ensure that complainant or supporter or witness is not punished by discharging, transferring, dismissing or otherwise for any misconduct, as a consequence to the complaint save with express permission in writing of the Internal Complaints Committee;

(g) if the situation so demands, immediately transfer the defendant.

(2) Every employer or owner shall take all necessary and reasonable steps to prevent and ensure that no woman is subject to sexual harassment in his workplace or educational institution by any third party and where any such sexual harassment occurs, the employer shall take all necessary and reasonable

steps to assist the aggrieved woman to redress the act of sexual harassment.

(3) The onus shall be on the employer or owner to prove that he had taken all reasonable measures to comply with the duties entrusted to him under this Act.

**24. Liability of Employer**—(1) Where an employer or owner,—

(a) fails to perform duties entrusted to him under section 23;

(b) fails to constitute an Internal Complaints Committee as required under section 4;

(c) protects a person found guilty of sexual harassment;

(d) in any manner pressurises the aggrieved woman or witnesses or supporters from initiating or participating in proceedings under this Act or pressurise her to withdrawing a complaint;

(e) fails to implement the order of the Internal Complaints Committee; or

(f) in any manner violates the provisions of this Act;

a complaint to this effect may be made to the Internal Complaints Committee or Special Officer, or the said Committee or Officer may take cognizance of the same *suo moto* and the matter will be dealt with by the said Committee or Officer in accordance with the procedure specified for dealing with complaints under this Act.

(2) In addition to the reliefs set out above, the Internal Complaints Committee or the Local Complaints Committee may direct the employer to pay a penalty, to be deposited in the "Sexual Harassment Fund" through the office of the Special Officer or compensation to the complainant or witness commensurate with the loss or injury suffered or damages caused to her by the above wrongful actions of employer or owner.

(3) In addition to the above, where any woman is subject to an act of sexual harassment due to the employer of or owner where the act took place, not having taken all necessary and reasonable steps to prevent the same, the aggrieved woman may

file a suit for damages, and other relief, against the employer in a civil court.

## CHAPTER IX

### *Appeal*

**25. Appeals Against Decisions/Reports of Complaints Committees or District Level Special Officer or Person from the Group of Experts**—(1) In taking any decisions and submitting any reports under this Act, Complaints Committees or District Level Special Officer and Person from the Group of Experts shall, for the purposes of this section, be deemed to be acting on behalf of the employer of the defendant, and where the defendant is himself the employer, then the said Committees/persons shall be deemed to be acting on behalf of the said employer.

(2) Any defendant aggrieved by a decision or report of a Complaints Committee or District Level Special Officer and person from the Group of Experts finding him guilty of sexual harassment, and/or against whom action has been taken by the employer, may:

(a) if he is a "workman" under Industrial Dispute Act, 1947:

(i) make a complaint in writing on points of fact and law, as if the decision had been taken by the employer to the Industrial Tribunal in whose jurisdiction his workplace falls, and on receipt of such a complaint, the Industrial Tribunal shall adjudicate upon the same as if it were a dispute referred to it in accordance with the provisions of the Industrial Disputes Act, 1947, and shall submit its award to the Appropriate Government and the provisions of the Industrial Disputes Act, 1947 shall apply accordingly:

Provided that where a defendant is aggrieved by any decision or report referred to in sub-section (2) and where the woman who was the victim of the sexual harassment was harassed at her workplace/in connection with her work, then any complaint referred to in subsection

(2) (a) (i) shall be filed in the Industrial Tribunal in whose jurisdiction the said woman's workplace falls.

(ii) file any other legal proceedings, on points of fact and law, as if the decision had been taken by the employer;

(b) if she is not a "workman" under industrial law, file proceedings, on points of both fact and law, before the forum/court before whom he would ordinarily file proceedings against a decision of, or action taken by, the employer.

(3) Any aggrieved woman who is aggrieved by a decision or report of an Internal Complaints Committee or a Local Complaints Committee/District Labour Officer and person from the Group of Experts taken under this Act, and/or action taken, or not taken by an employer or head of the educational institution in this regard, may:

(a) if she is a "workman" under industrial law:

(i) make a complaint in writing on points of fact and law, as if the decision had been taken by the employer, to the Industrial Tribunal in whose jurisdiction her workplace falls, and on receipt of such a complaint, the Industrial Tribunal shall adjudicate upon the same as if it were a dispute referred to it in accordance with the provisions of the Industrial Disputes Act, 1947, and shall submit its award to the Appropriate Government and the provisions of the Industrial Disputes Act, 1947 shall apply accordingly;

(ii) File any other legal proceedings, on points of fact and law, as if the decision had been taken by the employer.

(b) If she is not a "workman" under industrial law, file proceedings, on points of both fact and law, before the forum/court before whom she would ordinarily file proceedings against a decision of, or action taken by, the employer.

## CHAPTER X

### *Miscellaneous*

**26. Confidentiality**—Employers and others responsible for the implementation of this Act will recognize that confidentiality is important and will respect the confidentiality and privacy of complainants or defendants, to the extent reasonably possible.

**27. Services of Counsellor to be made available to the complainant**—On the request of a Complainant, a counsellor shall be made available to her, at the cost of the employer, at any time after the lodging of a complaint, whether before an Internal Complaints Committee or District Level Special Officer, which shall be in addition to any proceedings/enquiries which have been instituted under the Act.

**28. Withdrawal of Complaint**—(1) If at any stage after the filing of a complaint and during any proceedings in respect of it under this Act by the Complaints Committee, the aggrieved woman shall have the right to withdraw the complaint and the Committee/person shall permit her to withdraw the complaint and if an inquiry has commenced, shall discontinue the inquiry.

(2) If it is brought to the notice of the Complainants Committee, or the Committee is of the opinion that, pressure is being brought on the complainant or the witnesses to withdraw their statements or not go through with the complaint then the committee will record this.

**29. Complainant/Witnesses/Supporters not be penalized**—If a complaint of sexual harassment is dismissed by a Complaints Committee under this Act, no action whatsoever (including the recovery of any costs involved in investigating/enquiring into the complaint) may be taken in regard to the same against the complainant/witnesses/supporters by the employer.

**30. No court fees payable**—Where an aggrieved woman institutes any suit or legal proceedings in a civil court in respect of an act of sexual harassment which is unlawful under this Act, no court fees will be payable by the woman.

**31. Returns**—Every Internal Complaints Committee shall furnish from time to time to the District Special Officer concerned and every District Special Officer shall together with his return forward such return to the Central Government and to the State Government as they may require to monitor the effective implementation of the provisions of this Act.

**32. Employee's right to raise issues**—Every employee shall have the right to raise issues of sexual harassment at the worker's meeting and in any other appropriate forum and it shall be discussed thoroughly in the employer and employee meetings.

**33. Act not in derogation of any other Law**—The provisions of this Act shall be in addition to and not in derogation of the provisions of, any other law for the time being in force:

Provided that nothing in this Act shall effect any law, agreement, contract, terms and conditions of service or policy regarding sexual harassment at the workplace which applies to any woman employee or student on the date on which this Act comes into force, if any such law, agreement, contract, terms and conditions of service or policy regarding sexual harassment at the workplace is or are more favourable to the women concerned than the provisions of this Act.

**34.** (1) The appropriate Government may, by notification in the Official Gazette, make rules for carrying out the provisions of this Act.

(2) In particular and without prejudice to the generality of the foregoing power, such rules may provide for all or any of the following matters, namely:

(3) Every rule made by the Central Government under this Act shall be laid, as soon as may be after it is made, before each House of Parliament, while it is in session for a total period of thirty days which may be comprised in one session or in two or more successive sessions, and if, before the expiry of the session immediately following the session or the successive sessions aforesaid, both Houses agree in making any modification in the rule or both Houses agree that the rule should not be made, the rule shall thereafter have effect only in such modified form or be of no effect, as the case may be; so, however, that any such modification or annulment shall be without prejudice to the validity of anything previously done under that rule.

(4) Every rule made by the State Government under this Act shall be laid, as soon as may be after it is made, before each House of the State Legislature where it consists of two Houses, or, where such Legislature consists of one House, before that House.

## SCHEDULE I

The following item shall be added as Item 17 to The Fifth Schedule, Part I, of the Industrial Disputes Act, 1947:

"To dismiss, discharge or in any way adversely alter the service conditions of a female employee, (or any fellow employee who stands as a witness in this regard), on account of her making or having made an allegation of sexual harassment."

## SCHEDULE II

The following item shall be added as Item 11 to Schedule IV of the Maharashtra Recognition of Trade Unions & Prevention of Unfair Labour Practices Act, 1971:

"To dismiss, discharge or in any way adversely alter the service conditions of a female employee, (or any fellow employee who stands as a witness in this regard), on account of her making or having made an allegation of sexual harassment."

# Scheme of Short Stay Homes for Women and Girls

13

## 1. Objective

To provide shelter and facilities for rehabilitation of women and young girls who are deprived of social support due to family problems, exploitation, social ostracism, mental stress or other causes.

## 2. Target Group

Women and Girls who have left their homes on account of family tension or discord and are, as a consequence emotionally disturbed, victims of mental maladjustment, sexually assaulted victims and those facing social ostracism for a variety of reasons.

## 3. Implementing Agencies

1. Registered Voluntary Organizations (of at least 3 years standing)

## 4. Submission of Project Proposals

(i) Closing date for submission of Proposals to the State Governments 05-08-2004.

(ii) Scrutiny of proposals by State Governments from 06-08-2004 to 06-09-2004.

(iii) States to convene meetings of SLEC's between 07-09-2004 to 21-09-2004

(iv) Last date for reaching applications to Government of India 30-09-2004.

(v) Proposals received after the last date prescribed (i.e. 30-09-2004) shall be rejected.

(vi) Proposals sent by NGO's directly to this Department shall not be entertained.

(vii) Details of the Scheme can also be accessed at the Department's website www.wcd.nic.in. Further details are available with the State Social Welfare Boards/ Director, Women and Child Development/Social Welfare of State Governments.

Please type out and complete your application in accordance with the following format and forward it to the secretary, in-charge of the women and child development/social welfare department of the state concerned, along with all documents mentioned.

## FORMAT FOR APPLICATION

### I. Particulars About Organization

(i) Name of Implementing Agency/ Organization :

(ii) Address (with Pin code) :

(iii) Date of Registration :

(iv) Telephone No. (with STD Code) :

FAX : E-Mail :

(v) Financial Status :

| Sl. No. | Financial Year | Receipt and Payment | Income and Expenditure | Surplus OR Deficit |
|---|---|---|---|---|
| 1. | 2001-02 | | | |
| 2. | 2002-03 | | | |
| 3. | 2003-04 | | | |

(vi) Organization's Activities during the last three years :

(vii) Source of Funds :

(viii) List of Executive Committee Members with details of their Experience of working for Women's welfare (1/3rd of whom should be women) :

## II. Project Details

1. Target Group :
2. Full address of the proposed location of the Short Stay Home :
    - (i) District/Block :
    - (ii) Whether the location is in the District HQ/Tehsil HQ or Block :
3. Population of Town/City for the proposed Short Stay Home as per 2001 census :
4. Justification for setting up a Short Stay Home in the area :
5. Project Cost and Beneficiaries :

Further information regarding Recurring and Non-recurring costs can be obtained from the Director, State Social Welfare Board/Director, Women & Child Development Corporation, the State Governments or the Central Social Welfare Board or accessed through our website www.wcd.nic.in.

6. Details of facilities proposed to be made available in the Short Stay Home:

| | Number | Total Area (Sq. feet) |
|---|---|---|
| Rooms | | |
| Kitchen | | |
| Toilet/Bath | | |
| Store | | |
| Verandah | | |
| Carpet Area | | |
| Plinth Area | | |
| Open Space | | |
| Total | | |

(ii) Is the premise rented or rent-free. (Pl. furnish details thereof):

(iii) The location of the proposed Short Stay Home should be safe for beneficiaries. There should be security arrangements such as boundary walls, firefighting arrangements and external security lighting around the premises.

7. Details of likely beneficiaries:

## III. Documents to be Enclosed with Application Form

***Copy of :***

(a) Registration Certificate (duly attested by a Gazetted Officer)

(b) Memorandum of Association and Bye-Laws (duly authenticated)

(c) Audited Statement of Accounts (For preceding three years)

(d) Annual Report (For three preceding years)

(e) Constitution of the Board of Management with brief particulars of each member

(f) Justification for setting up a SSH in the area (Attach survey report, if any)

(g) A one page note on "How the Short Stay Home will be administered".

**IV.** Other Information, if any.

---

Government of India

MINISTRY OF HUMAN RESOURCE DEVELOPMENT

**(Department of Women and Child Development)**

Support to Training and Employment Programme For Women (STEP)

## GRANT OF FINANCIAL ASSISTANCE FOR SKILL UPGRADATION

### 1. Objective

To train and upgrade skills of women in traditional sectors, and to facilitate them to form viable groups in order to access credit, and establish market linkages.

### 2. Target Group

Women particularly from the Weaker Sections of the Society.

**3. Names of Trades**

Traditional sectors—(1) Agriculture, (2) Animal Husbandry, (3) Dairying, (4) Fishery, (5) Handlooms, (6) Handicrafts, (7) Khadi & Village Industries, (8) Sericulture.

**4. Implementing Agencies**

1. Registered Voluntary Organizations (of at least 3 years standing)
2. District Rural Development Authorities
3. Public Sector Undertakings/Organizations
4. Co-operatives
5. Federations

**4 (a). Eligibility Conditions**

Implementing agencies must be—

(i) Financially sound,

(ii) Have adequate experience in the sector, and

(iii) Facilities and administrative capacity to undertake and monitor the Project.

**5. Submission of Project Proposals**

(i) Closing date for submission of proposals to the State Governments: 31-07-2004.

(ii) Scrutiny of proposals by State Level Empowered Committees from 01-08-2004 to 31-08-2004.

(iii) States to convene meetings of SLEC's on or before 01-09-2004.

iv Last date for reaching applications to the Government of India—20-09-2004 along with the recommendations of the SLEC.

6. Proposals received after the last date prescribed (i.e. 20-09-2004) shall be rejected.
7. Proposals sent by implementing agencies directly to this Department shall not be entertained.
8. Details of the Scheme can also be accessed at the Department's website www.wcd.nic.in. Further details are available with the State Women's Development Corporations,

Director, Women and Child Development/Social Welfare of State Governments.

9. Please type out and complete your application in accordance with the following format and forward it to the secretary, in-charge of the women and child development/social welfare department of the state concerned, along with all documents mentioned. The information is to be forwarded as a project document.

## FORMAT FOR APPLICATION

### I. Particulars About Organization

(i) Name of Implementing Agency/ Organization :

(ii) Address (with Pin code) :

(iii) Date of Registration :

(iv) Telephone No. (with STD Code) :

FAX : E-Mail :

(v) Financial Status :

| Sl.No. | Financial Year | Receipt and Payment | Income and Expenditure | Surplus OR Deficit |
|---|---|---|---|---|
| 1. | 2001-02 | | | |
| 2. | 2002-03 | | | |
| 3. | 2003-04 | | | |

(vi) Organization's Objectives :

(vii) Source of Funds :

(viii) List of Executive Committee Members :

### II. Project Details

Details to be furnished as per tables below:

**Table – I**

| Location of Project Area | Name of Trade/Sector | Number of Beneficiaries* | Project Duration** | Source of Raw Material |
|---|---|---|---|---|
| | | | | |

* [Minimum 500 beneficiaries] ** [3 years]

**Table – II**

(Year-wise Cost of the Project)*

(Rs. in lakhs)

| Sl.No. | Items | 1st Year | 2nd Year | Total |
|---|---|---|---|---|
| 1. | Cost of stipend for training – (No. of beneficiaries x No. of months x Amount) | | | |
| 2. | Cost of Raw Material | | | |
| 3. | Cost of Trainer(s) | | | |
| 4. | Cost of equipment | | | |
| 5. | Administration and Establishment costs | | | |
| 6. | Contingencies | | | |
| 7. | Formation of SHGs/ Cooperatives | | | |
| 8. | TOTAL | | | |
| 9. | Government of India's Share [90% of the Total Project Cost] | | | |
| 10. | Implementing agency's share [10% of the Total Project Cost] | | | |

*Complete details to be given.

### III. Documents to be Enclosed with the Application Form

***Copy of :***

(i) Registration Certificate.

(ii) Memorandum of Association and Bye-Laws of Organization.

(iii) Audited Statement of Accounts (for preceding three years).

(iv) Annual Report (for three preceding years).

(v) Arrangements proposed for technical training and support including trainer's name and qualifications.

(vi) Outline Map of the Project Area.

(vii) Benchmark survey of intended beneficiaries.

(viii) Utilization Certificate and Statement of expenditure as certified by a C.A. (in respect of earlier project, if any).

(ix) Marketing Plan and Link up with Institutional Finance.

**IV.** Other Information, if any to be enclosed with the Project Document.

---

Government of India

MINISTRY OF HUMAN RESOURCE DEVELOPMENT

**(Department of Women and Child Development)**

Working Women's Hostel Scheme—Grant of Financial Assistance for Construction of Hostel Building for Working Women

**1. Objective**

To provide economical and safe accommodation to working women and girl trainees.

**2. Target Groups**

Working women and girls trainees, particularly from the weaker sections of the society.

**3. Implementing Agencies**

1. Voluntary Organizations/Public Trusts in the field of Women's Welfare/Social Welfare, Women's Education (of at least 3 years standing)
2. State Women's Development corporations.
3. Universities/Schools/Colleges of Social Work.
4. Urban Local Bodies.

**4. Submission of Project Proposal**

(i) Closing date for submission of proposals to the State Governments 14-8-2004.

(ii) Scrutiny of Proposals by State Governments from 16-08-2004 to 16-09-2004.

(iii) States to convene meetings of SLEC's on or before 15-10-2004.

(iv) Last date for reaching proposals to the Government of India accompanied by SLEC's recommendations—25-10-2004.

5. Proposals received after the last date prescribed (i.e. 25-10-2004) shall be rejected.

6. Proposals sent by NGO's directly to this Department will not be entertained.
7. Details of the Scheme can be accessed at the Department's website www.wcd.nic.in . Further details can also be had from the Secretary, Women and Child Development/Social Welfare, Director, Women and Child Development/Social Welfare of the State Governments.
8. Please type out and complete your application in accordance with the following format and forward it to the secretary, in-charge of the women and child development/social welfare of the state concerned, along with all documents mentioned.

**FORMAT FOR APPLICATION**

**I. Particulars About Organization**

(i) Name of Implementing Agency/ Organization :

(ii) Address (with Pin code) :

(iii) Date of Registration :

(iv) Telephone No. (with STD Code) :

FAX : E-Mail:

(v) Financial Status :

| Sl.No. | Financial Year | Receipt and payment | Income & Expenditure | Surplus OR Deficit |
|---|---|---|---|---|
| 1. | 2001-02 | | | |
| 2. | 2002-03 | | | |
| 3. | 2003-04 | | | |

(vi) Organization's Objectives :

(vii) Source of Funds :

(viii) List of Executive Committee Members :

**II. Project Details**

1. Target Group :
2. New or expansion project :
3. Location of Hostel :

4. Population of Village/Town/City/District : as per 2001 census
5. Project cost and no. of Beneficiaries :
6. Justification of the Project :

| Name of items | Estimated cost |
|---|---|
| Plinth Area | |
| Covered Area | |
| Civil Works | |
| Electrification | |
| Sanitation | |
| Contingencies | |
| Any other | |
| Total Cost | |

## III. Documents to be Enclosed with Application Form

***Copy of:***

(i) Registration Certificate

(ii) Memorandum of Association and Bye-Laws

(iii) Audited Statement of Accounts (for preceding three years)

(iv) Annual Report (for preceding three years)

(v) Plan and Estimates designed by a Registered Architect duly certified by the State PWD.

(vi) Location Plan showing contours/levels, building outline, landscaping, (wherever applicable) parking areas, access roads external lighting, etc.

(vii) A certificate stating that the design conforms to Town Planning Regulations, as well as to the building regulations, and has the approval of the competent authority.

(viii) The size of the drawings should not exceed A3 size.

(ix) Photographs of the site to be enclosed.

(x) A certificate from the organization stating that it owns the land where the hostel is proposed to be built and that it is free from encumbrances.

(xi) Accommodation in the WWH should, as a norm, be limited to 60 working women with variation upto 10 per cent.

(xii) Ideally, the carpet area of a room should be adequately spacious.

(xiii) The ideal building structure shoula not exceed ground floor plus two floors.

(xiv) The building should be accessible to physically challenged individuals. At least one room and one toilet should be provided for the physically challenged, as well as a ramp.

(xv) There should be one toilet and one bath for every 6-8 working women on an average.

(xvi) The structural safety of the building should be examined by the State PWD/CPWD, and a certificate appended.

(xvii) There should be a provision for a stand-by generator for security reasons.

(xviii) There should be security arrangements such as boundary walls, firefighting arrangements, warden's accommodation, chowkidar's quarters and external security lighting in the premises.

(xix) The cost of construction of the project would be worked out on the basis of State SOR. CPWD will verify the rates and compare them as per Plinth Area Rate of CPWD for the concerned state.

(xx) Please ensure that you have land available and it is suitably located for a Working Women's Hostel.

**IV.** Other Information, if any.

# Identification of Themes for Conducting Research on Issues Related to Women, Children and Nutrition

14

Broadly, the studies can be grouped in the following categories:

A. Profiles on various subjects based on published and unpublished official surveys, studies, analysis, etc.

B. Empirical research of selected issues and concerns based on structured sampling with a view to understand the changing scenario and their implications for social policy and other areas.

C. Benefit incidence analysis of some of the selected schemes on women and children implemented by various Ministries and Departments.

D. Evaluation studies of schemes and programmes of the Department.

E. Action Research on the various processes of empowering community, marginalized women, children in difficult circumstances.

F. Documentation and Directories.

## A. Profiles based on Available Materials

### *(a) Women of India*

The Department had brought out a statistical profile on Women in India in 1987. Two census reports have been published since then. There is a strong demand for publication of a new volume of this publication.

### (b) Children of India

Publication of NIPCCD on Statistical Profile on Children has similarly become dated and need to be revised.

### (c) Gender Profile of the States and Districts

While excellent situational analyses of Women of India are available, there is lack of adequate analytical information in most of the States regarding the situation of women, particularly at the districts and sub-district level. DANIDA had sponsored studies in a few States, which have become outdated. In the context of NFHS II and Census 2001 it is necessary to have a fresh look at the Gender Profiles of the States particularly at the districts and blocks, where significant intra-State differences still persists, but no organised information is available. These studies would facilitate block specific interventions. These studies would primarily look at the available statistical information, published as well as unpublished, as the primary sources and make an analysis of each district in the State.

### (d) Child Profile of the States and Districts

On the similar line State and district profile of children of India can be prepared, based on the latest available published and unpublished statistical information from various sources. Standard parameters of the study can be fixed by a group of experts on the subject and studies can entrusted to them.

### (e) Nutritional Profile of the Districts

National Institute of Nutrition had undertaken a study of nutritional profile of districts. Reports of about 125 districts are available, most of which have become dated. There are large parts of the country, particularly the demographically weak areas, where adequate information regarding nutritional status are not available. The National Institute of Nutrition or similar institute may be engaged for updating the studies in the already covered districts and undertaking fresh studies in the uncovered districts.

### (f) Women and the Economy

There has not been an adequate and proper assessment of women's contribution in Indian economy. Work Participation

Rate of Census 2001 continues to project a marginal role of women, although the Time Use Study had revealed an altogether different picture. It has become necessary to assess the contribution of women in various areas of the economy such as agriculture, dairy farming, handloom, handicrafts, etc. The Department may commission a few national level studies, which can analyse the available data to assess women's contribution in these fields.

## B. Empirical Studies

### *(a) Globalisation and its Impact on Women's Work*

There is very little information on the impact of globalisation on women's work in the informal sector. There are sporadic reports of fisherwomen losing jobs due to the entry multinational fishing trawlers, or traditional leather industry not able to stand in competition with modern companies with foreign collaborations, etc., but no systematic studies are available. It is proposed to sponsor a series of studies in selected areas like (a) Leather, (b) Fisheries, (c) Plantation, (d) Handloom, etc.

### *(b) Women's Work in New and Unconventional Areas*

Very little information is available on the new areas of women's work like Information Technology, Management, Military and Para-Military Services, Science, etc. The Department may sponsor a few studies in certain selected new areas to assess women's contribution in these fields.

### *(c) Atrocities against Women and Children*

The annual publication of National Crime Record Bureau is the only source of available information on atrocities against women and children in the country. It is the general perception that these reports do not fully capture the ground realities, since a large number of crimes against women and are not reported. Some of the recent reports of UNCHR, ICRW, Amnesty International, etc. have shown a large vacuum in the available information base on the subject. It may be worthwhile to commission a few studies in some select areas to assess the magnitude of crime committed against women, both within the family and outside, to find out the extent to which these get reported in the formal system and the various constraints in the delivery of justice. Studies can also sponsored to develop indicators to measure gender based violence.

### *(d) Sexual Harassment at work Places in Unorganised Sectors*

The extent and magnitude of this problem can be studied in some selected areas.

### *(e) Women's Self-Help Group Movement*

While the Self-Help Group Movement has picked up in a few States this is still at a nascent stage in most parts of the country, despite various incentives provided under different schemes of the Government. A few area specific empirical studies should be commissioned to see the strength and weakness of this movement in different parts of the country, with particular reference to find out whether the various programmes of different Ministries are working at cross-purposes. Specific policy and programme intervention that is required for effective synergy and convergence with various schemes and programmes need also to be studied.

### *(f) Studies on Female Infanticide and Foeticide*

The Department had commissioned studies in 8 States in the early nineties on female infanticide and foeticide. All the study reports had shown disturbing trends, which have now been confirmed in the Census 2001. Possibly the same organizations may be commissioned to study the problem in the same areas to see how the situation has aggravated over the decade and the specific reasons thereof. The study may also examine the impact of various interventions to arrest this trend and the reasons why these have failed to produce the desired results.

### *(g) Time Use Study*

Department of Statistics had undertaken Time Use Study in seven selected States on 18,000 households which came out with startling revelation. This study should be replicated on a larger canvass.

### *(h) Study of Crèches in Non-aided Sectors*

The crèches in the non-aided sector probably far outnumber the crèches sponsored by the Department, but not much information about their number, spread, structure, management and finances are available. Such a study has become overdue to develop a national policy on women's support services.

### *(i) Pattern of Employment of Higher Educated Women*

India has possibly the largest number of higher educated women who have preferred to remain without employment or are underemployment. Revolution in information technology has opened up the possibility of flexi space and timing modes of work participation. This phenomenon need to be studied through some micro studies.

## C. Benefit Incidence Analysis of Selected Schemes

The ongoing Gender Budget exercise has emphasised the importance of Benefit Incidence Analysis of selected schemes of a few Ministries and Departments to study the differential impact on male and females. It is suggested that the following major schemes of the Ministries of Health, Rural Development and Education may be taken up for such analysis through reputed research institutes:

(a) Sarva Siksha Yojana and its preceding schemes.

(b) Reproductive and Child Health Services.

(c) Swarn Jayanti Gramin Rojgar Yojana and its preceding and related schemes.

## D. Evaluation Studies of Schemes and Programmes

The impacts of various schemes and programmes of the Department or components thereof that have not been studied at length may be got evaluated through reputed research organizations. The suggested topics for evaluation in the next two to three years are as under:

(a) Balika Samridhi Yojana

(b) Kishori Shakti Yojana

(c) Condensed Course of Education for Girls

(d) Short Stay Homes

(e) Mini Anganwadis under ICDS

(f) Family Counselling Centres

### E. Action Research on the Processes Innovative Social Changes

A number of organizations are involved in various innovative activities for empowering marginalized women and children. The process of these activities provides useful learning experiences, which need to be documented, analysed and further, researched for their possible replication in other areas. Similarly implementation of various programmes through the involvement of community and panchayats in some States should be documented and researched. The Department may support a few such research programmes. Some of the illustrative topics of research could be:

(a) Rescue, Rehabilitation and Reintegration of Trafficked Women and Children.

(b) Integration of Mentally and Physically Handicapped Children in the Framework of Early Childhood Education system of the ICDS.

(c) Rehabilitation of HIV/AIDS affected women and children.

(d) Reintegration of Child Labour, Street Children, etc.

(e) Assessment and Effects of Community participation and Involvement of PRI/Local Bodies in the Implementation of ICDS.

### F. Documentation and Directories

The Department can support the following Directories, Bibliographies and other documentation works:

(a) Supreme Court and High Court Judgments on issues relating to Women and Children.

(b) Documentation of Dissertations on Women and Children of India in Indian and Foreign Universities.

(c) Directory of Voluntary Organisations working in the field of Women and Child Development.

# Women's Empowerment Year 2001

15

## Introduction

The Finance Minister in his Budget Speech of 2000-01 had announced that the year 2001 will be observed as "Women Empowerment Year". He had also announced setting up of a Task Force to chalk out specific programmes for observing the year 2001 as "Women Empowerment Year".

2. The announcement has been made in the context of an urgent need for improving the access of women to national resources and for ensuring their rightful place in the mainstream of economic development. The Government is committed to improve the status of women in India and towards this end, apart from the Constitutional guarantees; several schemes and programmes have been planned and executed from time to time. The declaration of the year 2001 as the "Women's Empowerment Year" is therefore, significant as it reiterates the Government's commitment to bring about equality for women in all walks of life.

3. The objective of the Women's Empowerment Year is to create large-scale awareness with the active participation of women themselves. The Department proposes to launch yearlong activities to bring about a change in the environment which will be conducive to develop self-confidence and assertiveness among women and children, especially girls.

## Task Force on Women and Children

4. In accordance with the announcement made by the Finance Minister in his Budget Speech for 2000-01, on 14th August,

2000, the Government (Department of Women and Child Development) has notified a Task Force under the chairpersonship of Shri K.C. Pant, Deputy Chairman of Planning Commission, consisting of individuals prominent in the field of women's issues. Secretaries of Central Ministries/Departments are special invitees to the meetings of the Task Force.

5. One of the terms of reference of the task force is to draw out a yearlong programme to celebrate the empowerment year. All Departments of Government of India must necessarily be involved in the planned activities. All activities need to be highly visible and supervised and supported to achieve maximum impact. The State Governments, Panchayati Raj and Urban Local Bodies would also be involved in the process. The activities envisaged during the next year would be at two levels—one programmatic, with the objective of intensifying ongoing initiatives in various sectors such as health and education with a special focus on women. At this level there would also be new initiatives to target underserved groups such as women in difficult circumstances, etc. At the other level, activities and programmes would aim to create/generate awareness through use of multimedia on the theme of women's empowerment. Some core messages would need to be focused on are domestic violence, education of girl children, nutrition and health, etc.

6. The Task Force has met twice and the main decisions are:

(a) Finalization of a logo and slogan on the theme of empowerment of women.

(b) Identification of several themes around which yearlong activities would be undertaken viz. Human Rights for women, Economic Empowerment of women, Social Empowerment of women, Women in difficult circumstances, Women and technology, Women and governance, Women and education, Women and health, nutrition, Women and media, Entrepreneurship in women.

(c) Participatory activities such as Poster designing/drawing competition for school and college students be organized.

(d) Separate category of film award on the theme of women's empowerment and telecasting movies on women's empowerment, organizing film festivals, etc.

(e) Finalization of yearlong activities for 2001.

7. A list of month-wise programmes to be taken up during the Women's Empowerment Year is given below:

**Women's Empowerment Year, 2001**

| Month and Theme | Event |
|---|---|
| **January** | |
| Human Rights for women | 1. Launch of the Empowerment year on 4-1-2001. A function will be organized which will include:<br>• Televised Address/Message by PM<br>• Award of Stree Shakti Puraskar.<br>2. Launch of an Integrated SHG based programme for women.<br>3. Meeting of AWWs at Block level in the 1st week to brief about the importance of the year, sensitization reg. Rights of Women, etc.<br>4. AWWs to convene meetings of women groups/mahila mandal at AWC, generate awareness as their rights.<br>5. National consultation meet for empowerment of adolescent girls—Kishori Shakti Yojana<br>6. Workshop on 'Empowerment of Women—Breaking New Grounds' by NCW for celebrating completion of 10 years of NCW (31-1-2001) |

(*Contd.*)

| Month and Theme | Event |
|---|---|
| **February**<br>Economic Empowerment of women | 1. National level seminar on property rights for women.<br>2. Expansion of banking facilities for women.<br>3. Micro credit Summit. |
| **March**<br>Social Empowerment of women | 1. Introduce legislation and amendments such as the Domestic Violence Bill, amendments to Indecent Representation Act, Sati, ITPA and NCW Acts.<br>2. IWD (8th March)<br>3. Two-day follow up Seminar on 'Forging partnership with judiciary, Police Administration and Media'.<br>4. Operationalise District level Committees on Violence against Women & Helplines.<br>5. Film Festival on Women.<br>6. Exhibition on 'Self-Help Groups and Women Empowerment'. |
| **April**<br>Women in difficult circumstances | 1. Launch of the Scheme for women in difficult circumstances.<br>2. Gender training for police officials, judiciary, revenue officials.<br>3. Activating the Monitoring Cell for trafficking under GOI. |

(*Contd.*)

| Month and Theme | Event |
|---|---|
| **May** | |
| Women and technology | 1. Technological Parks.<br>2. National Assessment on women friendly technology on Drudgery Reduction, Tools & Implements and income generation for women.<br>3. Exhibition on Women in Science (travelling).<br>4. Women in Information Technology. |
| **June** | |
| Women and Governance | 1. Teleconference to create a dialogue between MPs/MLAs and grass-root women.<br>2. Intensification of leadership training for women members of panchayats. |
| **July** | |
| Women and Education | 1. Campaign to ensure 100 per cent enrolment rates for girls by Panchayats/Urban bodies/NGOs.<br>2. Country-wide poster competitions at school and college level.<br>3. Sampoorna Shiksha Scheme.<br>4. Educational tours for girl students to create awareness. |
| **August** | |
| Women and Health | 1. Intensification of health camps at PHC level with a focus on anemia control and STI/RTI, towards safe motherhood for women.<br>2. Special programme on safe abortion.<br>3. Ongoing scheme for training of Dais will be implemented in 142 districts of 15 States where safe delivery rate is less than 30 per cent. |

(*Contd.*)

| Month and Theme | Event |
|---|---|
| **September** | |
| Nutrition | 1. Launch of National Nutrition Mission.<br>2. National Nutrition week—programme on nutrition.<br>3. Awareness campaign by M/o Health on nutrition.<br>4. South Asian Regional Meeting to take stock of progress towards gender equality: Challenges and Opportunities. |
| **October** | |
| Women and Media | 1. Film/documentary festival on women.<br>2. Sensitisation of Media-workshop.<br>3. National Sports Meet for Women. |
| **November** | |
| Entrepreneurship in Women | Mela month<br>1. Use of traditional melas, folk artists to propagate messages on women's empowerment.<br>2. Participation in IITF.<br>3. Delhi Haat.<br>4. Conference of women entrepreneurs. |
| **December** | |
| Vision for the future | 1. Commemorative book containing prominent women's view of the vision for the future.<br>2. National Convention on Future Strategies for Women.<br>3. Books on 'Women in India' on 5-7 subjects. |

# Gender Gap and the Millennium Development Goals

16

*Vibhuti Patel*

The Millennium Development Goals are a derivative of the Millennium Declaration of September 2000, which spells out the following values: freedom, equality, solidarity, tolerance, respect for nature, and shared responsibility. They are a clarion call of 189 governments, on behalf of their citizens, to "free our fellow men, women and children from the abject and dehumanizing conditions of extreme poverty, to which more than a billion of them are currently subjected. We are committed to making the right to development a reality for everyone and to freeing the entire human race from want" (Patel, 2006). These measures, collectively known as the Millennium Development Goals (MDGs), have become a prime focus of development work throughout the globe—a gold standard to which programs aspire, and by which they measure their work. They are as follows:

(i) Eradication of Poverty and Hunger,

(ii) Achievement of Universal Primary Education,

(iii) Promotion of Gender Equality and Empowerment,

(iv) Reduction of Child Mortality,

(v) Improvement of Maternal Health,

(vi) Combat HIV/AIDS, Malaria, T.B.,

(vii) Ensure Environmental Sustainability, and

(viii) Develop a Global Partnership for Development.

As articulated in the Millennium Declaration, the MDGs are benchmarks of development progress based on such fundamental values as freedom, equity and human rights and peace and security. MDGs can be achieved if all actors work together—heads of the nation states, civil society organizations, international financial institutions, global trade bodies and the UN system—and do their part. Poor countries have pledged to govern better, and invest in their people through health care and education. Rich countries must stick to their pledge to support the poor countries through aid, debt relief, and fairer and just trade. Only if there is commitment on the part of the rich as well as poor countries to fulfil these promises, all the MDGs could be achieved.

**Gender Concerns in MDGs**

All goals are expected to mainstream gender and MDG 3 has a special focus on gender and challenges discrimination against women by focusing on school education, ensuring that more women become literate, guaranteeing more voice and representation in public policy and decision making—political participation, providing improved job prospects—36% WPR, gender equality and the empowerment of women—win-win approach, food and nutrition security, women subsistence farmers, women as users, managers and storers of natural resources—climate change.

The MDGs explicitly acknowledge that gender—what a given society believes about the appropriate roles and activities of men and women, and the behaviours that result from these beliefs—can have a major impact on development, helping to promote it in some cases while seriously retarding it in others. MDG number 3 (out of 8) is specifically about gender, calling for an end to disparities between boys and girls at all levels of education. There is general agreement that education is vital to development, and ensuring that girls as well as boys have full opportunities for schooling will help improve lives in countless ways. Nevertheless, it would be wrong to conclude—as a casual reader of the MDGs might that gender equality in education is enough to bring development in society. Not surprisingly, then, the rules that regulate the behaviours and values of men that the relevance of gender to development is not confined to the educational sphere. Men and women, both, participate in nearly every aspect of life in communities throughout the world and women in a given society—that is, its gender system—have the potential to impact nearly every aspect of life. Therefore, while only one of the MDGs is specifically about gender, addressing gender is of critical importance to every MDG.

## Critique of the Indicators

The United Nations has suggested four indicators to measure Goal 3:

- the ratio of girls to boys in primary, secondary and tertiary education,
- the ratio of literate females to males among 15-24 year olds,
- the share of women in wage employment in the non-agricultural sector, and
- the proportion of seats held by women in national parliaments.

The first two are indicators of capabilities, the third is an indicator of opportunity, and the fourth is an indicator of agency. Although they represent all three domains of gender equality, they are not without their drawbacks. In addition, there may be other indicators that are better suited to tracking progress toward the MDG gender targets.

**Capability Indicators.** There are both substantive and technical concerns with the two capability indicators. The ratio of girls to boys in school reflects the input side of education, that is, how many girls and boys are enrolled in school, which is where most policy efforts have been directed. Getting girls and boys to school is clearly an important first step. Yet, the more important issue is school completion and student learning outcomes. The completion of 5 to 6 years of schools is necessary for mastery of basic competencies such as literacy and numeracy.

School enrolment ratios, whether on a gross or net basis, are poorly correlated with the rate of primary school completion; moreover, enrolment ratios are consistent with many different patterns of drop-out and retention. Finally, gender differences are brought into sharper contrast in the comparison of enrolment rates against completion rates.

Beyond the substantive issue of what should be the focus of the MDGs, there are other concerns with the proposed capability indicators. The ratio of girls to boys in school simply depicts the number of girls relative to boys in school. Enrolment rates, by contrast, give a picture of the number of students, boys or girls, enrolled in a given level of education relative to the population of the age group which should be enrolled at that level. Net enrolment rates, which take into consideration the appropriate age for each grade, are a good indicator of access to education, but they are not available for many countries. Gross enrolment rates are more widely available, but they include repeat students in the calculation and so will be higher than net enrolment rates. There are also concerns about the literacy indicator. This indicator was chosen to reflect the performance of the national education system, as well as the quality of the human resources within a country in relation to their potential for growth, contribution to development, and quality of life. Yet, the quality of the literacy data is suspect. Some countries collect literacy information using sophisticated and comprehensive techniques while others are not able to even provide the most basic information. In addition, because literacy is not a simple concept with a single universally accepted meaning, different countries measure literacy differently. The UNESCO definition ("A person is literate if s/he has completed five or more years of schooling") has been widely criticized partly because it assumes that people can be easily categorized as "literate" or "illiterate" or because adults with five or more years of schooling may still be functionally illiterate, while those with less than four years of schooling may have acquired literacy skills by non-formal means. Despite these limitations, this indicator is the best that exists across countries and over time.

**Opportunity Indicators:** The choice of indicator in the MDGs to measure progress in economic opportunity is the female share of non-agricultural wage employment. As noted in UNIFEM's Progress of the World's Women 2000, this is an indicator of the extent to which women have equal access to paid jobs in areas of expanding employment. As stated in the report, "Wage employment in industry and services usually puts some money directly into the hands of women themselves, unlike employment as an unpaid family worker on a family farm. Moreover, the pay is likely to be higher than the average pay for self-employment." The drawback of using this indicator is that it could be interpreted to also mean equality in income. A second drawback is that an increase in women's share of paid employment adds to women's total workload such that what women may gain in terms of cash they lose in terms of time (UNIFEM, 2000). Third, as Anker (2002) notes, this indicator only measures the presence or absence of work, and not the "decency" of work itself or the disadvantages women face—in access to employment (measured by unemployment rates), in returns to their labor (earnings or wages), in the types of jobs they hold (occupational segregation), and in security of employment (social protection). Finally, in grouping together all non-agricultural employment, the indicator can't distinguish between work which is formal or informal, full time or part time, and permanent or seasonal. There is ample evidence that women's participation in informal employment is as high as 80 per cent in some countries such as India, Uganda, Indonesia, among others (Charmes, 2000), and that women are more likely to predominate in part-time and seasonal jobs.

The ILO has proposed a series of indicators for equality in access to and fair treatment in employment as part of the ILO's decent work initiative (Anker, 2002). These indicators include gender-disaggregated unemployment rates, the female to male wages or earnings ratio (divided by years of school which controls for human capital), and occupational segregation by sex (the per cent of non-agricultural employment in male-dominated and female-dominated occupations and the index of dissimilarity), among others.

These indicators show a sobering picture of women's status in employment. For instance, in 1997 female unemployment rates were higher than male unemployment rates in all regions of the world for which data were available, although the gap narrowed in some regions (United Nations, 2000). Similarly, in no country for which data are available do women earn as much as men. For instance, in the manufacturing sector in 13 out of 39 countries, women earned up to 20 per cent less than men; in the other countries, the pay differential was even greater (*ibid.*). Approximately, half of all workers in the world are in gender-dominated occupations where at least 80 per cent of workers are of the same sex, a form of labor market rigidity that reduces employment opportunity and impairs economic efficiency (Anker, 2002). Occupational segregation is also associated with lower wage rates for women, as typical women's occupations tend to have lower pay, lower status and fewer possibilities for advancement than do male occupations.

Because of multiple data and other problems, it is difficult to recommend one global indicator to measure progress toward eliminating gender inequalities in access to assets and employment. Unemployment rates, for instance, are an important indicator of labor market performance in industrialized countries, but are of much more limited significance in low-income economies where the majority of the population engages in some form of economic activity—usually informal employment or self-employment. Occupational segregation indicators may not cover informal employment, and in some countries, they may not be correlated with other indicators of labor market disadvantage. And finally, data on the gender earnings gap—in both paid and self-employment—are currently not available for many countries. Of these three indicators, the gender earnings' gap is probably the best marker of gender equality in the labor market.

**Agency Indicators.** The United Nations has recommended that progress toward women's empowerment be tracked by the female share of seats in national parliaments. Currently, this is the only indicator that can be tracked on a global scale. It is an imperfect proxy for tracking aggregate levels of female empowerment because it says nothing about whether women have power in parliament to make decisions or whether or not they are sensitive to gender issues and can promote a gender equality legislative agenda. It has also been observed that greater progress has been made in municipal and local level elections than in national elections, so it would therefore be very useful to track progress that women are making at the local level. The International Union of Local Authorities has scattered data on municipal level institutions but aims to construct a global database on women in local government. At the individual level, indicators could include control over fertility and sexuality. Again, however, there is a paucity of such information for most countries. One barrier that stands in the way of women being able to use their capabilities, exploit opportunities, and exercise agency is violence. Worldwide, it has been estimated that violence against women is as serious a cause of death and incapacity among women of reproductive age as cancer, and is a greater cause of ill-health than traffic accidents and malaria combined. Therefore, another indicator of women's agency, albeit in a negative way, is the prevalence of physical violence in the past year experienced by women aged 15-49 at the hands of an intimate partner.

Measuring the true prevalence of gender-based violence presents several challenges. To accurately measure true prevalence of physical violence, the questions used to gather data must disaggregate specific acts of physical violence such as kicking, beating, hitting and slapping, information which can be hard to obtain because of its sensitive nature. Statistics available through the police, hospitals, women's centers, and other formal institutions often underestimate the levels of violence because of under-reporting. The WHO's World Report on Violence and Health, which presents data from 48 population-based surveys conducted in 35 developed and developing countries, and WHO's recent multi-country study on women's health and domestic violence lay a strong foundation for larger-scale data collection initiatives. Thus, although prevalence rates are a good indicator, they can't be used to track progress toward the goal since data are not currently available for a large number of countries.

### General Limitations of All Indicators

Beyond the specific issues associated with each indicator described above, there are a number of more general issues. First, the paucity of data on some indicators automatically restricts their use, despite the fact that there may be more valid indicators than the ones for which there is more data. Second, good ratios are not good enough because they say nothing about the absolute levels achieved. Third, national averages mask regional variation. Finally, few indicators exist that measure *quality* of progress toward the goal instead of just *quantity* of progress. The dearth of data and lack of standardization across countries limit a complete and accurate measurement of gender equality and empowerment. There are data gaps across all domains—capabilities, opportunity, and agency—but gaps are particularly prevalent in the domain of opportunity. For example, most of sub-Saharan Africa and South Asia are missing data on the share of women in wage employment in the non-agricultural sector. As noted earlier, even fewer have information on women's relative earnings. Lack of time-series data is an additional hindrance. Finally, data are often missing for countries that experienced violent conflict during the decade.

### Meeting the Goal of Empowering Women: Other Actions

Meeting the three targets will lay the foundation for women's empowerment because gaining power in society is dependent upon having capability, opportunity and influence over key decisions that affect life outcomes. However, achieving the goal of women's empowerment is not only about the content of interventions but about the process. The process of empowerment varies from culture to culture, but there are several types of changes that are considered to be central across cultures. Some of these changes include increased participation in decision-making, more equitable status of women in the family and community, increased political power and exercise of rights, and increased self-esteem.

Women can be empowered through development interventions. Some of the clearest evidence comes from evaluations of well-designed micro credit programs (Hashemi, Schuler, and Riley, 1996). In addition to gaining greater respect and legitimacy in the broader community—particularly from male members—because of their access to credit, the opportunity to have control over decisions about loan size, use of the loan, and so forth has been found to be empowering for women. Women borrowers have also gained experience and confidence as leaders of their Trust Banks (in the Philippines) and have gone on to be elected within their barangays in the Philippines and Mayor in Honduras (Cheston, 2002). A significant barrier to women's empowerment is gender-based violence. As mentioned earlier, the prevalence of violence against women can serve as an indicator of the level of empowerment of women in any given country. The lack of data currently makes this difficult to operationalise in the MDG context, but it does not reduce the urgency to address this problem.

At the country level, most initiatives to address violence have been legislative. Although the legislation varies, it typically includes a combination of protective or restraining orders and penalties for offenders. As with property rights, a formidable challenge are often the enforcement of existing laws. Procedural barriers and traditional attitudes of law enforcement and judicial officials undermine the effectiveness of existing anti-violence laws. Training programs for judicial and law enforcement personnel often go a long way to change such attitudes. Beyond training programs, the establishment of female-staffed police stations has been effective in making them more accessible to women. For the women who have experienced violence, a range of medical, psychological, legal, educational, and other support services is necessary.

Finally, to prevent violence, improving women's education levels and economic opportunities has been found to be a protective factor (Duvvury, 2002; Panda, 2002). The interventions noted above to improve women's economic opportunities thus become even more important. Ultimately, however, the threshold of acceptability of violence against women needs to be shifted upwards. To do that requires a massive media and public education campaign.

## Conclusion

Overall, the Convention to Eliminate All Forms of Discrimination Against Women (CEDAW) provides a useful international mechanism to hold countries accountable for meeting Goal 3. All nation states that have ratified the convention are obligated to take all necessary measures at the national level to implement the provisions within it, including providing legal protection against discrimination of women. In order to monitor progress made by nation states in advancing the agenda of CEDAW, each nation state is required to report to the Committee on the Elimination of Discrimination Against Women on specific measures that they have taken to advance the Convention's agenda. Each country is required to report within one year of acceding to the Convention and at least every four years thereafter, including whenever the Committee so requests. The Committee annually reports to the UN General Assembly and makes recommendations to nation-states based on an evaluation of the country reports. A recent study of the impact of CEDAW has shown that it provides a powerful instrument at the national and international levels for defining norms for constitutional guarantees of women's rights, for interpreting laws, mandating proactive, pro-women policies, and for dismantling discrimination overall (McPhedran et al., 2000). For CEDAW to be used effectively requires action at many levels and by many actors. Among the many factors identified by the study as being key to the effective utilization of CEDAW were the following: widespread awareness and knowledge of CEDAW; constructive dialogue between government representatives, CEDAW Committee members, and NGOs; governments recognizing how policy goals can be adapted to implement their stated commitment to CEDAW; and the systematic use of gender-specific indicators to assess the impact of governmental policies, laws, and budgets. The CEDAW mechanism be used to monitor progress toward the MDGs and to hold nation's accountable.

It is important that the women organizations advocating for sexual and reproductive rights develop ways to achieve progress on a range of issues within the framework established by the MDGs. They should ensure that a rights based approach be applied to development, both within the UN system and at the country level, that prioritizes equity, profound social changes, and sustainability, rather than simply the achievement of narrow quantitative targets.

The MDG campaign offers an opportunity to attend to the unfinished business of development by fulfilling the promises made by world leaders to reduce poverty, end hunger, improve health and eliminate illiteracy. Gender inequality fuels many of these ubiquitous challenges and is exacerbated by them. Conversely, gender equality and the empowerment of women can secure the future of women themselves, their households, and the communities in which they live. Relative to the past, current international development rhetoric places gender inequality high among the list of development priorities. Having an independent MDG goal on gender equality is a reflection of this new emphasis. The Millennium Development Goals are a derivative of the Millennium Declaration of September 2000, which spells out the following values: freedom, equality, solidarity, tolerance, respect for nature, and shared responsibility. They are a clarion call of 189 governments, on behalf of their citizens. World leaders who are currently doing performance appraisal must address the gender gap in the MDGs.

## References

Anker, R., I. Chernyshev, P. Egger, F. Mehran, and J. Ritter 2002. "Measuring Decent Work with Statistical Indicators." Policy Integration Paper No. 1. Geneva: ILO.

Charmes, J. 2000. "Informal Sector, Poverty and Gender: A Review of Empirical Evidence." Background Paper for the World Development Report 2001. Washington, D.C. World Bank.

Cheston, S. and L. Kuhn 2002. "Empowering Women Through Microfinance." New York: UNIFEM.

Commission on Human Rights 2003. Preliminary study on the impact of international economic and financial issues on the enjoyment of human rights submitted to working group on the right to development, February 3-14, 2003, Geneva.

Duvvury, N. and K. Allendorf 2001. "Domestic Violence in India: The Roles of Education and Employment." Paper presented at the Sixth Women's Policy Research Conference, The Status of Women: Facing the Facts, Forging the Future, June 8-9, 2001, Washington, D.C.

Patel, V. and M. Karne (co edited): *Macro Economic Policies and the Millennium Development Goals*, Gyan Publications, New Delhi, 2006.

# Gender Inequality in Development

*Vibhuti Patel*

17

Women's studies have challenged the conventional indicators of development that focus on urbanisation, higher education, mobility of labour, technological development, modernisation, infra-structural development, industrialisation, mechamisation in agricultural, white revolution, green revolution, blue revolution so on and so forth. Development dialogue of the last 32 years (1975 to the present) resulted into intellectual scrutiny with gender lens of

- The critique of trickledown theory
- Marginalisation thesis popularised by the UN as WID (Women in Development)
- 'Integration of Women' Approach known as Women and Development (WAD)
- Development Alternatives with Women (DAWN) at Nairobi Conference, 1985
- Gender and Development (GAD)—Women in Decision Making Process, 1990
- Adoption of CEDAW—Convention on all forms of Discrimination against Women
- Human Development Index, Gender Empowerment Measure, 1995
- Millennium Development Goals (MDGs), 2000
- Women Empowerment Policy, GoI, 2001
- Gender mainstreaming in planning, policy making and programme implementation

With the official recognition of subordinate status of women in economic, social, educational political and cultural spheres by all nation-states, two approaches became popular with regard to women in development process. First one was an instrumentalist approach influenced by Human Resource Development philosophy that supported investment in women so that their efficiency and productivity would increase which would increase their economic and social status. As against this, the second approach was guided by Human Development Concept that emphasised the quality of life or well-being aspect of investment in women. In this approach attainment of education, health, nutrition and better quality of life is considered to be an end in itself. Both approaches are interlinked (Sen, 1999).

### Definition of Gender Equality and Empowerment

Like race and ethnicity, gender is a social construct. It defines and differentiates the roles, rights, responsibilities and obligations of women and men. The innate biological differences between females and males are interpreted by society to create a set of social expectations that define the behaviors that are appropriate for women and men and that determine women's and men's differential access to rights, resources, and power in society. Although the specific nature and degree of these differences vary from one society to the next, they typically favor men, creating an imbalance in power and a gender inequality that exists in most societies worldwide.

### Definition of Gender Equality

According to the UN (2002), "equality is the cornerstone of every democratic society that aspires to social justice and human rights." The term gender equality has been defined in multiple ways in the development literature and has been the subject of great debate in the U.N. It often means women having the same opportunities in life as men, for instance equality of access to education and employment, which does not necessarily lead to equality of outcomes. Several experts have proposed conceptual frameworks for understanding gender equality. The United Nations Human Development Report (1995) refers to gender equality in terms of capabilities (education, health, and nutrition) and opportunities (economic and decision-making). Similarly, the World Bank defines gender equality in terms of equality under the law, equality of opportunity (including equality of rewards for work and equality in access to human capital and other productive resources that enable opportunity), and equality of voice (the ability to influence and contribute to the development process).

Three primary domains of equality between men and women emerge from both of these frameworks:

1. capabilities, access to resources and opportunities,
2. agency or the ability to influence, and
3. contribute to outcomes.

The capabilities domain refers to basic human abilities as measured through education, health and nutrition. It is the most fundamental of all the three domains and is necessary for achieving equality in the other two domains.

Access to resources and opportunities, the second domain, refers primarily to equality in the opportunity to use or apply basic capabilities through access to economic assets (such as land and property) and resources (such as income and employment).

The third domain, agency, is the defining element of the concept of empowerment and refers to the ability to make choices and decisions that can alter outcomes. Gender equality in this domain can only result from an equalizing in the balance of power between women and men in the household and societal institutions.

These three domains of equality are inter-related. Progress in any one domain to the exclusion of the others is insufficient to meet the goal of gender equality. While they are inter-related, the three domains are not necessarily dependent on each other. So, for instance, illiterate women may organize, thereby building their agency to influence outcomes for themselves and their households. Not surprisingly, women then use that agency to demand capability (better health or education) and opportunity (access to decent work). Similarly, women with capabilities (as measured by education) may have no economic opportunity, as is evidenced in many Middle Eastern countries.

Gender inequalities exist because of discrimination in the family and societal institutions and social, cultural, and religious norms that perpetuate stereotypes, practices and beliefs that are detrimental to women. Amartya Sen (2001) narrates seven forms of gender inequalities—mortality, natality, basic facility, special opportunity, profession, ownership and household.

Human rights conventions provide redress for discrimination. Among these, the Convention to Eliminate All Forms of Discrimination Against Women (CEDAW), adopted by the U.N. General Assembly in 1979, is the most universally accepted instrument for realizing gender equality and influencing cultural and traditional definitions of gender roles and family relations. The treaty has been ratified by 170 countries, including every nation in the Western Hemisphere except the United States, but its impact is dependent on political will and resources.

Economic institutions and policy can exacerbate existing gender inequalities instead of mitigating them. There is Convention to Eliminate All Forms of Discrimination Against Women (CEDAW), adopted by the U.N. General Assembly in 1979, a strong tendency to see the market as a liberating force for women. While modern markets can and do undermine some of the pre-existing forms of culturally-determined gender inequality, they also incorporate and transform pre-existing inequalities into new ones (Elson and Pearson, 1997). Commercialised new reproductive technologies are posing major threat to women's survival chances in India and China by encouraging existing patriarchal biases of son preference and sex selective abortions of female fetuses (Patel, 2002).

Laws and policies play a significant role in determining the extent of gender inequality that exists in a society. They can serve to protect women's rights or to reduce them. For example, in many countries, women still lack the legal right to inherit or own property and, in many others, violence against women is not considered a criminal offense. Without transformations in economic relations or the implementation and enforcement of legal rights and protection, gender equality and the empowerment of women can remain an elusive goal.

### *Definition of Empowerment*

The concept of empowerment is related to gender equality but distinct from it. Empowerment is a process that marks change over a period of time and requires that the individual being empowered is involved as a significant agent in that change process. Several experts agree that an empowered woman is one who has the agency to formulate strategic choices and to control resources and decisions that affect important life outcomes. The core of the concept of empowerment lies in the ability of the woman to control her own destiny. For example, only empowered woman can oppose pressure to undergo sex selective abortion of female foetus (Patel, 2002). This implies that to be empowered women must not only have equal capabilities (such as education and health) and access to resources and opportunities (such as land and employment), they must also have the agency to use those rights, capabilities, resources, and opportunities to make strategic choices and decisions (such as is provided through leadership opportunities and participation in political institutions).

## Gender and the Process of Economic Development

The incorporation of subsistence economies into 'modern' market economies has brought into question the traditional gender-based division of labour as an organizing principle in the rural and urban sector because of the basic injustice it perpetuates. Women end up doing the least skilled work and are underpaid or are expected to contribute to survival needs of the family without any corresponding benefits. Esther Boserup (1971) in her pioneering work brought to fore African women's crucial contribution towards food security and explained the political economy of polygamy in Africa that allowed men to concentrate and centralize economic resources through unpaid and backbreaking labour of women and children in the subsistence economy that did not have much animal resources or mechanisation for cultivation of land.

## Economic Basis and Functioning of Patriarchy and Matrilineal Societies, Structures and Systems

Patriarchy thrives on control of women's sexuality, fertility and labour for male hegemony over economic resources. Analytical tools provided by Gender Economics (GE) are extremely useful to deal with the socio-economic and legal issues concerning marriage, divorce, custody of children, guardianship rights, alimony, maintenance, property rights of mother, sister, daughter, legally wedded wives and her child/children, co-wives and their children, keeps and their children and the issues concerning adoption. GE has a special significance in the subsistence economy, which uses the kinship networks, institutions of polygamy and polyandry for concentration and centralisation of wealth and capital by either the patriarchs or the matriarchs. Domestic animals, women and children are the main assets in the subsistence sector where collection of fuel, fodder, water are important components of daily life over and above agrarian chores, live-stock rearing and kitchen gardening.

GE has drawn heavily from all mainstream disciplines and innumerable social movements of the last three decades. GE provides insights to examine budgets of Government Organisations (GOs) and Non-Government Organisations (NGOs) from the point of view of gender justice. Priority areas encompass all aspects of human development—women's education, health and nutrition, skill development, accounts, financial and commercial viability, legal standing, asset and corpus building. GE contextualises day-to-day survival struggles of women in the family, in the households, in the community and in the micro, meso and macro economy with the perspective of power relations which control women and girl children's sexuality, fertility and labour.

To explain this concept, I would like to give some examples from women's lives:

## Control of Women's Sexuality

(i) Dress code which, restricts mobility of women and girls, does not allow her to do those chores which require flexible body movements, reduces her efficiency and employability in non-conventional occupations.

(ii) "Tool" as a phallic symbol, not being allowed to be used by women as menstruation is supposed to have a contaminating influence. Hence, hostility towards women who ride bicycles, drive cars and scooters, operate machines and use ploughs for farming, wheels for pottery, saw for carpentry.

(iii) Women being treated as repository of custom and tradition and cultural practices, dedicated as *devdasis, jogtis* and forced to undergo series of masochistic fasting, scarification and self-infliction of pain which make them unemployable and perpetually dependant on the patriarchs. They enjoy only subversive power of men's comfort women that too, is mediated by men, as women don't have any legal rights. In the commercial context, the same happens to women beneficiary of *Maitri-Karar* (friendship contract) and *Seva-karar* (Service contract) with economically, politically and socially powerful men.

(iv) Need for male escorts, bodyguards for dainty, sickly and weak women who see their identity as anorexic women. Billion-dollar beauty business thrives by controlling young women so that they are incapable of using their body for manual chores. Here, women's insecurity about their looks is used by the cosmetic industry.

(v) Women eating last, the least and the left over. Nourishing and balanced diet as a male prerogative. Daughters and brides kept on starvation diet. Food secure middle-aged women as honorary men.

Inference of (i), (ii), (iii), (iv) and (v) is subordinate social status of women reflected in declining sex ratio. As per 2001 Census there were 933 women per 1000 men in India. NFHS III, published in 2007 has reported very high mortality and morbidity rates for women in India.

**Control of Women's Fertility**

(i) Women being treated as male-child producing machine. Customary practices of female infanticide and neglect and abandonment of girl child, scientific techniques of sex determination tests are used for female foeticide, pre-conception elimination of female embryo with the help of sex-preselection techniques.

(ii) Population policies targeting women for unsafe contraceptives and harmful hormone based contraceptive researches, which violate bodily integrity and dignity of married and unmarried girls and women.

(iii) Laws on prostitution penalising and persecuting women victims of sexploitation that is running a parallel economy of as much as 200 billion rupees.

(iv) Social boycott of unwed mothers. 'Illegitimate' children being stigmatised by society and deprived of economic, social and educational opportunities. They are further marginalised in the economy, which is undergoing massive structural adjustments and instability. Facilities like identity card, ration card and other legal documents which are a must for citizenship rights are not provided to them.

Inference of (i), (ii), (iii) and (iv), can be named as brothel model of economic development which thrives on unpaid and invisiblised labour of women. It perpetuates the vicious circle of child marriage, child prostitution and child labour (CP, CM and CL). Super-exploitation of female headed household and domestic workers get sanctity in this model. Women have to shoulder an added burden of 'double standard of sexual morality' along with the burden of the vicious circle of poverty, prostitution and unemployment.

**Control of Women's Labour**

(i) Use of women in the economy for the occupations that are extensions of housework, i.e. 3 Cs (cooking, cleaning and caring). Only 8 per cent of women are in the organised sector which guarantees protection of labour legislation and ERA (Equal Remuneration Act). Ninety-two per cent of women are in the informal sector that does not guarantee job-security, regular income and personal safety.

(ii) Demonisation of highly qualified, efficiency plus and career women. Witch hunting of intellectually independent and verbally articulate women workers, employees, technicians and decision-makers.

(iii) Sexual harassment as a major occupational hazard to crush the confidence of women and to keep them in the state of perpetual terrorisation, humiliation and intimidation.

Inference of (i), (ii) and (iii), can be limited opportunities for women and ghettoisation of women in non-challenging, routinised and low-status jobs known as "women prone industries" in the official discourse. Most of the economic activities done by majority of women are non-marketed and non-monetised and reward for labour does not reflect the value of their labour. In such a situation to gauge economic worth of their work Time Use studies are the most effective tools to identify their opportunity costs.

## Market, Mobility and Women

Globalisation induced mobility of women has posed new problems for women in the labour market. Hence, efforts at empowerment of women by 550 feminist economists who are functioning in 31 countries under the banner of International Association of Feminist Economics to provide DAWN (Development Alternatives with Women) gain tremendous importance in the contemporary context of discourse on Human Development. According to them, the most pressing issues are as follows:

(i) **Economic profile of special needs population**—Women in poverty groups and female headed households (divorced, deserted, widowed, separated women), home-based workers, women workers in the family enterprise, self-employed women and women entrepreneurs demand affirmative action from the state.

(ii) **Analysis of nature of occupational diversification among women, industrial classification**—Implications of office automation, computerisation, flexi-time, job-sharing, tele working, and part time work.

(iii) **Effects of structural adjustment on market segmentation**—Segmented factor market affects self-employed women directly when they want to buy raw material and other services. Segmented labour-market has direct bearing on the daily grind of women workers in the informal sector. Segmented product market makes unorganised women workers and women's collectives without networking insecure and vulnerable as sellers (Kabeer, 2000).

(iv) **Economic basis of customary laws and the family laws**—When the customary laws get codified, we must be vigilant about the fact that women's interests are not sacrificed. Women's land rights and property rights need special mention at the time of codification of personal laws.

(v) In mega development projects, which displace the native population, care must be taken to see to it that women get equal share in monetary compensation, land-rights and right to shelter. The same applies to the social and natural disaster management programmes.

(vi) Political economy of GET RICH QUICK formula in the name of dowry, *sati* (widow burning), *bhootali* (witch hunting) for land grab, house-grab or to deprive women of their legitimate property rights demands serious attention. Violence against women in the private and public domain must be recognised as serious threat to human development.

(vii) **Women's empowerment by men decision-makers**—In a situation where women's agency is virtually non-existent, the benevolent patriarchs wedded to the cause of women's empowerment become project coordinators who must be gender sensitised.

Gender Bias in Theories of Value, Distribution and Population has been a major bone of contention. Neoclassical analysis based on law of marginal utility in consumer analysis, marginal cost in the product pricing and marginal productivity have come under severe scrutiny. In the area of home economics, Nobel Laureate Gary Backer's model of 'competing interests' in distribution of resources in the households and higher 'opportunity cost' of men as 'bread-earner' and women as 'home-maker' is criticized by women's studies scholars as sexist and statusquo-ist. Amartya Kumar Sen and Martha Nassbaum have put forward a concept of 'cooperative conflict' in the theory of distribution and have advocated proactive measure to enhance women's capabilities.

### Feminist Criticism of Development Indices and WID-WAD-GAD

Conventional indicators of development such as modernization, technological development, mechanization, automation, urbanization, industrialization are critiqued by women's studies as they have bypassed and marginalized women. They have provided three approaches to understand women's role in the micro, meso and macroeconomy (Patel, 2002).

There has been a coexistence of three approaches for women's development. Women in Development (WID) model explains the reasons for women being treated as beneficiaries of the crumbs thrown at them, in the margin of the economy, consumer and an auxiliary labour force to be utilised in the crisis period and eased out the moment men are ready for take over. The discourse revolved around the economic growth paradigm. Women and Development (WAD) model integrates women in the development work as active change agents. Affirmative action by the state and pro-active approach by the civil society through NGOs and women's groups are advocated by these models for empowerment of women against the forces of patriarchal class society. NGOs-voluntary organisations implementing this approach have become powerful force during 1990s. Gender and Development (GAD) model is based on an understanding of gender relations and empowers the weak (he or she). Gender is socially constructed and gender relations are power relations. Here power is an important analytical category. Explicit measures of gender inequalities are sex-ratio, literacy rates, health and nutrition indicators, wage differentials, ownership of land and property.

## Visibility of Women in Statistics and Data System

For effective execution of macro policies such as National Perspective Plan for Women, Women Empowerment Policy, State Women's Policy, etc. we need an accurate database, area studies and time allocation studies, studies on energy expenditure and food consumption patterns among women of different communities, public utility services such as safe transport, public urinals, and women's room in the office. Gender economists have done pioneering work to understand demographic profile of women and sex-ratio. Formulation of gender aware data system on literacy, education level, employment and earnings, health and well-being, sources of livelihood helps proper planning and policy making for empowerment of women. Inter-district, inter-state and cross country comparisons of women's empowerment are obtained from Gender related Development Index (GDI). GDI owes its origin to its precursor, the HDI (Human Development Index), three main components of which are per capita income, educational attainment and life-expectancy which is a proxy for health attainment. Gender disparities are measured keeping these three indicators into consideration. An additional measure, gender empowerment measure (GEM) has been formulated to take into account aspects relating to economic participation and decision-making by women. The indicators used in GEM are share in income, share in parliamentary seats and an index that includes share in administrative and managerial jobs and share in professional and technical posts. This exercise is done with a philosophical understanding that without engendering, human development is endangered.

## National Human Development Report (HDR), 2001

The first HDR prepared by the Planning Commission of India revealed that gender disparity across the states had declined in 2002. The report has given Gender Equity Index (GEI) in which Bihar has the most abysmal record of 0.49.GEI of U.P. and Assam is between 0.5- 0.59. Maharashtra, Orissa, Rajasthan, West Bengal figure in the GEI bracket 0.6-0.74. The group in the topmost bracket, i.e. 0.75 + is composed of the North Eastern states except Assam, Southern states and Himachal Pradesh. The HDR has not seriously taken into account, the declining sex ratio, especially the juvenile sex ratio (0-9 years) while estimating various development indices. The report has used eight indicators to map the human development of states. It has provided diagrammatic representation of human development in the form of development radars comprising eight indicators, namely incidence of poverty, per capita consumption expenditure, life expectancy at age one, infant mortality rates, intensity of formal education, literacy rates, access to safe drinking water, proportion of households with *pucca* houses. The central thesis of HDR has been economic prosperity in terms of high per capita income does not necessarily lead to overall human development. Declining sex ratio in the prosperous states like Punjab, Haryana, Gujarat and Maharashtra prove the point.

### State and City Human Development Reports

Several states in India have prepared HDRs. For example, Maharashtra, Tamil Nadu, Kerala, West Bengal, Karnataka, Delhi, Gujarat, so on and so forth. HDR for Mumbai is in pipeline. In all these reports, there is a need to focus more on the impact of budgetary allocations on women's well-being and women's development. Gender budgeting as a tool for ensuring gender sensitive human development has been accepted as a mandate by nearly 60 countries.

### Gender Equality and Development

Gender equality has three aspects: equal opportunities, equal treatment and equal entitlements for both, men and women. It is directly linked with human development.

The WID discourse deconstructs the economic growth paradigm and focuses on women specific statistics and indicators, policies and schemes, plan allocation and programmes on health, education and employment.

WAD (Women and Development) model integrates women in the development work as active change agents. Affirmative action by the state and pro-active approach by the civil society through NGOs and women's groups are advocated by this model for empowerment of women against the forces of patriarchal class society. NGOs-voluntary organisations implementing this approach have become powerful force during 1990s.

GAD (Gender and Development) model is based on an understanding of gender relations that empowers the weak (he or she). Gender is socially constructed and gender relations are power relations based on caste, class, ethnicity, race and religion. Here power is an important analytical category.

## Conclusion

Explicit measures of gender inequalities are sex ratio, literacy rates, health and nutrition indicators, wage differentials, ownership of land and property. The implicit measures of gender inequalities are those embedded in relations of power and in hierarchies and are more difficult to measure. Located in the household, in custom, religion, and culture, these intra-household inequalities result in unequal distribution of power, control over resources and decision-making, dependence rather than self-reliance, control rather than autonomy and unfair, unequal distribution of work, drudgery and even food. Current development debate has resulted into generation of Meaningful Indicators of Women and Development. In 2004, India ranked 127 in Human Development while in Gender Development Index India's rank was 78. Comparative data of 130 countries regarding gender-related development index (GDI) reveals that gender-equality does not depend entirely on the income level of society. The human development approach which focuses on demographic, health, education, employment and human rights issues of women provides realistic insights to address women's concerns.

## References

Boserup, Esther (1970) *Women's Role in Economic Development*, New York: St. Martins Press.

Elson, D., and R. Pearson (1997) "The Subordination of Women and the Internationalization of Factory Production." in Visvanathan, J., L. Duggan, L. Nisonoff, N. Wiegersman, eds. *The Women, Gender & Development Reader*. London: Zed Press.

Patel, Vibhuti (2002) *Women's Challenges of the New Millennium*, New Delhi: Gyan Publications.

Sen, Amartya Kumar (2001) "Many Faces of Gender Inequality", Chennai: *Frontline*, Vol. 18, Issue 22, Oct. 27-Nov. 09.

# Gender Sensitization*

18

Gender disaggregated data is the basis for gender sensitive policy formulation and programme planning. The need for gender statistics in formulating policies and programmes can hardly be over-emphasized. The Census of India is a veritable mine of information on demographic, social and economic aspects of population. It is the only source of population characteristics at the lowest administrative levels; village in rural areas and ward in urban areas.

Conceptually, information collected at the census is gender neutral and compiled and tabulated for both men and women separately. The Questionnaire and Instruction Manual for collection of information in the field have been carefully designed to avoid any bias on the basis of gender. The training of Census functionaries also focuses on this aspect of neutrality. Evaluation of Census data indicate that while the coverage error for females was slightly higher in 2001 Census, than that for males, in the Censuses prior to 2001, there was a need to improve the data regarding the economic activity of females.

Towards this end, the last three decades have seen special efforts. In Census 1991, emphasis was laid on netting of women's contribution in the economic activities. Main emphasis was on unpaid work done by women. Question on 'Work' was amplified to include unpaid work in family farm and family enterprise. This was followed by publicity campaigns on television, radio

---

*http://censusindia.gov.in/Ad_Campaign/drop_in_articles/03-Gender_Sensitization.pdf

and the print media to generate awareness. This had a significant impact that was reflected in the female work participation rate, which improved from 19.7 per cent in 1981 Census to 22.3 per cent in 1991. However, the data continued to show regional disparities in gender statistics on Work Participation Ratio and adult Sex Ratio.

During Census 2001, special efforts were made to address gender concerns. Gender sensitization activities were initiated right from the stage of planning. These included modifications in the instruction manuals, special modules on gender, media campaigns and other modes of mass mobilization to raise awareness on the vital issue. Great emphasis was laid on the need to ensure that each question should be canvassed for each individual member of the household and that women's individuality should not be compromised or conditioned by any bias. Possible causes for gender bias creeping in the data collection and dissemination were evaluated. At the same time changes were made in the wording of questions and focused training was thought of to reduce gaps in understanding and to ensure accurate information and coverage to the extent possible.

With a view to review the past experience and fine-tune the strategies it is pertinent to understand gender gaps in data. The National Workshop on Gender mainstreaming held on 30 July 2010 looked at data sets on key gender indicators and deliberated on all sensitive issues, which could affect accurate netting in the field due to any prevailing cultural or other bias, shared local concerns of States/UTs and proposed a strategy to improve gender statistics in Census 2011. A national consultative workshop held in July 2010 was followed by number of group workshops which had participation of different DCOs and UN agencies supporting this initiative.

Gender mainstreaming activities of Census 2011 encompassing gender responsive training and publicity is an outcome of detailed data analysis and subsequent deliberations and consultative processes involving different stake holders.

Some of the key parameters concerning gender disaggregated data in Census are highlighted below:

- The overall growth rate during the 1991-01 has been 23.1 per cent for female population, which is slightly higher than that of male population (22.2%) at the national level. The trend is similar in case of rural and urban areas. In majority of the states also this trend was noted which in fact has been reversal of trends seen during 1981-91 when female population growth was lower as compared to male population growth.
- The Census 2001 also registered a higher sex ratio (i.e. females per thousand males) of population (933) over the Census 1991 (927), an increase of 6 points at national level. In 23 States/Union Territories, increase in the sex ratio of total population was observed as compared to 1991. Similar trends were seen in rural and urban areas of 23 and 25 States/UTs respectively. The increase was more pronounced in 7+ age group not only at national level but also in 29 states.
- Notwithstanding increase in the overall value of sex ratio of total population, the child sex ratio in the age group 0-6 has plummeted from 945 in Census 1991 to 927 in 2001 at the national level. The trends were alarming in some of the major States like Punjab, Haryana, Gujarat, Himachal Pradesh, Uttarakhand and the Union Territories of Chandigarh and Delhi. 477 districts comprising of 70 per cent of total districts (593) had shown a decline in the value of child sex ratio (0-6) and in 118 districts child sex ratio had fallen below 900. This shortfall of girl child population in early childhood may reflect in higher age groups in the years to come.
- The female work participation (i.e. percentage of female workers to total female population) at the National level increased from 22.3 per cent in 1991 to 25.8 per cent on 2001, however increase was distinct in the category of marginal workers. Similar trends were seen in many states while male Work Participation Ratio remained almost unchanged during 1991-01. In the 15-59 age group 80.7 per cent male population was

economically active against 40 per cent females during 2001 Census. Despite increasing trends, the gaps in female workers are noted in certain districts at the 2001 Census. As many as 36 districts reported less than 10 per cent female work participation rate. A point to be noted in the context of work and non-work is that the Census does not define these concepts. It is the National System of Accounts that does so. The Census merely enumerates as per the definition laid down. Controversies regarding the netting of work especially of females in the Census are therefore misdirected.

The post-Enumeration Survey of Census 2001 has shown that while there was no gender bias in coverage, the overall omission rate was 23.3 per thousand persons, which is higher than that in the Census 1991 (17.6 per thousand). The first and foremost aim of Census 2011 would be to ensure complete coverage without omission or duplication. An analysis of the net omission rate per thousand populations in selected age groups has shown a relatively higher female omission rate up to age of 24 years in rural areas. It is also noticed that the male/female gap in omission rates show a sizable differential of eight and six percentage points in the 60+ age group in rural and urban areas respectively. There is a need to focus on these age groups and ensure that the gap is narrowed if not eliminated.

The Juvenile Sex Ratio and Sex Ratio at Birth are vital parameters and it would be the endeavor of the Census organization to net these accurately.

In addition to the basic count, special efforts will also be taken to accurately net the socio-cultural, demographic and economic characteristics, which, inter alia, would include correct netting of head of the household, age, age at marriage, marital status, literacy, and economic activities in unorganized and unpaid work. A number of activities involving female workers and real pictures of women at work have been added in the Instruction Manual to help probing about the female economic pursuits. The gender component will be an integral part of all training programmes.

Special focus will be directed towards areas that returned abnormal gender parameters such as sex ratio, literacy and female work participation at Census 2001, by developing special gender modules and training strategies for sensitization of Census functionaries. These efforts would be more focused in 262 districts, which have returned very low gender parameters as per 2001 Census. These districts will have Gender Master Trainer Facilitators (GMTFs) who will support Master Trainers and impart special training to enumerators with the aid of special modules and kits specially devised for training at different levels. This module will focus to reduce stereotypes and apathy with the help of handouts on Gender and Data Sheets to make 2011 census a gender responsive Census.

It is equally important to create awareness among the general masses about the gender issues to facilitate correct reporting of information about each member specially women. Steps will also be taken to reach out to respondents through gender sensitive publicity campaigns and outreach programmes. The ultimate aim will be to create an environment that will sensitize both enumerators as well as respondents.

## Contributors

**Vibhuti Patel,** Director, PGSR and Professor and Head, Department of Economics, SNDT Women's University, Churchgate, Mumbai-400020. Email: vibhuti.np@gmail.com

**Nishta Paul,** National Law School of India University, Bangalore. E-mail: nishta.paul@gmail.com

**Bhabani Shankar Nayak,** Doctoral Research Fellow, Development Studies, Development and Environment (CDE), University of Sussex, UK. E-mail: b.s.nayak@sussex.ac.uk

**Geeta Sinha,** Master in Gender and Development, Institute of Development Studies (IDS), University of Sussex, UK.

**Parthasarathi Mondal,** Assistant Professor, Centre for Development Studies, Tata Institute of Social Sciences, P.B. 8313, Deonar, Mumbai-400088.
E-mail: pmondal@tiss.edu
E-mail: mondal_parthasarathi@hotmail.com

**Arpana Nath,** Indian Institute of Technology, Guwahati.
E-mail: aparna@iitg.ernet.in

**Pallav Mukhopadhyay,** Department of Journalism and Mass Communication, University of Calcutta, West Bengal.